THE MEAN SEASON

The Attack on the Welfare State

Fred Block Richard A. Cloward
Barbara Ehrenreich Frances Fox Piven

PANTHEON BOOKS   NEW YORK

Library of Congress Cataloging-in-Publication Data
The mean season.
1. Economic assistance, Domestic—United States.
2. Public welfare—United States. 3. United States—
Social policy. 4. Welfare state. I. Block, Fred L.
HC110.P63M42   1987   361'.973   86-43126
ISBN 0-394-55338-1
ISBN 0-394-74450-0 (pbk.)

Manufactured in the United States of America

468975

Book Design by Quinn Hall

THE MEAN SEASON

CONTENTS

ACKNOWLEDGMENTS

THIS BOOK IS A collective effort. The idea emerged through a series of conversations over several months in which we clarified the complementary aspects of our work—and discovered some disagreements as well. And as our chapters took form, we passed successive drafts back and forth for advice. Certainly, each of us is responsible for the chapters that bear our name, but just as certainly, some of the credit or blame must be shared.

We owe a special debt to several people who facilitated this collaboration. Jim Shoch helped us to find each other and to recognize our shared agenda. Claus Offe met with us at an early stage and provided ideas and encouragement. Finally, André Schiffrin, managing director of Pantheon, shaped the book in important ways by his substantive suggestions and by the strength of his editorial commitment.

We are also grateful to a number of other people who helped us formulate the ideas in the individual chapters or who commented on particular drafts. These include Richard Duboff, Greg Duncan, Larry Hirschhorn, Jerry Jacobs, Carole Joffe, Michael Katz, Karl Klare, David Plotke, Sam Preston, Mark Stern, and the members of the Mellon Seminar on Work and Welfare at the University of Pennsylvania. Fred Block also wishes to thank the German Marshall Fund of the United States for their financial support in the final stages of completing his chapter. Barbara Ehrenreich wishes to thank the Institute for Policy Studies for their continuing collegial support.

INTRODUCTION

*Fred Block, Richard A. Cloward, Barbara Ehrenreich,
and Frances Fox Piven*

OVER THE LAST DECADE, the welfare state has become
the target of a concerted ideological attack. From the expanding
network of conservative think tanks and foundations on up to the
president himself, the same themes are reiterated: that social welfare measures are a drag on the economy, an incentive to immoral-
ity, and a cruel hoax on the needy themselves. In the process, even
the phrase "the welfare state" has been discredited. Conservatives
employ it as a term of invective, while liberals, the erstwhile advocates of the welfare state, have been hesitant to defend it.

What has been momentarily forgotten, in the disarray created
by the conservative attack, is that the welfare state is the only
defense many people have against the vicissitudes of the market
economy. Capitalism, from the beginning, has confronted people
with the continual threat of economic dislocation: downturns in
the business cycle periodically throw millions out of work; shifting
patterns of investment plunge some regions (or industries) into
depression while others boom; long-term structural changes in the
economy—such as the shift away from agriculture and, more recently, from heavy manufacturing—leave millions stranded with
obsolete skills and scanty resources. The only sure "logic" of the
market is change and disruption; and for many of us, the only
protection lies in the programs of the welfare state.

Thus, for example, unemployment insurance and other income
maintenance programs mitigate the impact of the business cycle.

Medicare and Social Security help the elderly survive in an economy that has little use for them. A host of special programs protect children and single mothers from destitution. Whatever its shortcomings, the American welfare state has blunted the most damaging effects of the market economy; and this alone represents an enormous human achievement.

The conservative assault has also generated confusion about just *whose* achievement it is. To listen to the current, one-sided discussion, one might conclude that social welfare programs had been created *de novo,* some twenty or so years ago, by a handful of "new class" professionals in the universities, foundations, and federal bureaucracies. In fact, the modern welfare state is the product of decades of political effort by ordinary Americans to gain some control over their lives in the face of massive economic disruptions. The foundations of the welfare state were laid in the Great Depression of the 1930s, when millions of Americans struggled to win the most basic forms of economic protection: the right to unionize, minimum-wage laws, business regulation, and income support programs such as unemployment insurance. The next period of welfare state expansion was in the 1960s, when black Americans uprooted by the rapid modernization of southern agriculture demanded and won greater protections for the very poor, including increased income benefits, job programs, and health insurance.

The impact of these welfare state programs extends far beyond their immediate beneficiaries. For all of us, in many ways, life has been made a little more humane through the protection of the elderly, the disabled, the young, and the very poor. Working people, in particular, benefit from the existence of a "safety net" that helps shield them from the harsh terms employers often seek to impose in a market economy, especially during periods of economic downturn and uncertainty. Without a safety net, low-paid, unorganized workers would face the choice of acquiescence to employer demands or the risk of joblessness and its traditional consequence—hunger. Even better-paid, unionized workers depend on the welfare state to guarantee that periodic mass layoffs will not lead to destitution and homelessness. Thus the welfare state is an achievement not only because it reduces the misery of a minority in need, but because it eases the chronic insecurity of the majority.

Yet the American welfare state is in many ways a flawed and fragmented creation, especially when compared to the more gener-ous welfare states of the European capitalist societies. The inadequacies of our welfare state reflect a second historical factor in its formation: American social programs were shaped not only by the struggles of poor and working people but by the relatively greater resistance of business in the United States. We have an inadequate, patchwork system of health insurance (Medicaid for the poor, Medicare for the elderly, and so forth) because medical business interests have successfully opposed a comprehensive, uni-versal system of national health insurance. We have grossly inade-quate, subpoverty income support programs (especially Aid to Families with Dependent Children) because employers have suc-cessfully fought to keep benefits below the minimum-wage level. In general, welfare state programs represent an uneasy compro-mise between the demands of the economically vulnerable and the resistance of the economically powerful.

The current ideological attack on the welfare state is a con-tinuation of the repeated efforts of the American business elite to limit the gains not only of the most vulnerable, but of the majority of working people. In fact, the contemporary arguments against the welfare state are remarkably similar to those that have been employed decade after decade by business interests and their intel-lectual representatives. As in the past, they warn that any interfer-ence with the "laws" of the market harms the very people who were intended to benefit: limit the prerogatives of employers—through minimum-wage legislation, health and safety standards, or unemployment insurance—and you will slow economic growth, reducing prosperity for everyone. Attempt to help the most needy and you will only succeed in undermining their morality, family life, and self-respect. And so forth. The arguments are ancient and reflect the historic clash of interests that has shaped the welfare state itself.

But if the ideological attack on the welfare state echoes the past, the economic circumstances that it grows out of are new and deeply challenging. The American economy is undergoing a structural transformation which may turn out to be as profound in its consequences as the earlier shift from an agricultural to an industrial economy. One element of this transformation is the "globalization" of the economy, as capital becomes increasingly mobile and as foreign competition directly challenges core American industries such as autos and steel. Another element is the new computer technology, which holds both the promise of vastly increased productivity and the threat of massive job loss. For better or for worse, we are headed toward a postindustrial economy in which the kinds of jobs that have traditionally been the mainstay of the American working class will be scarce or nonexistent.

The central political question, then, is who will bear the hardships associated with the transition to a postindustrial economy. Will the new technology and new international division of labor lead to an improved standard of living for the average person—for example, through shortened and more flexible hours of work? Or will the final result be widespread poverty and desperation?

Already, the business community has made its answer plain. It has launched a broad-scale attack on working-class standards of living, including intensified union-busting, demands for concessions in wages and benefits, and the imposition of a greater tax burden on the poor and the middle class relative to the rich. At the same time, business has accelerated the decline of American industry by recklessly diverting capital away from productive investments and into financial speculation. As a result, the class contours of American society have begun to change for the first time in the post–world war era: the affluent control a greater share of wealth and income than ever before; the poor are becoming both poorer and more numerous; and the middle class, faced with stagnating wages and diminishing middle-income employment, is shrinking.

The current attack on the welfare state is of a piece with the overall business offensive against labor. While employers have been pressing for concessions from their workers, business interests have supported an administration that is openly hostile to the welfare state. Thus, precisely at a time when the jobs and industries that once provided economic security to American workers are vanishing or endangered, so too are the social programs that have offered at least some guarantee of subsistence in hard times. Just as we embark on what could be a turbulent transition to a new kind of economy, with the possibility of ever more plant closings and unemployment, we have become, as a nation, least prepared to endure the shock of transition without extensive human suffering.

Herein lies the tragedy of our present circumstances. What we need is no less than a new social compact to enable people to cope with a rapidly changing economic environment. What we are likely to get, if conservative business interests prevail, is a return to the untrammeled market as the singular organizing principle governing the lives of poor and working people. The need for an expanded and reformed welfare state has perhaps never been greater, but the ideological opposition to the welfare state has never been so intense, so well organized, and so powerfully represented.

The strength of the opposition is nowhere better reflected than in current discussions of "welfare reform" that center entirely on workfare—plans to drop individuals from the welfare rolls unless they agree to take available employment or sign up for training programs. There are differences between the various workfare plans with respect to the quality and quantity of the training opportunities offered, the level of coercion in requiring individuals to take particular jobs, and the determination of how quickly a mother must agree to place her small children in child care so that she can participate in work or training. Yet all of the workfare plans reinforce the dominance of the market by pressuring participants to take whatever jobs happen to be available, at whatever wages employers see fit to offer.

The current fixation on workfare as the solution to poverty is ironic in view of the fact that a growing number of the poor are working full time at jobs that do not pay enough to keep families above the poverty level. Moreover, forcing hundreds of thousands of welfare recipients into an already overcrowded labor market will only weaken further the economic position of low-wage work-ers. Supporters of workfare rarely address the fact that the unem-ployment rate is approximately 7 percent, and has remained at that level even during the expansionary phase of the business cycle. Yet workfare advocates always emphasize that they want to put an end to dependency by allowing the poor to earn a paycheck. No men-tion is made of the debilitating effects of dependency on the low-wage labor market, though there is nothing ennobling about being forced to please an employer in order to feed one's children. The same can be said of the periodic bouts of involuntary unemploy-ment that are a routine feature of the lives of most low-wage workers.

Yet liberals have been in the forefront of recent calls for work-fare. In general, liberals have offered only timid and infrequent rebuttals to conservative attacks on the welfare state. Instead of advancing a strong and principled defense of the welfare state, liberals seem to have fallen into theoretical and moral disarray. Part of the problem lies with the liberal intelligentsia, who were totally unprepared for a re-emergence of conservative opposition to the welfare state. They had, we believe, succumbed to a kind of complacency bred by theory. Most analysts, whatever their other disagreements, had come to take for granted that expanded welfare state programs were an inevitable concomitant of economic growth and urbanization. Consistently, and not unreasonably, a good deal of the work done by left and liberal social welfare analysts was critical of the programs, fastening on their inadequa-cies and neglecting their achievements. This critical tradition—which certainly had its place in periods of social welfare expansion—left many of the liberal intelligentsia unprepared to respond to the conservative assault with a strong defense of the welfare state.

But this alone cannot account for the failure of erstwhile liberal intellectuals to rise to the defense of the welfare state. There has also been an undeniable element of spinelessness in the face of the renewed fashionability of right-wing or "neoconservative" ideol-ogy. To be sure, liberal academics reject the simplistic slogans of the right, but just as often they have been willing to jump on the bandwagon, preaching the virtues of "free enterprise" or the merits of workfare as a solution to poverty.

The consequences of this intellectual vacuum have been serious. Many ordinary people, in a variety of circumstances, have organized to protect themselves from the rightward drift of public policy and the business offensive against labor: industrial workers have attempted to resist plant closings and wage concessions; farmers have fought against foreclosures; women's groups have fought to preserve social programs whose beneficiaries are largely women and their dependent children. But all of these efforts have been weakened by the absence of an intellectual framework to give them coherence and legitimacy. Struggles have remained disconnected, and for the most part narrowly defensive, lacking a positive agenda beyond the preservation of the status quo. An ideological framework for resisting the right need not, of course, come from intellectuals alone. But it is difficult for any social group to develop a coherent alternative to the rightward drift when not only the business elite and the government but also the intelligentsia agree that it is futile to oppose the logic of the market.

We see this book as one part of the larger effort to construct an ideological framework for democratic resistance to market domination. We have tried to develop the kind of principled defense of the welfare state that has so far been absent from current political debate. We do this primarily by dissecting the right-wing ideas that have come to dominate public policy. For the most part our task here is a critical, oppositional one; we have not sought to lay out a program for the reconstruction of the welfare state. But we hope that this book will help to open up the space for a broad and genuine debate about that process of reconstruction.

THE ESSAYS THAT make up this book approach the problem in very different ways, making use of different kinds of arguments and different types of data. The first two essays, written by Frances Fox Piven and Richard Cloward, are a direct response to conservative attacks on social welfare, particularly such programs as Aid to Families with Dependent Children. Piven and Cloward begin by placing these attacks in a historical context, showing that the current opposition to social welfare reiterates earlier arguments and earlier class dynamics. They continue by revealing the flawed empirical basis of recent charges that blame the welfare system for a worsening of poverty and family disorganization. They conclude with an indictment of the scholarly research on welfare and poverty, showing how that literature has framed research questions far too narrowly. They insist that as long as the dominance of the market remains a premise of such research, it will be impossible to frame adequate policies to protect the poor.

The third essay, by Fred Block, challenges currently dominant views about the relationship between social welfare expenditures and problems of the American economy. Block demonstrates that there is little empirical basis for claims that high social welfare spending has sapped the strength of the American economy or that austerity is a precondition for further economic advance. He argues instead that the conservative account offers the wrong prescriptions for the more complex problems of an increasingly post-industrial economy. Block's conclusion is that an expansion of social welfare spending might well be the best way to restore the vitality of the American economy.

The final essay, by Barbara Ehrenreich, focuses on some of the central ideas in the rhetoric the right has used to attack the welfare state. She shows how the right has used the idea of a liberal "new class" and the notion of "permissiveness" to undermine popular support for social welfare. Ehrenreich's analysis goes on to illuminate the social terrain that has made the right's claims somewhat plausible. She argues that the right has succeeded in redirecting popular anxiety aroused by the consumer culture against safer targets such as the poor and the government. She demonstrates how the appeal of these conservative ideas results from the failure of liberals to oppose or challenge the logic of the market and the commodification of all of social life.

THE MEAN SEASON

The Historical Sources of the Contemporary Relief Debate

Frances Fox Piven and Richard A. Cloward

D URING THE LAST DECADE, criticism of American social welfare programs has grown more and more clamorous. Analysts compete to advance what are purported to be new insights, presumably gleaned from contemporary experience, showing that social welfare programs are in fact harmful to those whom they are supposed to help, driving them deeper into poverty. Yet for all the uproar, almost nothing new is being said. The "theory" that welfare harms the poor is centuries old, and always gains ascendancy when programs that aid the poor are under serious political assault, as they clearly are today. Indeed, the contemporary attack on social welfare is being scripted by a history of conflict over relief that goes back to the sixteenth century.

Historically, attacks on welfare were usually precipitated by sharp economic dislocations associated with periodic market downturns or with the introduction of new forms of production. Viewed from the bottom, market downturns obviously meant material hardship, as well as destruction of the resources on which community and personal life depended. Shifts in the market for goods and in methods of production had similar effects when they entailed the massive displacement of workers and the uprooting of communities and families. In the wake of such disturbances, people often mobilized to demand protection from the market forces that were destroying their way of life, and sometimes life itself. At such junctures, elites frequently responded by granting relief or welfare on a large scale.

But while maintaining social peace might require that relief be expanded, this concession was problematic from the perspective of elites precisely to the extent that it shielded working and poor people from the market. The very dislocations that precipitated protest from below often generated new opportunities for profit which relief obstructed. When working people were shielded by social provision, they were more likely to resist the hardships imposed by the changing forms of production and the changing terms of profitability.

In the past as today, the public discussion of social welfare ignored these large-scale economic dislocations, and the divergent class interests involved. Market downturns left huge numbers of the work force unemployed and drove the wages of those still working far below subsistence. Entire trades were destroyed when new machines and new ways of organizing production were introduced; families were pauperized and villages decimated. But the institutional changes that swept away the life supports of the poor, and the role of dominant classes in promoting those changes, were typically ignored, buried in a veritable barrage of reports that piously argued that relief programs were not good for the society and were even worse for the poor.

The present debate over social welfare in the United States reiterates the historical debate with remarkable exactness. As during earlier periods, high-minded and disinterested charges are being brought against welfare state programs (in our time mainly by intellectuals attached to corporate-funded think tanks). This chapter places these contemporary charges against the American welfare state in the context of the long history of conflicts over social welfare.

IT IS ONLY DURING the last half-century that the United States has become, in the modern sense, a "welfare state." This term has diverse meanings, reflecting in part different national traditions, and sometimes it is used to embrace virtually all state interventions in the economy and society. We use it here in the much narrower sense of government programs that provide income supports to groups deemed to be at risk in the market (such as the aged), or programs that protect people against specified contingencies, such as unemployment or sickness or marital breakdown.[1] Because social programs were inaugurated later here, and because expenditure levels remained lower than in most other affluent Western nations, the United States is often thought of as a welfare state laggard. Nevertheless, despite the late beginning and despite often strident opposition, the national programs first established in the depths of the Great Depression did endure, and were eventually expanded and elaborated. By the mid-seventies, welfare state expenditures accounted for 7.7 percent of the gross national product, and in 1985 the U.S. Census reported that 31 percent of the population and 47 percent of households received benefits from federal social insurance or means-tested programs.[2] Feldstein (1985: 94) estimates that social programs of all kinds now cost more than $300 billion a year, compared to $19 billion twenty years ago, and account for half of all federal government spending on nondefense programs.[3]

The expansion of welfare benefit programs has reduced poverty and inequality in the United States in two ways. First, the programs directly distribute income to the poor. Tax revenues gathered from those who are at least somewhat better off fund programs that provide income and services to those who are worst off. It is true that the *redistribution* effected through this tax-and-transfer mechanism has been very limited (Devine and Canak

[1] Wilensky's definition, for example, is broader: "The essence of welfare is government protected minimum standards of income, nutrition, health, housing and education, assured to every citizen as a political right" (1975:1). However, the very sweep of this definition introduces troublesome ambiguities, for it embraces a range of public services, including education, which may or may not have the effect of ensuring minimum living standards. See Alber (1985) for a knowledgeable discussion of alternative definitions of the welfare state.

[2] *New York Times,* April 17, 1985. The largest source of these benefits was, of course, the Social Security program. Consistent with these data, Caplow et al. (1982: 26–29) returned to Middletown and found that a solid majority of families receive federal benefits today, compared to only one-third even during the depths of the Great Depression.

[3] After adjusting for inflation, there has been a sixfold increase in real outlays between 1965 and 1985, and an increase in the share of the GNP absorbed by the social programs from 2.9% to 7.7% (Feldstein 1985: 94).

1986). Governments typically fund relief programs for the poor by taxing the middle class rather than the rich, and the United States is certainly no exception. Nevertheless, the most extreme destitution was relieved, and as social welfare spending increased, the poverty rate dropped, from 30 percent in 1950 to a low of 11 percent in 1973. Danziger and Plotnick (1982: 45) estimate that in 1976, three-quarters of those who would otherwise have fallen below the poverty line were lifted out of poverty by cash and in-kind transfers. Moreover, it is not only the very poor whose position has been improved. The expansion of the welfare state effectively counteracted a marked upward trend in the income inequality that was being generated by the market during the three decades after World War II (Reynolds and Smolensky 1977; Danziger, Haveman, and Plotnick, 1981; Plotnick and Skidmore 1975).

The other way that welfare state programs reduce poverty is by strengthening the bargaining position of working people, particularly those with little leverage in the labor market. The social programs remove people from the work force, with the result that the ranks of the reserve army of labor are thinned. We tend to overlook this effect because, once freed of the obligation to sell their labor, groups such as the aged or the disabled come to be defined as "unemployable." But before the protective programs were established, many of the aged and the disabled did work; and prior to Aid to Families with Dependent Children and the food stamp program, most impoverished mothers and their children also foraged for whatever work they could get. Programs that make it possible for millions of the old or the disabled or impoverished mothers to survive without work or the search for work obviously tighten labor markets, and thus buttress the bargaining power of those who remain in the labor force in contests over wages and working conditions.

The existence of social welfare also affects power relations in the labor market in a less direct way. When working people are made more secure by sources of income that do not depend on the market, when they know they can turn to unemployment or relief benefits, they are likely to become a little bolder and more demanding in their dealings with employers. The availability of social provision thus strengthens the position of workers by making them more secure, and this is especially important for nonunionized low-wage workers, who are otherwise close to the precipice of sheer want.

Of course, other economic and political conditions also bear on the relative power of workers and may offset the effects of welfare state programs. For example, the expansion of the welfare state in the United States in the late 1960s and early 1970s was rapidly followed by a series of sectoral and locational changes in the pattern of investment which shifted employment growth from high-wage industrial jobs to low-wage service jobs, and from the Rust Belt central cities (where many of the poor, especially the minority poor, had concentrated) to the Sun Belt and the metropolitan fringe. Moreover, the expansion of social welfare was followed rapidly by the influx of baby-boom workers and of greater numbers of women into the labor market, by the decline in union membership and strength, and by the erosion of the legislative protection of the minimum wage. Equally important, the effects of an expanded welfare state in strengthening workers have been offset by an aggressive employer campaign to drive down labor costs. Thus the welfare state has not been the sole or even the main determinant of worker power in the last two decades, but rather has helped to partially offset the factors that were eroding worker power. Even this, of course, is a major achievement.

We emphasize, however, that *the achievements of the welfare state are largely the result of the fact that social welfare programs generate what are called, in the current debate, "work disincentives."*[4] We underline this point because it is exactly the reverse of conservative charges against welfare state programs. As attempts to slash these programs have gained momentum in the last decade, so have public claims that they are ineffective and even worsen the poverty they are intended to alleviate, precisely because they discourage work efforts or generate work disincentives. These claims are so egregious that they might well be called the Great Relief Hoax. They are a hoax because they contradict what might other-

---

[4] See Stigler (1946) for one of the earliest contemporary formulations of this problem.

wise be obvious: that people whose labor is of little value in the market are better off when they receive income protections, and that most other workers are also better off when they no longer have to compete with such vulnerable workers. But the Great Relief Hoax is not an invention of our time. It has a very long history.

ECONOMIC DISLOCATION AND DEMANDS FOR RELIEF

The first relief programs that could reasonably be construed as predecessors to the modern welfare state emerged with the breakdown of traditional agricultural economies and the rise of capitalist markets. Public arrangements for the relief of the poor—arrangements the Webbs (1963: 29) called the "new statecraft dealing with destitution"—were forged in Northern Europe and England in the first half of the sixteenth century, in the wake of severe economic disturbance and social strife. The forces that would shape social provision over the succeeding centuries were already apparent. Economic dislocation and the attendant disruption of social life not only led to vagrancy and crime among the poor but sometimes made them "unruly" and demanding, and relief programs were everywhere designed to restore order by providing aid.

As capitalist labor markets spread, social strife over poor relief periodically intensified. More and more people were drawn or forced out of traditional agriculture and into wage labor, out of the villages and into the cities. They became totally dependent on market employment for their subsistence, and were thus totally exposed to the often terrible vicissitudes of the market. When periodic downturns or massive market shifts left large numbers unemployed (a term that was not even invented until markets in human labor were established on a large scale), or forced wages below subsistence, people often mobilized in threatening protests and demanded aid. Thus in the late eighteenth and early nineteenth centuries, in the aftermath of accelerating enclosure, rising grain prices, the destruction of the handloom weaving trade, and other market developments, the English countryside seethed with insurgency. And for a long time, even after capitalist markets were well established, the poor were strengthened in their demands for social protection by the precapitalist idea of a social compact between rich and poor, a compact that obligated the rich to provide for the poor at times of great need in exchange for their service and deference. This pressure from below frequently forced the expansion of relief, and in England it was sufficiently threatening to sustain relatively liberal relief-giving for long periods.[5]

Even in the United States, where the idea of a social compact was weaker, and where employers were not politically restrained by the power of an aristocratic class with roots in a traditional landed economy, pressures from below for social protection could not be ignored at times of widespread economic hardship.[6] The most dramatic of these surges appears to have occurred in the mid-nineteenth century, in the midst of the decades-long wave of immigration from famine-ridden Ireland and on the eve of industrialization. Annual reports compiled by Katz (1986: 37) from the state of New York, for example, show that the outdoor relief rolls jumped from 11,937 in 1840 to 63,764 in 1850 to 174,403 in 1860, while the poorhouse population increased as well.

The contemporary American welfare state was also initiated, and then expanded, in response to pressure from below. The massive unemployment of the Great Depression stimulated a wave of protests demanding "bread or wages." Local government authorities, their revenues depleted by the economic collapse, were both stymied in responding to these demands and fearful of resisting them. To cope with their dilemma, they lobbied in an increasingly alarmist spirit for federal emergency relief measures, until then unprecedented in the United States. In the spring of 1933, only weeks after he took office, Franklin Roosevelt pushed a relatively

---

[5] See Piven and Cloward (1985: chap. 2) for an extended discussion of the relationship between the displacement of people from traditional agricultural economies and the emergence of relief.
[6] Much of the history of popular political struggles over poor relief in the United States before the Great Depression remains to be written. The historical studies remain sparse. See Mohl (1971) on New York City before 1825. See Katz (1986, chap. 1) for a brief overview of popular demands for relief in the United States. Some references to demands of the unemployed for relief can be found in Gutman (1976: 60–61); Foner (1947: 162); Feder (1936: 32–5, 52); and Reznick (1933: 31).

liberal relief program through the Congress—the first step in the creation of the contemporary American welfare state. Within eighteen months, 20 million people, fully 16 percent of the population, were receiving relief payments (Piven and Cloward 1971: chap. 2; Patterson 1981: chap. 4).

In the 1960s, there was a new upsurge from below, this time composed of blacks displaced from southern agriculture. As mass protests escalated, threatening to disrupt the precarious regional and racial accommodations on which national Democratic leaders relied, the Kennedy and Johnson administrations responded by liberalizing and expanding the programs initiated in the 1930s, as well as by introducing new programs in housing, health, and nutrition. Furthermore, a good many corporate leaders went along with this liberalization, at least for a time. Not only were they chastened by black riots in the biggest cities of the nation, but the fantastic economic expansion in the period following World War II had softened business opposition to social programs. Indeed, commentators began to refer to the emergence of a new domestic accord between capital and labor. One important feature of that accord was the acceptance of expanded welfare state programs, which some analysts began to call the "social wage" in recognition of working-class stakes in the welfare state.

EMPLOYER OPPOSITION TO RELIEF

Except at moments when widespread insurgency from the bottom threatened social peace, economic elites resisted the demands of the poor. For one thing, the wealthy resented the cost of relief, as evidenced by recurrent complaints about the poor rates or the tax rates. But the opposition was as deep and persistent as it was because employer groups feared that relief provided to particularly vulnerable groups—the unemployed or the aged or the very young—would have far-reaching effects on all working people. Employers understood that by shielding working people from some of the hazards of the market, social programs blunted market sanctions and thus reduced the still formidable power of employers over workers. Moreover, for just this reason, the very *idea* of social provision was dangerously subversive of market ideology.[7] Because the stakes were high, struggles for social protection from below were always answered by resistance from above. Accordingly, once a measure of social peace was restored, employers pressed to restrict and reshape the programs. They exerted themselves to lower benefits, to tighten eligibility criteria so fewer people would receive benefits, and to attach such punitive conditions to the receipt of aid that few people would willingly apply for it. Such measures were intended, of course, to restore the compulsion to sell labor on whatever terms the market offered.

Furthermore, new market conditions sometimes provoked employer opposition even to long-established relief programs, usually as part of a larger campaign to increase worker discipline. This was especially likely when employers were confronted by intensified competition. To maintain or restore profits, they tried to extract more from their workers, whether by speeding up the pace of work or lowering wages or both. And they tried to strip workers of social protections in order to make them acquiesce to these new conditions. Conflicts over relief, in short, have always been at the heart of broader class conflicts over power in market relations.

Even in the sixteenth century, it was apparent that a good deal was at stake in the organization of relief arrangements, that relief was not merely a modest system of redistribution, but that the extent of relief and the methods by which it was distributed affected power relations between classes. Accordingly, from the start enormous energy and inventiveness were invested in devising relief programs that carefully scrutinized and categorized supplicants (the impotent versus the able-bodied, the resident

[7] The meaning of the growth in the relief rolls in the mid-nineteenth century, and of subsequent attacks on relief, is sometimes muddied by the issue of the use of relief as political patronage. Thus Katz (1986: 36) writes that as the relief rolls grew, so did "a complex network linking the poor, some local businessmen and professionals, and ward politicians in an exchange of welfare, cash and votes." But this thesis should be treated with caution, given the ease with which outdoor relief was subsequently eliminated in the big cities where patronage politics was well established. By contrast, Civil War pensions, a form of social provision that tended to reach the somewhat better off, were indeed widely used as patronage, and steadily expanded in the closing decades of the century. This was during the very period in which the virtual elimination of outdoor relief in the big cities of the nation was justified by the argument that relief was susceptible to patronage abuse. On Civil War pensions, see Keller (1977: 506).

versus the vagrant), hedged in the giving of aid with elaborate conditions, subjected recipients to strict disciplinary regimens and close surveillance, and exposed them to public rituals of degradation as "paupers." Otherwise, it was feared that social provision would encourage the poor to shun work, or rather, to shun the kinds of work and the terms of work for which they were deemed fit.

Efforts to shape relief arrangements so they would not intrude on market relations virtually define the history of social welfare, or at least the history of elite efforts to shape the programs. Thus the stratagem of requiring those who received aid to enter workhouses was recurrently attempted and recurrently fell into disuse, partly because the poor themselves were outraged by these institutions (and sometimes tore them down), but also because the better off objected to the higher costs of indoor relief.[8] As the outdoor relief rolls were slashed during subsequent decades, total costs actually rose because substantial numbers remained in the far more costly poorhouses (Katz 1986: 37).[9] Moreover, costs aside, manufacturers were always wary of the possibility that the workhouse, or any organized work-relief program, would nurture nascent forms of social production to compete with the market. In effect, strident opposition by manufacturers to useful production ensured that work-relief programs would be costly, since whatever goods were produced could not be marketed. Under these constraints, after a flurry of reform enthusiasm, enforced work usually degenerated into meaningless tasks like breaking stones. And the workhouse, no matter that it was proclaimed a "House of Industry" by Benthamite reformers, became a place so unspeakably vile no one would enter it except on penalty of starvation. That, from the perspective of reformers, was in a way its virtue. As we have said elsewhere,

---

[8] This problem was first delineated by T. H. Marshall (1964) some decades ago when he explored the tensions between the capitalist markets and the social rights that had come to be associated with citizenship.

[9] In 1870, New York State spent an average of $109.59 for each of its 15,343 poorhouse inmates, and an average of $8.96 for each of the 101,796 people who received outdoor relief (Katz 1986: 293–4, n. 29).

What begins as a great expansion of direct relief, and then turns into some form of work relief, ends finally with a sharp contraction of the rolls. . . . Meanwhile, the few who [are] allowed to remain on the rolls . . . [are] . . . once again subjected to the punitive and degrading treatment which has been used to buttress the work ethos since the inception of relief. (Piven and Cloward 1971: 348)

Thus, in the 1830s, the English ruling class mobilized a largely successful attempt to eliminate outdoor relief. In part, they were reacting to the fact that the relief rolls had swelled steadily over the previous century, absorbing large numbers of the rural poor who had been displaced from agriculture. In part, they were acting to satisfy the need for a willing labor force to serve in the emerging factory system; in Polanyi's words, "industrial capitalism was ready to be started" (1957: 102). All that was required for the great industrial takeoff was an unimpeded market in human labor.

In place of outdoor relief, the New Poor Law Commissioners of 1834 called for the workhouse.

Into such a house none will enter voluntarily; work, confinement, and discipline, will deter the indolent and vicious; and nothing but extreme necessity will induce any to accept . . . the sacrifice of their accustomed habits and gratifications. (Piven and Cloward 1971: 33–4)

If relief was available only in places so feared and hated, then the rising manufacturing class of England could be assured that no one who could possibly work would turn to relief. Willingness to enter the workhouse was thus, in itself, an infallible test of eligibility.

A broadly similar mobilization against relief occurred in the United States in the closing decades of the nineteenth century. American communities had more or less replicated the English parish-based poor-relief system, with its combination of the workhouse or almshouse and aid to at least some of the poor in their own homes (as well as variable local arrangements for indenturing or auctioning off paupers, practices that were more likely in small towns than in big cities). With these arrangements, American communities also replicated the conflicts that pervaded the English system. Accordingly, periodic efforts to stem pauperism by replacing outdoor relief with poorhouses or workhouses began with colonial development (Mohl 1971; Alexander 1983; Katz 1986: chap. 1). These "reforms," while perhaps more successful than in England, were nevertheless limited in their application because it was widely understood by local elites that the often turbulent poor would not submit to the almshouse or the workhouse.

Beginning in the mid-1870s, in the wake of the relief expansion that had begun some three decades earlier, public outdoor relief came under sustained and concerted attack. The attack was part of a larger effort by industrialists to cope with the reckless expansion and falling prices of the period (Gordon, Edwards, and Reich 1982: 106 and *passim*). Moreover, these were the years of the great railroad strikes, and the specter of an insurrectionary working class loomed large. Spurred by their own need to survive in an era of fierce competition, industrialists struggled to reduce production costs, mainly by mechanizing to eliminate skilled workers and gain more control over the production process. Accordingly, they attacked unions and recruited millions of immigrants to flood the labor market, in an effort that Gordon, Edwards, and Reich characterize as the "homogenization" of the labor force. And to deter resistance to the changing terms of work, they also inaugurated —in partnership with the new charity organization societies—a largely successful campaign against public outdoor relief in most of the big cities of the country.

The corporate-funded charity organization society movement took its lead from a society established in London in 1869. Thereafter, the movement spread rapidly as similar societies were inaugurated in most big American cities.[10] The Charity Organization Society of New York, established in 1882, listed among its patrons such names as William Waldorf Astor, August Belmont,

[10] Reznick (1956: 297) reports that by 1883 there were 25 charity societies, and the number more than doubled in the following decade.

Andrew Carnegie, J. Pierpont Morgan, and Mrs. Cornelius Vanderbilt (Brandt 1908: 266). The main goal of this movement was to eliminate outdoor relief on the grounds that it supported all manner of wicked behavior among the lower orders, especially malingering. In place of outdoor relief, the charity organization societies recommended a closely controlled, scientific philanthropy dedicated to correcting the moral turpitude they believed was the cause of poverty. However, a local clergyman, writing to Frederic C. Howe, a trustee of the Cleveland Charity Organization Society, saw it rather differently:

> Your society, with its board of trustees made up of steel magnates, coal operators, and employers is not really interested in charity. If it were, it would stop the twelve-hour day; it would increase wages and put an end to the cruel killing and maiming of men. It is interested in getting its own wreckage out of sight. . . . Christ himself might have been turned over by you to the police department as a "vagrant without visible means of support." (Cited in Bremner 1956: 54)

While reform campaigns against outdoor relief had occurred before in the United States, never were these efforts as vigorous or uncompromising as in the late nineteenth century. Public outdoor relief was suspended in New York City in 1874, except for the provision of coal in the winter, and was simply eliminated in Brooklyn in 1878 and in Philadelphia in 1879. In the next few years, funds for relief were slashed in Providence, where expenditures dropped from $150,051 in 1978 to $7,333 a year later; in Cleveland, outlays were cut from $95,000 in 1878 to $17,000 in 1880. Comparable cuts were made in Chicago and Washington. The New York Association for Improving the Condition of the Poor even opposed "soup houses" because they did not distinguish between those who were deserving and those who were not. By the turn of the century, public outdoor relief had virtually been eliminated in the big cities, although the campaign was less effective in many smaller towns (Mohl 1983: 41–2; Keller 1977).

Employer concern with relief mounted again in the early 1930s, as the rapid implementation of the new emergency relief program helped calm the protests that had generated it. Earlier, in the panicked months of 1932, some prominent business leaders had themselves called for national emergency relief measures (although businessmen were riled when the new federal relief agency tried to create jobs on public projects for the unemployed: they protested the added costs, and were indignant at the prospect of government intrusion into their markets[11]). But once the panic of 1932 subsided, businessmen and southern planters began to complain of the disruptive effects they thought federal minimum relief payments were exerting on local wage rates (Piven and Cloward 1971: chap. 3).

Accordingly, and true to the historic pattern, Roosevelt terminated emergency relief in the mid-1930s. In its place, he proposed a new work relief program for the able-bodied, as well as an intricately fashioned set of measures (incorporated in the Social Security Act) which provided benefits for some of the unemployed and for some of the old, the disabled, and orphaned children. The political pressures that shaped these measures were the same dualistic pressures that have always shaped welfare state programs. On the one hand, and especially in the still-tumultuous 1930s, there were pressures from those who were still poor, often desperately poor. As Domhoff says in his explanation of the act, "distress and discontent [were] bubbling up from the lower levels within the depression-ridden society" (Domhoff 1970: 217; see also Piven and Cloward 1971: chap. 3, and 1977: chap. 2). On the other hand, employer objections to liberal emergency relief mounted, helping to prompt new legislation.

Until this time, business had consistently rejected proposals for old-age or unemployment insurance. But once federal legislation seemed inevitable, at least some big-business leaders were willing to play a role in molding it. Some provisions of the Social Security

---

[11] See the discussion of business opposition to work relief during this period in Piven and Cloward (1971: 80-4); see Esping-Anderson (1986) for a general discussion of the sources of this opposition in aspects of the modern welfare state which promote the "decommodification" of production.

bill originated in the work of a number of business-backed policy groups, including the Business Advisory Council of the Department of Commerce (headed by Gerald Swope of General Electric), Industrial Relations Counsellors (the consulting firm created and controlled by John D. Rockefeller, Jr.), and the American Association for Labor Legislation, which had been largely responsible for crafting the Wisconsin unemployment plan on which part of the act was modeled. Not surprisingly, a number of these "business statesmen" came from the retail sector, which had a stake in measures that promised to sustain mass purchasing power during economic downturns. A few leaders from such capital-intensive industries as oil also lent some support to the bill, since they did not depend on low-wage labor (see Ferguson 1984 for this argument).

But large manufacturers that did depend on low-wage labor, as well as smaller businesses generally, opposed the act. The chambers of commerce and the National Association of Manufacturers were adamant in their opposition, as were organized agricultural interests, particularly southern plantation owners who relied on an ample supply of cheap labor. Moreover, these southern interests carried great weight in the New Deal and particularly in the Congress, where both the House Ways and Means Committee and the Senate Finance Committee were chaired by southerners (Alston and Ferrie 1985a: 105).[12]

The intricate provisions of the Social Security Act, particularly when contrasted with the liberal federal emergency relief program it replaced (or even when contrasted with the staff recommendations on social security), can be understood as a compromise between the conflicting needs to quell unrest and to ensure a supply of low-wage labor. The legislation carefully restricted eligibility for old-age and unemployment insurance: whole categories of workers, including agricultural workers, were excluded from coverage in both programs. Among those in eligible categories, only workers with a personal history of steady employment qualified, and

---

[12] For a more general discussion of the role of the South in the New Deal, see Key (1984); Tindall (1965); Piven and Cloward (1977: chap. 5); Alston and Ferrie (1985b).

benefits were pegged to former earnings. Since unemployment insurance was the more market-sensitive program because it provided aid to able-bodied adults in their prime, the states were ceded considerable authority in eligibility determination, in setting benefit levels, and in specifying the duration of coverage, an arrangement that made the program more sensitive to local labor-market conditions and employer demands. The result was a system of social provision that in some ways actually underlined market sanctions and incentives while in other ways straining against them: protection against adversity was extremely modest and could be earned only through work, and the stratification of the labor market was at least partially reproduced in the schedule of program benefits.

The effort to design social programs that meshed with the market was even more evident in the "categorical programs" that provided aid for some of the impoverished not covered by old-age or unemployment insurance. The categorical programs singled out as eligible only those of the poor who were unlikely to be of much value as workers (the aged, the orphaned, and the blind). Control over the setting of benefit levels and the administration of these restricted programs was lodged in the states or localities, where local employers could use their influence to gain whatever additional restrictions were needed to ensure that the programs would mesh precisely with the requirements of local labor markets. As Quadagno says, "a 'states-rights' agenda served to maintain the confidence of the . . . business community" (1984: 645). Southern congressmen who packed the House Ways and Means Committee even succeeded in eliminating language requiring states to set old-age-assistance grant levels so as to provide "a reasonable subsistence compatible with decency and health." Their fear was that funds for the elderly would reach younger members of black families, who would then be less pliant workers.[13]

---

[13] See Piven and Cloward (1971: 115–16). See also Alston and Ferrie (1985a) and Quadagno (1984: 643). See Weir (1986) for a different explanation of unemployment policy that generally emphasizes the impact of constraints arising from administrative and electoral-representative arrangements. See also James Patterson (1967: 144–5) and Richard Bensel (1984: 168) for a discussion of the conflicts generated by the patronage implications of relief expenditure.

These carefully designed arrangements led over time to the institutionalization of a series of welfare state programs so closely "market-conforming" as to make the United States notorious among Western democracies for the narrow and niggardly protections it provided. Until the 1960s, even those of the aged fortunate enough to be covered by Social Security pensions earned through work—the Old Age and Survivors and Dependents Insurance (OASDI) provisions of the Social Security Act—received benefits so low that many of them remained in poverty, and many remained in the labor force as well.

The expansion of the welfare state that was widely considered part of the class accord in the period immediately following World War II was once again interrupted by employer opposition, this time prompted by the economic convulsions of the 1970s. Analysts dispute the reasons for the onset of rapid inflation and declining corporate profit rates. But whether the causes lay in the inflationary impact of the Vietnam War, the oil-price shocks, or the longer-term problems associated with the declining competitiveness of the American economy, it is clear that American business sought to reduce the impact of these instabilities with a renewed assault against the working class. Employers mobilized to cut wages, slash workplace protections, crush unions, and discredit the very possibility of worker power with an ideological campaign threatening capital flight if workers resisted the new demands.

As during earlier periods, the effort to restrict or eliminate welfare state protections is an important part of the business mobilization against the working class. In part, the intent is to redistribute income upward: sharp tax cuts are implemented for the rich, and the revenue losses are to be at least partly offset by cuts in the social programs. In part, the intent is to reduce the labor-market power of workers by intensifying economic insecurity.

CONTEMPORARY EMPLOYER OPPOSITION

To better appreciate the reasons for the current mobilization against the welfare state, it is worthwhile to review some of the estimates made of the work effort that is in a sense "lost" as a consequence of the expansion of the social programs. Overall, it is clear that expansion of the programs has removed millions of people from the labor market, resulting, of course, in a "tighter" labor market than would otherwise exist. Consider the effects of Social Security payments on the work-force participation of the aged. OASDI benefit expenditures reached $182 billion in fiscal 1986, or 4.4 percent of GNP and one-third of federal outlays on nondefense items (Feldstein 1985: 102). In 1948, half of all men over sixty-five were in the labor force. As Social Security expanded, the proportion dropped to 20 percent. Meanwhile, with the enactment of optional retirement at sixty-two, the proportion of men aged sixty-two to sixty-four who were labor-force participants fell from 80 percent in 1961 to 60 percent in 1978 (Burhauser and Tolley 1978: 449–53).[14]

Social welfare measures have had similar if less dramatic effects on the labor-force participation of other groups. The expansion of the disability programs from 687,000 recipients in 1960 to 4,352,-000 in 1975 appears to be correlated with a sizable drop in the labor-force participation not only of relatively older workers but even of prime-age men forty-five to fifty-four years old. Ellwood and Summers (1986) report that 4 percent of these prime-age men were out of the labor force in 1960, but 9 percent in 1980; for blacks, the percentage of nonparticipants had gone from 7 percent to 16 percent. Mead (1986: 133–4) draws on a Congressional Budget Office (1982) study to blame relatively generous benefits for the fact that the disability rolls doubled between 1969 and 1976, and that the proportion of recipients returning to work each year fell. In 1977, 28 percent of those on the disability rolls received the equivalent of over three-fifths of their prior earnings, while 14 percent actually received more than 100 percent, a result made possible by the fact that disability benefits are scaled to family size, while wages are not. Moreover, disability recipients receive Medicare, and often also receive income from other programs, such as veterans' benefits. Mead concludes, not without indignation, that the

---

[14] For a concise review of some studies of the work-disincentive effects on the aged of Social Security benefits, see Danziger, Haveman, and Plotnick (1981).

main role of disability programs has been to let poorer, older, and less skilled workers retire early.[15] Of course, these data probably also reflect the increased use of disability benefits to cope with the involuntary unemployment resulting from deindustrialization, which has left many displaced workers trapped in communities where there are no longer even low-wage jobs to be found. However—and this is Mead's point and the point of the critics generally—without recourse to programs like disability, many of these displaced industrial workers would be quicker to take whatever employment they could get.

Or consider unemployment insurance. In the decades since 1935, coverage has been extended to more workers and benefits have been liberalized, largely by congressional action extending the duration of coverage during periods of high unemployment. In the recession of 1973–74, for example, the basic 26-week period of coverage was extended to 65 weeks (and many workers displaced from jobs by foreign competition also received benefits under the Trade Adjustment Assistance Act). As a result, two out of three of the 12 million unemployed received benefits during that severe downturn. Again, there are disputes about the precise effects of unemployment insurance on work effort. However, almost all studies agree that the availability of unemployment benefits increases the length of unemployment spells.[16] Mead cites a government survey conducted in 1976 to show that unemployment benefits not only substantially extended the length of time out of work but also raised the wage expectations of the unemployed:

> The average worker who had lost or left a job was prepared to enter a new one only if it paid 7 percent *more* than his or her last position. While 35 percent of these jobless were willing to return to work for less than they formerly earned, 38 percent demanded more money. Even after fifty weeks out of work the average respondent persisted in expecting nearly as high a wage

[15] Parsons (1980) and Leonard (1979) also report large disincentive effects of the disability programs. However, Haveman and Wolfe (1981) found significantly smaller disincentive effects.
[16] Danziger, Haveman, and Plotnick (1981) review these studies. See also Feldstein (1974), and Garfinkle and Plotnick.

as in his or her old job. If the jobless demanding a wage increase were defined as voluntarily unemployed and excluded from the statistics, unemployment as officially measured would drop by more than a point, more than three points for nonwhites. (Mead 1986: 72)

Disincentive effects were also found when the federal government sponsored a series of guaranteed-income experiments. Low-income families in the experimental groups were provided with income and were compared with control groups in several locations, including New Jersey, Seattle, Denver, rural Iowa, North Carolina, and Gary, Indiana.[17] While the level of experimental benefits varied between sites and among test groups, it was relatively generous compared to the means-tested programs. And as is to be expected, the benefits reduced work effort. In New Jersey, husbands reduced work effort by 5 percent and wives by 25 percent; Seattle and Denver, which had more generous income supports, showed work-effort reduction of 9 and 20 percent by husbands and wives respectively.

By now, the research literature on work-disincentive effects is voluminous. In an exhaustive review of over 100 of these studies, Danziger, Haveman, and Plotnick (1981) concluded that the major income-transfer programs, including those for the elderly, have reduced the total annual hours of work in the economy by an estimated 4.8 percent (see also Masters and Garfinkle 1978). Lampman's estimate is somewhat higher, about 7 percent of total hours worked, and he also points out that the reduction is concentrated among groups with relatively low productivity (1979). These percentages are, however, more significant than they might at first seem. They suggest that if the programs were eliminated, and if employment did not expand faster than the work force, the increased search for jobs by former beneficiaries could raise the unemployment level by 5 to 7 percent.

The Reagan administration's efforts to slash the programs should be viewed in the light of these effects. The immediate

[17] New Jersey, Seattle, and Denver were the largest experimental sites.

consequence of program cuts has been to expand the number of people searching for employment, and to lower the terms on which they will accept employment.[18] The other and more pervasive consequence is to weaken workers generally in their relations with employers. Thus when the duration of unemployment benefits was slashed despite widespread industrial displacement, the proportion of the unemployed who received benefits fell from two-thirds to one-third—the lowest level since the Great Depression. Inevitably, those still working fear the prospect of job loss more, and because they do are more likely to concede to employer demands. Those who are already without work are forced more quickly to underbid each other in the competition for jobs. Meanwhile, the termination of the Comprehensive Education and Training Act removed 400,-000 people from public service jobs, and a relentless purge of the disability rolls succeeded in removing nearly half a million people, although vigorous lobbying and litigation resulted in the restoration of 291,000 cases to the rolls.[19]

Cuts in AFDC, Medicaid, and food-stamp benefits have similar effects on many low-wage service-sector workers, particularly part-time, temporary, and home workers, who are less likely to be covered by unemployment or disability insurance. Moreover, workers with these protections turn to the means-tested programs when their unemployment benefits are exhausted or when they find their disability benefits terminated. Without these residual protections, the worker's fear of being fired that buttresses employer power is intensified. The Reagan administration has worked

---

[18] A study by the congressional Office of Technology Assessment found that of the 11.5 million workers who lost jobs because of plant shutdowns or relocations between 1979 and 1984, only 60% found new jobs, and of these, 45% had taken pay cuts, often sharp pay cuts (*New York Times*, February 7, 1985).

[19] The criteria defining medical eligibility were eased in the 1960s and 1970s, and vocational factors were introduced in determining suitability for employment, so that, for example, functionally illiterate people were judged disabled if they were physically unable to perform manual labor. Critics charged that as a consequence the disability rolls had become populated by many people who could in fact work, and in 1980 the Carter administration obtained legislation authorizing a general case review. The Reagan administration used this legislative authorization to purge the rolls by imposing stricter medical criteria and eliminating any consideration of vocational or occupational factors. At this writing, the Reagan administration is asking the Supreme Court to rule that it has the authority to eliminate vocational criteria. If it is successful, perhaps more than a million of the disabled could be removed from the rolls.

hard to cut the means-tested programs. It has repeatedly demanded reductions in program budgets, albeit with mixed success.[20] (In point of fact, AFDC recipients have suffered most from
the failure of the states to raise benefit levels to keep pace with
inflation, as we will note in the next chapter. But this process was
well under way when Reagan took office.) The Reagan administration has also vigorously advocated forced-work programs for
AFDC recipients, and workfare programs are now being implemented in about thirty states. And it has twice floated proposals
for radically restructuring the AFDC and nutritional programs by
devolving administrative and fiscal responsibility to the states.
Such a move would make these programs more vulnerable to
business pressures, since businessmen can and do bargain with
state and local officials for tax and policy concessions as the price
of locating in one place or another.[21] The original administration
decentralization proposal in 1981, dubbed a "New Federalism,"
was allowed to die when the governors voiced loud objections. But
the administration is trying again. An internal administration
memo explains the current effort at decentralization with the disin-
genuous argument that "individual needs for public assistance can
be assessed most effectively at the level of government closest to
the need."

The elimination of any federal standards, which in the past
lifted benefit levels particularly in low-wage and low-benefit states,
is said to be justified on similar grounds: "Because individual needs
vary, public assistance benefits should not be tied to a federally-
determined standard." Lest this talk about individual needs lead
anyone to forget the main issue, the memo takes care to reaffirm

---

[20] After implementing the first round of administration cuts in 1981, the Congress resisted the
draconian cuts subsequently proposed. The actual reductions were not anything like the crippling
cutbacks the Reagan administration had demanded. A report prepared by the Urban Institute
estimated that through 1984, AFDC outlays were down 14% compared to the 28% the Reagan
administration wanted, and food-stamp outlays were also down 14% compared to the administration's attempted cut of 52% (Palmer and Sawhill 1984: Table 6.1). Even these more modest cuts
forced hundreds of thousands deeper into poverty. See U.S. House of Representatives, Committee
on Ways and Means (1985).
[21] For a more extended discussion of the political significance of decentralization efforts, see Piven
and Cloward (1985: 128–32).

the old principle of less eligibility: "No worker should be able to better his financial condition by reducing or quitting work and collecting public assistance, and public assistance should not make a non-worker financially better off than a worker."[22] To guarantee the implementation of this principle, the administration proposes to decentralize the programs. The funds from 59 existing programs that provide services and benefits to the poor would become available for state and local experiments to "reduce dependency" on government assistance. Over time, this strategy could facilitate massive cuts in federal funding.

The persistence and shrewdness of the administration in this and other efforts to cut welfare state programs reveals its seriousness of purpose. And that purpose is an old one. The social programs are the focus of business opposition in the eighties for much the same reason they have always been. The existence of the programs, whether poor relief or unemployment insurance, provides working people with a measure of security, and therefore with a measure of power.

THE BRIEF AGAINST SOCIAL PROVISION

Whether the object is to curtail benefits recently won or to whittle away long-established protections, employer campaigns against relief or welfare must necessarily also be public relations campaigns of considerable sensitivity, particularly in the contemporary United States, where electoral-representative arrangements require that a good many working people be persuaded to support (or ignore) policies that are against their own interests. Naturally enough, such campaigns do not explain the questions of class power that are at issue, or deal with the way changing economic relations are affecting the circumstances of different classes. Instead, campaigns against social provision invariably take the form of public arguments that relief is in fact injurious to everyone, and especially to those who receive it.

---

[22] These quotations are from an undated memo circulated privately by the White House Welfare Reform Task Force entitled "Public Assistance to Alleviate Poverty."

The paradigmatic case against relief was developed in England in the early 1830s at a time when English manufacturing interests were slashing outdoor relief in order to force displaced agricultural workers into the newly forming industrial proletariat. Accordingly, the great liberal thinkers of the day, such as Townsend, Malthus, Bentham, and Burke, discovered that the well-being of the nation demanded that poor relief be abolished, or at least be sharply restricted.

> Scholars proclaimed in unison that a science had been discovered which put the laws governing man's world beyond any doubt. It was at the behest of these laws that compassion was removed from the hearts, and a stoic determination to renounce human solidarity in the name of the greatest happiness for the greatest number gained the dignity of secular religion. The mechanism of the market was asserting itself and clamoring for completion: human labor had to be made a commodity. (Polanyi 1957: 102)

No doubt the English ruling class drew comfort from the theory that it was not the economic dislocations of the previous century which were responsible for the misery of the poor, but the giving of relief itself. As the Poor Law Commission of 1834 said, outdoor relief, by repealing the "law of nature by which the effects of each man's improvidence or misconduct are borne by himself and his family," had generated a "train of evils: the loss of self-respect, responsibility, prudence, temperance, hard work, and the other virtues that had once sustained him. It was this degradation of character, more than material impoverishment, that defined the pauper" (Himmelfarb 1985: 162–3). As in so many other matters, Alexis de Tocqueville summed up the core of the what was and continues to be the elite wisdom:

> Any permanent, regular, administrative system whose aim will be to provide for the needs of the poor will breed more miseries than it can cure, will deprave the population that it wants to

help and comfort, will in time reduce the rich to being no more than the tenant-farmers of the poor, will dry up the sources of savings, will stop the accumulation of capital, will retard the development of trade, will benumb human industry and activity, and will culminate by bringing about a violent revolution in the State, when the number of those who receive alms will have become as large as those who give it, and the indigent, no longer being able to take from the impoverished rich the means of providing for his needs, will find it easier to plunder them of all their property at one stroke than to ask for their help. (1968: 25)

If these warnings have a familiar ring, so should the use to which they were put, in a "barrage of publicity and polemic." Ten thousand copies of the official report of the Poor Law Commissioners were sold, and another ten thousand distributed without charge. Similarly, the volumes of testimony the commission had collected were widely disseminated, and all this in the context of a larger publicity campaign involving "hundreds of lesser-known pamphleteers, justices of the peace, clergyman, magistrates, Members of Parliament, landowners, economists, philanthropists, and reformers" (Himmelfarb 1985: 154–5). To the accompaniment of this chorus of approval, the Poor Law Commissioners recommended, and the Parliament enacted, a series of reforms that attempted to make the workhouse the main form of relief in England. As Polanyi sums it up, "Psychological torture was coolly advocated and smoothly put into practice by mild philanthropists as a means of oiling the wheels of the labor mill" (1957: 82).

The broadly similar campaign against outdoor relief in the United States toward the end of the nineteenth century was accompanied by similar charges against social provision. The arguments were of course already familiar from earlier attacks on poor relief for fostering idleness and improvidence, as well as from the highly publicized English campaign for the New Poor Law. Still, the attack on outdoor relief that began in the 1870s was far more serious and sustained than earlier efforts to slash relief, and the rhetoric that accompanied it was more strident. This was, after all, the era of Herbert Spencer and the flowering of social Darwinism.[23] Blithely ignoring the massive disruptions associated with rapid industrialization, large-scale immigration, urbanization, and recurrent severe depressions, reformers pinpointed public outdoor relief as the source of the travails of poverty and social disorganization in late-nineteenth-century cities. They also produced the "data" to confirm it. Katz (1986: 86–8) describes a survey of 12,614 poorhouse inmates conducted by Dr. Charles S. Hoyt, secretary of the New York State Board of Charities, in 1874–75. It became the most widely quoted document on pauperism in the late nineteenth century, and purported to show that most inmates were long-term paupers, presumably destroyed by idleness and dependency. In fact, Hoyt reached this conclusion by administering his questionnaire only to the "fixed population" (and not to short-term inmates) as well as by including inmates of insane asylums and orphanages attached to some of the poorhouses in his sample, all of which greatly exaggerated the persistent use of relief and its deleterious effects.

No one expressed the outlook of the reformers better than Josephine Shaw Lowell, leader in the establishment of the New York State Charities Aid Association, member of the New York State Board of Charities, founder in 1882 of the New York Charity Organization Society, and in all these capacities, a leader in the campaign to abolish outdoor relief. In the midst of the depression of the 1880s that followed fast on the heels of the devastating depression of the 1870s, she declared relief to be responsible both for low wages and for poverty:

> All systematic dolegiving is proved not to be charitable. . . . Almsgiving and dolegiving are hurtful even to those who do not receive them, because they help to keep down wages by enabling those who do receive them to work for less than fair pay. No greater wrong can be done . . . to all working people. . . .

---

[23] For a discussion of the dominant intellectual views of the time, see Haskell (1977).

Almsgiving and dolegiving are hurtful to those who receive them because they lead men to remit their own exertions and depend on others. . . . false hopes are excited, the unhappy recipients of alms become dependent, lose their energy, are rendered incapable of self-support. . . . The proof that dolegiving and almsgiving do break down independence, do destroy energy, do undermine character, may be found in the growing ranks of pauperism in every city, in the fact that the larger the funds given in relief in any community, the more pressing is the demand for them. . . . Better leave people to the hard working of natural laws than to run the risk of interfering with those laws in a mischievous manner. (Lowell 1972: 3–6)

Lowell also thought that each case of poverty "is to be *radically* dealt with; that in finding fellow beings in want and suffering, the cause of the want and suffering are to be removed if possible, even if the process be as painful as plucking out an eye or cutting off a limb" (1972: 6, emphasis in original). The gruesome metaphor takes on meaning when it is recalled that prominent reformers (although not Lowell herself) recommended breaking up families—for example, by institutionalizing young children so their impoverished mothers could seek employment—as a "solution" to pauperism.[24] In fact, with the constriction of outdoor relief, many impoverished families themselves tried to place their children in orphan asylums, hoping to retrieve them when times were better.

From the depression that began in 1873, the country rolled from one economic collapse to another at intervals of only a few years. In 1874, the American Iron and Steel Institute estimated at least 1 million unemployed. By 1878, labor advocate William G. Moody estimated half the work force was either wholly or partially unemployed (Mohl 1983: 36). In the 1880s, the numbers of unemployed again reached close to a million, while 5.5 million new immigrants, many recruited by commission agents for industrial-

[24] See Bremner (1956) for the most influential study of the period. See also Katz (1986, especially pp. 72–8) for a discussion of the views of S. Humphrey Gurteen, another leader in the charity organization movement. See also Pumphrey and Pumphrey (1983) on the practice of institutionalizing the children of impoverished mothers.

ists, poured into the country. Even those lucky enough to find employment remained miserably poor. Foner reports, for example, that in the 1880s a family of four needed, at the barest minimum, about $720 a year for subsistence. Many workers, even better-paid male workers, earned much less. Government data showed that the average worker earned only a little more than a dollar a day in 1883. If the worker was exceptionally fortunate and employed year round, this would yield an annual income of less than half the subsistence minimum (Foner 1955: 20).

As for relief, Katz (1985: 47–48) reports that before outdoor relief was eliminated in Brooklyn in 1878, the practice consisted of distributing meager amounts of food (flour, potatoes, or rice but no "luxuries" such as tea or sugar) or coal, but never both in the same week. The average family probably received aid for only a very few weeks each year. Similarly, in his study of poverty in Boston, Huggins (1971: 146–7) shows that during the winter of 1893–94, when a new economic crisis caused widespread desperation, an estimated $9 was distributed to each male applicant for the whole winter season. Under these conditions, it is reasonable to surmise that neither the giving nor the withholding of relief had much to do with the moral decline of the poor which so preoccupied the reformers.

These brute economic facts notwithstanding, what Keller (1977: 504) calls the "chilling social Darwinist assumptions" held sway among the reformers. It was not the economy that needed correcting. On the contrary, as a reformer reviewing the problem of unemployment in the dark year of 1894 observed:

> In this country, despite all assertions to the contrary, there is generally work enough for everybody who is willing to work, at wages which with proper economy will enable the worker to lay something aside for a rainy day. (Shaw 1894: 29)

Rather, what was of concern to the reformers was interference with the natural laws—conceived in moral as well as economic terms—which demanded the survival of the fittest. "Hard times," Albert Shaw worried, "increase . . . the number of unworthy persons who ask aid," and he went on to assure his readers, in a review of charity society efforts in a dozen cities, that very little charity was being given at all (1894: 31). Outdoor relief, echoed the New York State Board of Charities, speaking much as did state charity boards elsewhere, is "injurious and hurtful to the unfortunate and worthy poor, demoralizing in its tendencies, a prolific source of pauperism and official corruption, and an unjust burden upon the public" (Mohl 1983: 45).

Opposition to federal emergency relief and work relief in the early 1930s sounded some of these same, by now classical, themes. In a message to Congress in 1931, as the catastrophe of the Great Depression swept through the country leaving millions unemployed, Hoover reiterated his opposition to any "government dole" with the extraordinary assertion, in the midst of a worldwide economic collapse, that the "breakdown and increased unemployment in Europe is due in part to such practices" as government relief for the unemployed (cited in Piven and Cloward 1971: 53). Similarly, in a message to Congress January 4, 1935, Roosevelt declared that emergency relief, with its relatively inclusive coverage and liberal grant levels, would be terminated. In 1935, unemployment remained at historic levels, and the economy had made only a feeble recovery. Nevertheless, Roosevelt echoed the age-old theory that relief was a major source of the malaise: "Continued dependence upon relief induces a spiritual and moral disintegration fundamentally destructive to the national fiber. . . . We must preserve not only the bodies of the unemployed from destitution but also their self-respect, their self-reliance and courage and determination" (Schlesinger, 1960: 267–8).

In the next chapter, we examine at length the contemporary rhetoric of relief reform. Here we want only to remind the reader of the close resemblance between the historic antiwelfare arguments and current charges against the welfare state, pithily captured by Nathan Glazer in his pronouncement "Our efforts to deal with distress themselves increase distress" (1971: 52). Charles Murray (1984: 68) advances the identical thesis that the expansion of social provision in the sixties and seventies had the perverse consequence of increasing poverty. Kaus (1986: 68) worries about the "effect of welfare in sustaining the underclass, umbilical-cord style." The historic contentions echo repetitively through all of these contemporary complaints.

THE APPARENT CREDIBILITY OF THE CHARGES

Why has the argument that social welfare is injurious to the poor been persuasive even at times when the programs were so small as to make the charges dubious for that reason alone? Part of the answer is in the sheer weight of well-funded propaganda. Another part is that, whether in Tocqueville's day or ours, a crude sort of evidence can usually be found to make these charges credible simply by scrutinizing the poor. Ordinarily, patterns of life among people at the bottom do not draw much attention; they are left to cope as best they can, and their coping generally includes behavior that is "deviant" according to official society. Attacks on social provision become the occasion for publicizing these patterns of life among the poor. Thus out-of-wedlock births are "discovered" by Tocqueville in nineteenth-century rural England, or by social scientists among blacks in twentieth-century America, and proclaimed to be new pathological trends, which are then attributed to social aid.

Nor does the existence of huge and presumably neutral systems of government information make the contemporary poor less susceptible to these politically motivated "discoveries." At first glance, it might seem that virtually everything that can be counted is being counted, analyzed, and reported in any case. But not quite so; the data systems are pliant. A recent example, which we will have occasion to discuss in more detail in the next chapter, is instructive. For many years, the Census had used a coding procedure that did not identify unmarried mothers when they lived in a larger household with their parents. With the rise of a public outcry about welfare and illegitimacy in the 1970s and 1980s, the Census coding procedures were altered so that unmarried mothers were sure to be identified, and the numbers reported doubled in two years (Bane and Ellwood 1984: 3, fn.1).

This is not to say that the evidence of disorganization is entirely or even mainly an artifact. Symptoms of disorganization among the poor may very well escalate during periods of relief conflict, not because of the availability of aid, but as a consequence of the economic and social dislocations that led to the expansion of relief-giving in the first place. Because these disorganizing trends coincide with the expansion of relief-giving, critics can generally find the "proof" of their contention that relief is harmful to the poor.

Thus the fluctuations in the economy which lead to material hardship and demands for relief also deprive people of the basic resources needed to sustain community and personal life. Not only market downturns but also economic growth can mean rapid shifts in the kinds of workers required, or the places in which they are required. Such dislocations not only reduce wage income for many people; they can also wipe out other resources on which social life is constructed, as when enclosure eliminated the common lands in eighteenth-century England, or when downtown business leaders joined together in urban renewal projects that displaced the poor and working class from their homes and communities in twentieth-century American cities. The costs of these market developments for people at the bottom go beyond material hardship to the rupture of ties to place, kin, community, and culture which make a coherent social and personal life possible. As a result, symptoms of social disorganization do mount. While the relief that is sometimes given at such times mitigates hardship, it can hardly repair the ruptures that result from economic dislocation. But the giving of aid does provide the occasion for invoking the spurious theory that it is relief itself that causes social and personal disorganization.

In fact, while Tocqueville abhorred "legal almsgiving," his understanding of the relationship between poverty and relief was far more complicated than the use of his opinions by latter-day intellectuals such as Himmelfarb (1985: chap. 6). Tocqueville was at some pains to make clear that the root causes of poverty were not in indiscriminate almsgiving but in the destructive effects on the poor of what he called "industrialization." Poverty was the result, in other words, of the creation of a class of workers exposed to the insecurities of the market, a development that created both great wealth and great misery. His solution was a prescient call for intervention in the economy to prevent the rapid displacement of population and promote more balanced and stable economic development (1969: 26).

But perhaps the most important reason that the charges against welfare seem to make sense is the strength of the cognitive model on which they draw, a model that gives the particular charges a coherence and persuasiveness they would otherwise lack. The model is continuously alluded to by the reformers when they speak of the "natural law" that is violated by "legal almsgiving." Natural law in England and the United States is, of course, *laissez-faire*. It is the set of ideas that asserts that not only goods but money, land, and labor are all commodities, and as commodities must be regulated, not by governments or communities, but by the market "law" of supply and demand. To do otherwise, to intrude through public action on market processes, is to court disaster by disrupting the workings of natural law. Once this mythic conception of how society is organized gained ascendancy, it became a powerful ideological resource in the periodic campaigns against social protections.

MARKET-CONFORMING PROGRAMS AND THE DEGRADATION OF THE PAUPER

There is a final, perhaps ironic point to be made about the consequences of employer-led assaults on social provision. These assaults result in programs so punitive and stigmatizing that they do indeed come over time to produce some of the demoralizing effects attributed to the fact of social provision itself. When Tocqueville (1968: 19) declaimed about the "degraded condition into which the lower classes have fallen" as a result of relief, there was perhaps this truth in his observation: people kept in misery by penurious levels of aid, and then forced to accept the degraded identity of the pauper in exchange for that aid, are likely to be stripped of their energy and morale.

Consider, for example, the institution of the workhouse or the almshouse. The workhouse was self-consciously designed to deter people from asking for aid. The method of deterrence was simply to make conditions so repugnant that the poor would strive at virtually any cost to avoid the dreaded state of the pauper. Thus workhouses and almshouses were awful: bad and insufficient food, decrepit and filthy quarters into which all sorts of unfortunates, including the diseased and frequently the insane, were indiscriminately crowded together. The fact that the receipt of aid was conditional on incarceration, and incarceration under these vile physical conditions, also made inevitable the total social degradation of the pauper. Other rituals of the workhouse, such as the separation of family members and the strict penal regimen, virtually ensured that result. The terror inspired by the workhouse did no doubt induce most of the poor to endeavor somehow to survive by their own exertions, and probably also ensured that many did not survive at all. As for those of the very young or the crippled or the sick or the old who had no other option than "the house," their physical and social degradation became an object lesson in what it meant to fail in the labor market. "The Poor Law," says Hobsbawm, "was not so much intended to help the unfortunate as to stigmatize the self-confessed failures of society" (1968: 69). A high price was paid for this social lesson in the torment inflicted on the enfeebled people who were incarcerated. Moreover, to the extent that the able-bodied also turned to the workhouse, the experience must surely have been extremely debilitating, both physically and psychologically. But the damage thus done was not attributed to the awful conditions of the workhouse or the extraordinary measures through which paupers were made into social pariahs, but rather to the insidious effects of relief itself.

Polanyi's seminal work on the English Speenhamland system has contributed to this confusion. Despite his sharp criticism of the institutional arrangements that produced a "self-regulating market" in land, commodities, and labor in the nineteenth century, and his empathy with the poor who were the victims of the campaign to commodify human labor, Polanyi nevertheless saw the spread of relief in England after 1895 as the major source of the destitution of the poor.

Although it took some time till the self-respect of the common man sank to the low point where he preferred poor relief to wages, his wages which were subsidized from public funds were bound eventually to be bottomless, and to force him upon the rates. Little by little the people of the countryside were pauperized; the adage, "once on the rates, always on the rates" was a true saying. But for the protracted effects of the allowance system [that is, poor relief] it would be impossible to explain the human and social degradation of early capitalism. (1957: 80)

Under the Speenhamland plan—which some historians claim was not in fact so widely practiced as Polanyi thought[25]—the poor-relief authorities guaranteed "the right to live" by requiring that the poor offer themselves to employers for whatever wages they could get, and by then supplementing the wages with relief benefits keyed to family size and the price of bread. As Polanyi (1957: 97) says, the Speenhamland system was "started as aid-in-wages, ostensibly benefitting the employees, but actually using public means to subsidize the employers. For the main effect of the allowance system was to depress wages below the subsistence level." The confusion in Polanyi's analysis arises from the failure to distinguish firmly between the effects on wages and morale of guaranteeing the "right to live," and the effects on wages and morale of the forced-work aspect of the Speenhamland plan. At a time when there was an enormous surplus of labor in rural England, the work demanded of those who were living on the parish must indeed have driven wages down, and this together with the general upheaval in rural life caused by the spread of markets must surely have been demoralizing. But income guarantees of themselves, stripped of the forced-work requirements, would have had quite the opposite effect. By removing large numbers of the rural population from the labor force at a time of labor surplus, relief payments unconditioned by work would have raised the price of labor and perhaps

---

[25] This is not a settled issue. See Blaug (1963) and Block and Sommers (1984).

introduced a measure of stability into the life of the rural poor at a time of wrenching instabilities. Polanyi acknowledges this possibility only very indirectly when he says that had it not been for the introduction of the anticombination laws (laws prohibiting unions) at the same time as the Speenhamland system spread, its results might have been quite different. That is a reasonable supposition. But even in the absence of worker organization, relief payments themselves, had they been severed from the forced-work component of the system, would have set a floor under rural wages. It thus seems reasonable to think that it was the use of the relief system to force the rural poor to work at any wage—"work relief" in contemporary language—that caused the general deterioration in wages and morale which many observers reported in southern England, where the plan was apparently implemented more widely.

The lesson for contemporary welfare policy seems to us clear. Market-oriented relief reforms help to produce the demoralizing effects on recipients that are attributed to the fact of social provision itself. Nowhere is this more evident than in the elaborately crafted arrangements of the contemporary American "means-tested" programs. These arrangements, which reflect a history of employer opposition, do indeed debilitate and demoralize the people who receive benefits. It is not receiving benefits that is damaging to recipients, but rather the fact that benefits are so low as to ensure physical misery and an outcast social status. Even these benefits are given only under close surveillance (including, until recently, midnight raids, "suitable-home" laws, and "man-in-the-house" rules) and are conditioned on modern rituals of degradation such as publicized "hot lines" encouraging relatives, friends, and neighbors to report information on welfare recipients—all of which surely have disabling and demoralizing effects.

The history of employer-backed relief reform also casts light on the contemporary campaign to replace cash assistance with varieties of mandatory work programs. Experience suggests it is unlikely that many people will actually be employed in such programs. Costs alone, and particularly the high costs of child care for AFDC mothers, would preclude it. Forced-work programs are significant, not because they are likely to be implemented on a large scale, but because the introduction of punitive and stigmatizing workfare programs will deter people from applying for aid at all, much as the threat of the workhouse deterred people from becoming supplicants. The implications of Mead's uncompromising declaration in favor of forced work should be considered in this light:

> The solution must lie in public authority. Low-wage work apparently must be mandated just as the draft has sometimes apparently been necessary to staff the military. Authority achieves compliance more efficiently than benefits. . . . Government need not make the desired behavior worthwhile to people. It simply threatens punishment (in this case, the loss of benefits) if they do not comply. (1986: 84–5)

Even more chilling is Kaus's call for the abolition of all social welfare benefits for the poor and their replacement by subminimum-wage jobs. The New Poor Law Commissioners of 1834, who promoted a forced-work system where paupers were made to break stone or move woodpiles from one place to another in exchange for their porridge, could not have said it better.

> Workfare should not be a short-term program to existing welfare clients, but a long-term program to destroy the culture of poverty. In this "hard" view, what's most important is not whether sweeping streets or cleaning buildings helps Betsy Smith, single teenage parent and high school dropout, learn skills that will help her find a private sector job. It is whether the prospect of sweeping streets and cleaning buildings for a welfare grant will deter Betsy Smith from having the illegitimate child that drops her out of school and onto welfare in the first place—or, failing that, whether the *sight* of Betsy Smith sweeping streets after having her illegitimate child will discourage her younger sisters and neighbors from doing as she did. (Kaus 1986: 27)

Kaus is almost surely right about the deterrent effects he anticipates for his proposal. As we said fifteen years ago in *Regulating the Poor,* work relief is designed to spur people to offer themselves to any employer on any terms. And it does this by making pariahs of those who cannot support themselves. This object lesson in the virtues of work is accomplished by the terrible treatment accorded those who do not work (1971: 34). The resulting immiseration and degradation of the pauperized poor then becomes yet another justification in the campaign against social provision.

REFERENCES

Alber, Jens. 1985. "Continuities and Changes in the Idea of the Welfare State." Paper prepared for a conference, "The Future of the Welfare State," sponsored by the New School for Social Research and the Friedrich Ebert Foundation, New York, December 5–6, 1985.

Alexander, John K. 1983. "The Functions of Public Welfare in Late-Eighteenth-Century Philadelphia: Regulating the Poor?" Pp. 15–34 in Walter I. Trattner, ed., *Social Welfare or Social Control? Some Historical Reflections on "Regulating the Poor."* Knoxville: University of Tennessee Press.

Alston, Lee J., and Joseph P. Ferrie. 1985a. "Labor Costs, Paternalism, and Loyalty in Southern Agriculture: A Constraint on the Growth of the Welfare State." *Journal of Economic History* 14(1): 95–117.

———. 1985b. "Resisting the Welfare State: Southern Opposition to the Farm Security Administration." In Robert Higgs, ed., *The Emergence of the Modern Political Economy.* Greenwich, Conn.

Bane, Mary Jo, and David T. Ellwood. 1984. "Single Mothers and Their Living Arrangements." John F. Kennedy School of Government, Harvard University, Cambridge, Mass. Mimeo.

Bensel, Richard. 1984. *Sectionalism and American Political Development, 1880–1980.* Madison: University of Wisconsin Press.

Blaug, Mark. 1963. "The Myth of the Old Poor Law and the Making of the New." *Journal of Economic History* 23: 151–84.

Block, Fred, and Margaret R. Sommers. 1984. "Beyond the Economistic Fallacy: The Holistic Social Science of Karl Polanyi." Pp. 47–84 in Theda Skocpol, ed., *Vision and Method in Historical Sociology.* Cambridge: Cambridge University Press.

Brandt, Lillian. 1908. *The Charity Organization Society of the City of New York, 1882–1907.* Twentieth Annual Report for the Year Ending September Thirtieth, Nineteen Hundred & Seven.

Bremner, Robert H. 1956. *From the Depths: The Discovery of Poverty in the United States.* New York: New York University Press.

Burhauser, Richard V., and G. S. Tolley. 1978. "Older Americans and Market Work." *The Gerontologist* 18(5): 449–53.

Theodore Caplow et al. 1982. *Middletown Families: Fifty Years of Change and Continuity.* Minneapolis: University of Minnesota Press.

Congressional Budget Office. 1982. *Disability Compensation: Current Issues and Options for Change.* Washington, D.C.: Government Printing Office.

Danziger, Sheldon H., Robert Haveman, and Robert D. Plotnick. 1981. "How Income Transfer Programs Affect Work, Savings, and the Income Distribution: A Critical Review." *Journal of Economic Literature* 19: 975–1028.

Danziger, Sheldon H., and Robert D. Plotnick. 1982. "The War on Income Poverty: Achievements and Failures." Pp. 31–50 in Paul Sommers, ed., *Welfare Reform in America.* Hingham, Mass. Kluwer-Nijhoff Publishing.

Devine, Joel A., and William Canak. 1986. "Redistribution in a Bifurcated Welfare State: Quintile Shares and the U.S. Case." *Social Problems* 33(5): 391–406.

Domhoff, G. William. 1970. *The Higher Circle: The Governing Class in America.* New York: Random House.

Ellwood, David T., and Lawrence H. Summers. 1986. "Poverty in America: Is Welfare the Answer or the Problem?" Pp. 78–105 in Sheldon H. Danziger and Daniel H. Weinberg, eds., *Fighting Poverty: What Works and What Doesn't.* Cambridge, Mass.: Harvard University Press.

Esping-Anderson, Gosta. 1986. "Institutional Accommodation to Full Employment: A Comparison of Regimes." In H. Keman and H. Palokeimo, eds., *Government Responses to the Contemporary Economic Crisis.* Beverly Hills, Calif.: Sage Pubns. In press.

Feder, Leah H. 1936. *Unemployment Relief in Periods of Depression.* New York: Russell Sage Foundation.

Feldstein. Martin. 1974. "Unemployment Compensation: Adverse Incentives and Distributional Anomalies." *National Tax Journal* 27: 231–44.

———. 1985. "The Social Security Explosion." *Public Interest.* 81: 94–106.

Ferguson, Thomas. 1984. "From Normalcy to New Deal: Industrial Structure, Party Competition, and American Public Policy in the Great Depression." *International Organization* 38(1): 41–94.

Foner, Philip S. 1947. *History of the Labor Movement in the United States.* New York: International Publishers.

———. 1955. *History of the Labor Movement in the United States. Vol. 2.* New York: International Publishers.

Garfinkle, Irwin, and Robert Plotnick. Undated. "How Much Does Unemployment Insurance Increase the Unemployment Rate and Reduce Work, Earnings, and Inefficiency?" Discussion Paper no. 378-76. Institute for Research on Poverty, University of Wisconsin, Madison.

Glazer, Nathan. 1971. "The Limits of Social Policy." *Commentary* 52(3): 51–58.

Gordon, David M., Richard Edwards, and Michael Reich. 1982. *Segmented Work, Divided Workers: The Historical Transformation of Labor in the United States.* Cambridge: Cambridge University Press.

Haskell, Thomas. 1977. *The Emergence of Professional Social Science.* Urbana: University of Illinois Press.

Haveman, Robert H., and Barbara L. Wolfe. 1981. "Have Disability Transfers Caused the Decline in Older Male Labor Force Participation? A Work-Status Rational Choice Model." Institute for Research on Poverty, University of Wisconsin, Madison. Mimeo.

Heclo, Hugh. 1986. "The Political Foundations of Antipoverty Policy." Pp. 312–40 in Sheldon H. Danziger and Daniel H. Weinberg, eds., *Fighting Poverty: What Works and What Doesn't.* Cambridge, Mass.: Harvard University Press.

Himmelfarb, Gertrude. 1983. *The Idea of Poverty: England in the Early Industrial Age.* New York: Vintage Books.

Hobsbawm, Eric J. 1968. *Industry and Empire: The Making of Modern English Society.* Vol. 2, *1750 to the Present Day.* New York: Pantheon Books.

Huggins, Nathan Irving. 1971. *Protestants Against Poverty: Boston's Charities, 1870–1900.* Westport, Conn.: Greenwood Publishing Co.

Katz, Michael B. 1986. *In the Shadow of the Poor House: A Social History of Welfare in America.* New York: Basic Books.

Kaus, Mickey. 1986. "The Work Ethic State." *New Republic,* July 7, pp. 22–33.

Keller, Morton. 1977. *Affairs of State: Public Life in the Nineteenth Century.* Cambridge, Mass.: Harvard University Press.

Key, V. O. 1984. *Southern Politics in State and Nation.* Knoxville: University of Tennessee Press.

Lampman, Robert. 1979. *Focus* (University of Wisconsin) 4(1): 3.

Leonard, J. 1979. "The Social Security Disability Program and Labor Force Participation." Working Paper no. 392. National Bureau of Economic Research, Cambridge, Mass.

Lowell, Josephine Shaw, "Uplifting the Pauper." 1972. Pp. 3–11 in David Rothman and Sheila Rothman, eds., *On Their Own: The Poor in Modern America.* Reading, Mass.: Addison-Wesley Publishing Co.

Marshall, T. H. 1964. *Class, Citizenship, and Social Development.* Garden City, N.Y.: Doubleday & Co.

Masters, Stanley, and Irwin Garfinkle. 1978. *Estimating the Labor Supply Effects of Income-Maintenance Alternatives.* Madison: Institute for Research on Poverty, University of Wisconsin.

Mead, Lawrence M. 1986. *Beyond Entitlement: The Social Obligations of Citizenship.* New York: Free Press.

Mohl, Raymond A. 1971. *Poverty in New York, 1783–1825.* New York: Oxford University Press.

———. 1983. Pp. 35–50 in Walter I. Trattner, ed., *Social Welfare or Social Control? Some Historical Reflections on "Regulating the Poor."* Knoxville: University of Tennessee Press.

Murray, Charles A. 1984. *Losing Ground: American Social Policy, 1950–1980.* New York: Basic Books.

Palmer, John, and Isabel Sawhill, eds. 1984. *The Reagan Record: An Assessment of America's Changing Domestic Priorities.* Cambridge, Mass.: Ballinger Publishing Co.

Parsons, Donald O. 1979. "The Male Labor Force Participation Decision: Health, Declared Health, and Economic Incentives." Ohio State University, Columbus. Mimeo.

Patterson, James T. 1967. *Congressional Conservatism and the New Deal.* Lexington: University of Kentucky Press.

———. 1981. *America's Struggle Against Poverty, 1900–1980.* Cambridge, Mass.: Harvard University Press.

Piven, Frances Fox, and Richard A. Cloward. 1971. *Regulating the Poor: The Functions of Public Welfare.* New York: Pantheon Books.

———. 1977. *Poor People's Movements: Why They Succeed, How They Fail.* New York: Pantheon Books.

———. 1985. *The New Class War: Reagan's Attack on the Welfare State and Its Consequences.* Rev. and enl. ed. New York: Pantheon Books.

Plotnick, Robert, and Felicity Skidmore. 1975. *Progress Against Poverty: A Review of the 1964–1974 Decade.* New York: Academic Press.

Polanyi, Karl. 1957. *The Great Transformation: The Political and Economic Origins of Our Time.* Boston: Beacon Press.

Pumphrey, Muriel, and Ralph E. Pumphrey. 1983. "The Widows' Pension Movement, 1900–1930: Preventive Child-Saving or Social Control?" Pp. 51–66 in Walter I. Trattner, ed., *Social Welfare or Social Control? Some Historical Reflections on "Regulating the Poor."* Knoxville: University of Tennessee Press.

Quadagno, Jill. 1984. "Welfare Capitalism and the Social Security Act of 1935." *American Sociological Review* 49(5): 623–47.

Reynolds, Morgan, and Eugene Smolensky. 1977. *Public Expenditures, Taxes, and the Distribution of Income: The United States, 1950, 1961, 1970.* New York: Academic Press.

Re, Samuel. 1933. "The Depression of 1819–1822, a Social History." *American Historical Review* 39: 28–47.

———. 1956. "Patterns of Thought and Action in an American Depression, 1882–86." *American Historical Review* 21(2): 284–307.

Schlesinger, Arthur M., Jr. 1960. *The Age of Roosevelt.* Vol. 3, *The Politics of Upheaval, 1935–36.* Boston: Houghton Mifflin Co.

Shaw, Albert. 1894. "Relief for the Unemployed in American Cities." *Review of Reviews* 9: 29–37.

Stigler, George. 1946. "The Economics of Minimum Wage Legislation." *American Economic Review* 36.

Tindall. George B. 1965. *The Emergence of the New South.* Baton Rouge: University of Louisiana Press.

Tocqueville, Alexis de. [1835] 1968. "Memoir on Pauperism." Pp. 1–27 in Seymour Drescher, ed., *Tocqueville and Beaumont on Social Reform.* New York: Harper Torchbooks.

U.S. House of Representatives. Committee on Ways and Means. Subcommittees on Oversight and on Public Assistance and Unemployment Compensation. 1985. *Children in Poverty.* Washington, D.C.: Government Printing Office.

Webb, Sidney, and Beatrice Webb. 1963. *English Poor Law History.* Pt. 1, *The Old Poor Law.* Hamden, Conn.: Archon Books.

Weir, Margaret. 1986. "The U.S. Federal Government and Unemployment: Policy Innovation in the New Deal and the Great Society." In Project on the Federal Social Role, Working Paper no. 8: *Unemployment.* National Conference on Social Welfare, Washington, D.C.

White House Welfare Reform Task Force. Undated. "Public Assistance to Alleviate Poverty: Proposed Demonstration Program." Mimeo.

Wilensky, Harold I. 1975. *The Welfare State and Equality: Structural and Ideological Roots of Public Expenditures.* Berkeley: University of California Press.

The Contemporary Relief Debate

Frances Fox Piven and Richard A. Cloward

THE INTELLECTUAL FOUNDATION for a major attack on the AFDC program has been built over the past two decades. Edward Banfield's book *The Unheavenly City* (1970) helped put the cornerstone in place with the argument that the poor were doomed to poverty by their inability to defer gratification, and that interventions by "do-gooders" were therefore useless. The conservative thesis began to take fuller form in Nathan Glazer's 1971 article "The Limits of Social Policy" and in Susan Sheehan's 1976 depiction of the life of a Puerto Rican AFDC mother and family. Martin Anderson's *Welfare* (1978) was extremely influential, especially his general conclusion that the welfare system has "created a new caste of Americans—perhaps as much as one-tenth of this nation—a caste of people almost totally dependent on the state, with little hope or prospect of breaking free. Perhaps we should call them the Dependent Americans" (p. 56). And after Reagan launched the attack on the relief programs in 1981, four additional works appeared which extended and consolidated the rationale for the conservative mobilization: George Gilder's *Wealth and Poverty* (1981), Ken Auletta's 1982 book *The Underclass*, Charles Murray's *Losing Ground* (1984), and Lawrence M. Mead's *Beyond Entitlement: The Social Obligations of Citizenship* (1986).

These works fit the pattern of antiwelfare rhetoric laid out centuries ago. Increases in the types and amounts of social spending in the late 1960s and early 1970s are summed up. Then the point is made that conditions among the poor deteriorated: family breakdown, out-of-wedlock births, weakened attachments to the labor force, crime and delinquency, poor school performance, and deeper poverty. With this correlation established, it is "obvious" that welfare is the cause of disorganization and poverty. So many more dollars spent in one year, so much more disorganization and poverty in the next. The remedies, too, run true to the classical formulae. Slash or dismantle the programs; or at the least, orient them more strictly to the market—for example, by requiring recipients to "work off" relief payments.

This period of relief conflict has some distinctive features, however. Nothing has been so striking as the steadfast popular support of the social programs. Public opinion surveys show that a large majority of Americans approve of the social programs; in fact, approval has been growing during the Reagan years. Programs for the aged enjoy virtually unanimous favor, partly because the elderly themselves constitute a significant fraction of national opinion polls, and because they are organized to protect their interests. Furthermore, these programs substantially relieve adult children of responsibility for their aging parents, so the nonelderly also have a major stake in them. And despite anxieties about the future solvency of the Social Security system, working-age people hope these benefits will be available to them at retirement.

Americans also believe in the fairness of providing the unemployed and disabled with financial assistance. And there is even considerable support for the poor-serving programs, such as AFDC, which were generally scorned in the past. To be sure, since the Great Depression the polls have consistently shown that about three in four favor the *idea* of helping the poor (Davis 1986). But there was also strong public antipathy to the particular government programs for the poor, especially to AFDC. That has changed. Most people agree that the Reagan administration's cuts have hurt the poor, and they have become more supportive of the means-tested programs as efforts to cut them continue. The Heritage Foundation, for example, reported poll findings in 1985 showing that "three in four Americans think that poor people who receive welfare and food stamps need the assistance," they are more positive toward these programs than three years earlier, and "fewer people criticized government aid for fostering dependence among the poor."[1] The Federal Advisory Commission on Inter-Governmental Relations reported 1982 poll results showing that "the public, if faced with necessity to accept cutbacks in state and local government services, would prefer cuts in assistance to parks and recreation, colleges and universities, and streets and highways over aid to the needy. Only 7 percent favored cuts in services to the needy."[2] None of this is to say that these preferences are necessarily salient. The way most people vote, for example, is determined mainly by the state of the economy, not by the state of the social programs. But if the Reagan administration had actually succeeded in making Social Security voluntary, or in eliminating or substantially slashing the major programs for the poor, disabled, and unemployed, there might well have been a reaction in the election of 1984.

Even with these qualifications, popular support constitutes a major obstacle to the success of the attack on the welfare state, as we predicted it would at the outset of the Reagan era (Piven and Cloward 1982). Despite some administrative restructuring and budget cuts, the income-maintenance programs remain basically intact. We thought the current campaign would fail mainly because of changes in American political culture associated with the political economy of an advanced industrial society. In particular, beginning with the Great Depression, the enlarging role of government in the economy has undermined the legitimacy of traditional *laissez-faire* ideas and given rise to a greatly strengthened popular belief that the state is responsible for economic well-being. It is this popular economic conviction which poses the main political obstacle to the business community's determination to slash social provision.

Public opinion presents a similar challenge to intellectuals al-

---

[1] *New York Times,* September 23, 1985: 38. For general summaries of the national polls, see Lipset (1985 and 1986), and Navarro (1985).
[2] Cited in Navarro (1985: 6); see also Davis (1986) and Shapiro and Patterson (1986) for detailed analyses of poll data pertaining specifically to welfare.

lied with the attack. This is probably the main reason why so much of their writing about social provision has veered away from programs where the idea of economic rights is most firmly established, as is true of Social Security and, to a lesser extent, of the unemployment and disability programs. The main attack has narrowed down to welfare and the nutritional subsidies for the poor, programs about which the public is more ambivalent. Despite the sympathy for the impoverished expressed in the public opinion polls, the AFDC program and its beneficiaries remain vulnerable to the classical stereotypes associated with pauperism, and it is these stereotypes that conservatives are attempting to revitalize. Moreover, unlike elderly or disability claimants, AFDC recipients are unorganized and are therefore unable to respond to charges effectively. The narrowing of the debate over the welfare state to AFDC is obscured by the sweeping titles or subtitles of the conservative literature, such as Glazer's "Limits of Social Policy" or Murray's "Social Policy 1950–1980." But it is the AFDC and the nutritional programs with which these works largely deal. In effect, the propaganda mobilization against the welfare state is based on a strategy of tarring it with the AFDC brush.

Whether the critics intend it or not, singling out AFDC inevitably becomes an attack on minorities. A majority of the women and children on AFDC are blacks and Hispanics; the charges are not so much against "dependent Americans" as against "dependent minority Americans." Race is a deep and fiercely divisive factor in American political culture. The attack on the welfare state reflects this division and draws strength from it. In this sense, the AFDC brush being used to tar the welfare state is indeed black.

Racial undercurrents in the attack on the welfare state also reflect contemporary racial tensions, for blacks are at the very center of domestic political conflicts. The postwar black protest movement was largely responsible for creating the political pressures that led to the expansion of social spending, as well as to the weakening of racial barriers in access to employment, housing, and education. Many of these gains activated and exacerbated white racism, and helped bring on a political backlash in the years since. The writing of some of the critics of government programs for the poor reflects that backlash. Murray's work is an outstanding example. In a book devoted to the causes of poverty, he singles out affirmative action for discussion: among the social policy innovations of the 1960s, affirmative action was the "priority one" (1984: 44). The idea took hold in the sixties, he says, that it is not enough to create "equality of opportunity"; instead, government should promote "equality of results." But it is altogether unclear what affirmative action has to do with poverty, even with black and Hispanic poverty. The black and Hispanic poor generally find employment in the low-wage sectors of the job market, which are already disproportionately populated by minorities. And what possible bearing could affirmative action have on the attachment of the white poor to the labor force, or on their propensity to form single-parent families? If affirmative action benefitted anyone, it was blacks and Hispanics already in the middle class, or those poised to enter it. In short, the question is why affirmative action is being brought into discussions of poverty at all.[3] It is difficult to escape the conclusion that the purpose is to discredit the welfare state by associating it with an issue that continues to generate intense racial antagonism.[4]

THERE IS ANOTHER WAY in which the current attack on the welfare state is distinctive. Intellectuals involved in past cam-

[3] Murray claims that many of the reforms in the 1960s represented sharp breaks with past practice. One was the break with "the principle that government should not support employed people" through programs like food stamps for which the working poor are eligible (1984: 45). But this is nonsense. Government has supported the incomes of working people in various ways since the New Deal, housing subsidies being a major example. Nor is there any evidence that these traditional income supplements worsened the long-term economic circumstances of the beneficiaries (who, in the earlier years of public housing, were mainly members of the white working class). Agricultural subsidies are another large example of traditional subsidies to working people.

[4] Overall, blacks and whites hold quite different views on the question whether institutional arrangements in the United States are racist. Hochschild summarizes the contrasting outlooks as revealed in public opinion polls:

> Many whites want to believe that that the enormous achievement of . . . equal opportunity has improved the status of blacks so much that prejudice and discrimination, and their economic and political consequences, are declining and even disappearing. Many blacks, however, contend that it has merely provided a formal shell of equal opportunity, leaving most blacks where they have always been [except that whites no longer perceive a problem]. (1986: 2–3)

paigns against relief were usually in the service of the employing class and were often members of it, so that the employers' outlook permeated inquiries into the causes of poverty. There were few to speak for the poor and to represent their interests in the forums of opinion. There were no investigators to amass data to test the interpretations that made up the elite consensus. But that is no longer entirely true. What distinguishes the current attack is the existence of an intellectual opposition that has generated a formidable body of competing evidence and interpretation.

This opposition was fostered by several institutional developments. One was the expansion of higher education in the postwar period. It is no longer just philanthrophists, philosophers, and poor-law commissioners who are taken to be authoritative observers of the poor; to this array have been added economists, sociologists, and political scientists. This alone would by no means have guaranteed the rise of dissenting intellectual opinion. Claims about academic freedom notwithstanding, funding matters mightily, in the university as elsewhere. What did spur the growth of oppositional intellectual work on the welfare state was the flow of resources provided by the growth of the welfare state itself. As one of the participants in this process says, "The War on Poverty and related efforts to create a Great Society [had] a major impact on the academic community in the United States. . . . A major social science research effort grew up beside, and partly because of, the War on Poverty" (Haveman 1986: 8).

In the 1960s and 1970s, government provided universities with grants and contracts to train vast numbers of personnel to staff the social programs, to conduct demonstrations and social experiments that might lead to new policy and programmatic initiatives, and to conduct research investigations as an aid to program planning and evaluation, as well as to supply evidence that would be helpful in coping with charges against the programs. These studies of the welfare state became academically respectable and legitimate. The scholars who engaged in them were skilled methodologists, they generated new and useful bodies of data, and they published a prodigious number of sophisticated reports on a wide range of welfare state issues, some of which challenged traditional assumptions about welfare. Indeed, the scope and complexity of the work produced on both sides of this debate is itself a major achievement, considering that only a few decades ago the subject of welfare was dominated almost entirely by rhetoric alone.

Two of the centers that have contributed most to this development are the Institute for Social Research at the University of Michigan and the University of Wisconsin's Institute for Research on Poverty. Over the years, these institutes, and collaborating researchers located elsewhere in the academic world, have published literally hundreds of studies of different aspects of social welfare policy. These findings became the main basis for a debate when the business mobilization against the welfare state got fully under way after the election of 1980. The most recent important publications include Greg Duncan's *Years of Poverty, Years of Plenty* (1984), published by the University of Michigan's Institute for Social Research, and *Fighting Poverty* (1986), a compilation of recent research studies edited by Sheldon H. Danziger and Daniel H. Weinberger, which was jointly sponsored by the University of Wisconsin's Institute for Research on Poverty and the U.S. Department of Health and Human Services.

By the 1970s, the political implications of the rise of this oppositional establishment had become evident to corporate leaders, and they began to augment the flow of resources to conservative scholars and institutes as well as to fund new research institutes that have as one of their primary purposes the production of evidence and analysis in support of the contention that social spending is a destructive force in the lives of poor people. The American Enterprise Institute was created in 1970 and the Heritage Foundation in 1973. In 1977, the Manhattan Institute was formed, and it has since been responsible for supporting the preparation of the two most important books justifying the business mobilization against the welfare state: Gilder's *Wealth and Poverty* and Murray's *Losing Ground.* Moreover, under the Reagan administration, government funds are more likely to be channeled to conservative investigators.

Most of the evidence on which both sides of the debate draw is provided by greatly expanded systems of governmental data collection. By now, virtually everything is counted, and with a technical sophistication never before known. Public agencies in the fields of population, health, education, labor-force participation, and law enforcement—to mention only a few—regularly release data on family income, family organization, employment, school achievement, crime, and much else. In principle, all of these data are in the public domain. But taken alone, data mean little. It is the analysis and interpretation of them that matters. The significance of the emergence of an oppositional intellectual establishment is that it, too, has access to these data, and can challenge the way the critics analyze and interpret them.

The point of these interrelated developments is not only that the scientific examination of the consequences of social spending has become a major enterprise; it is that the enterprise is not wholly controlled by the business class. There is, as a result, a debate, and it reflects broad differences in outlook. The defenders tilt toward structural explanations rooted in larger social and economic processes. The critics generally prefer "cultural" theories that attribute poverty to attitudes and behavior, especially to a "culture of dependency" ostensibly induced by the very effort to cure poverty itself. We turn, then, to the highlights of the debate.

WELFARE AND FAMILY CHANGES

One main charge by the critics is that social spending has generated a virtual epidemic of poor families headed by women. The evidence they cite in support of this charge is mainly about black families. By 1983, the proportion of single-parent families among whites had moved up to 12 percent, and that among Hispanics to 23 percent. For blacks, however, the figure was 42 percent. In all of the data describing the range of processes leading to female headship, blacks stood out. In 1980, one-third of all live births among white teenagers were outside marriage, but 85 percent of black births were. Compared to white women, black women have higher rates of separation, and lower rates of remarriage following divorce. Finally, there has been a sharp fall in the rates of marriage among younger black women as compared to younger white women.[5] For all these reasons, families with female heads are becoming predominant among the black poor (Wilson and Neckerman 1986).

The main case against AFDC is based on the apparent correlation between the growth of black families headed by women and the growth in the AFDC rolls. The rise in this family form is alleged to have occurred in the late 1960s and early 1970s, and it was in those same years that the AFDC rolls rose rapidly. In both 1940 and 1950, the proportion of black families headed by women was 18 percent, and it rose modestly to 22 percent by 1960. But then the proportion shot upward, reaching 28 percent in 1970 and 35 percent in 1975 (Wilson and Neckerman 1986: 235, table 10.1). Consistently, the AFDC rolls in 1960 included only about 750,000 families, and then they too shot upward, reaching 2.5 million in 1970 and 3.5 million in 1975.

To the critics, these parallel trends make for an inescapable conclusion. The expanded availability of AFDC after the mid-1960s caused female-headed families to form on an unprecedented scale by encouraging illegitimacy, separation, and divorce. However, this explanation leaves two large questions unanswered.

First, is it credible to think that the family system of the poor was transformed from a two-parent to a one-parent system in less than a decade? The AFDC rise was extremely precipitous. Between 1960 and the early 1970s, the rolls rose from 750,000 to more than 3 million, and about 75 percent of that increase took place *after* 1965. If AFDC was responsible for the rapid growth in female headship, then it produced that effect in little more than five years, and that is not a reasonable conclusion. More likely, as we will argue, *a large reservoir of poor families headed by women had already formed, and unprecedented numbers of them applied for AFDC in the 1960s because they came to think of welfare as a right.*

Second, if AFDC was responsible for the growth of families

[5] All of these trends continued in the late 1960s and 1970s, raising the illegitimacy ratios for both blacks and whites, but especially for blacks. For example, among women age 20–24, the proportion never married among whites rose from 29 to 47% between 1960 and 1980; among blacks, from 30 to 69%. Among women aged 25–29, the proportion among whites rose from 9 to 18% over these two decades, and from 13 to 37% among blacks (Wilson and Neckerman 1986: table 10.3).

with female heads, as the critics charge, why should that effect have been so much greater for blacks than for other groups? This question has not even been raised, much less answered. Just to raise it makes clear that the availability of AFDC did not uniquely affect blacks, although other forces did. *We will maintain that the growth of black single-parent families had been set in motion by a series of social and economic upheavals that did in fact specifically affect blacks, and that these upheavals were under way long before the AFDC rise.*

One of the striking characteristics of the present debate is the extent to which the social and economic antecedents of the rises in *both* black single-parent families and the AFDC rolls have been ignored. The tendency is to treat social spending as if it were the only influence on the lives of the poor. The 1940s and 1950s were years of a mass exodus by blacks from the rural South, and migration has always been associated with the weakening of family life. Moreover, even though the black middle class expanded during these decades, many newly urban blacks were in severe economic straits.[6] Between 1954 and 1964, the national nonwhite unemployment rate ranged between 10 and 13 percent (Bureau of Labor Statistics 1969: 11). Subemployment rates, which count the number unemployed for 15 weeks during the year as well as those working at extremely low wages, were first calculated in 1966, and showed a nonwhite rate of 22 percent compared to a white rate of 8 percent (Bureau of Labor Statistics 1967: 97). In nine of the major central-city ghettos to which blacks had migrated, the nonwhite subemployment rate averaged 33 percent in 1966. Had this measure been calculated during the recessions of the late 1950s, the rate would

---

[6] There is substantial evidence of black economic progress. A Rand Corporation study found that black male wages increased 52% faster than white between 1940 and 1980. The ratio of black male wages to white male wages rose from 43% in 1940 to 73% by 1980. The Rand study also shows that the racial wage differential has practically disappeared in the South, where the majority of blacks still reside. Taken together, these trends have led to the growth of a black middle class that now outnumbers the black poor. These are impressive indicators of change. However, future progress may be slower. An important cause of past progress, according to the Rand study, was the postwar migration from the low-wage South to the higher-wage North, an impetus to economic improvement that will not be repeated. The fact that 40% of black families are now headed by females is another barrier to economic progress.

have been much higher. Furthermore, black migrants concentrated in urban areas that experienced little or no economic growth in the early 1960s. For example, New York, Chicago, Philadelphia, Baltimore, Newark, and Los Angeles all showed less employment gain than the national average of 7 percent between 1963 and 1965. New York and Los Angeles showed no gain at all (Bureau of Labor Statistics 1968: 17).

The combined impact of migration and these urban economic conditions on family structure was plain enough. Between 1940 and 1965, the rate of live illegitimate births among unmarried black women between the ages of fifteen and forty-four rose from 3.6 to 9.8 percent; for whites, the illegitimacy rates were only 0.4 percent and 1.2 percent in these two years. Furthermore, the ratio of these illegitimate births to all live births also began to rise, although the reasons were complex, such as a rise in the proportion of young people, a falling fertility rate among the married, and a falling rate of marriage.[7] Consequently, between 1940 and 1965 the ratio of illegitimate births to all live births for blacks rose from 17 to 26 percent, but the illegitimacy ratio for whites only moved up from 2 to 4 percent. By 1966, just as the AFDC explosion was about to occur, 42 percent of black families with incomes under $3,000 had come to be headed by females, compared to 23 percent of white families (Bureau of Labor Statistics 1967: 70–4). In other words, by the mid-1960s huge pools of impoverished families headed by women had built up in the cities. *However, the full extent of this buildup was not noticed.*

In earlier decades, it had been common for single mothers and their children to live with their parent or parents in three-generation families with the result that the census undercounted them. Family members were typically described by their relationship to the extended-family head—single mothers were described as daughters, for example. Many single-parent subunits thus remained unidentified, and therefore uncounted. This measurement

---

[7] These figures include widows, and families whose male heads were in the armed forces or absent for reasons other than divorce or separation. Rates of separation and divorce were sharply differentiated by race: for example, of all families headed by females in 1966, 46% of black women were separated or divorced, compared to 31% of white women (Bureau of Labor Statistics 1967: 70).

problem was recognized only recently. As we noted in chapter I, when Census coding procedures were changed between 1981 and 1983, *the number of subunits identified actually doubled* (Bane and Ellwood 1984, fn. 1; Ellwood and Bane 1986: 151–2).

No one has yet tried to estimate the extent to which under-counting has distorted the data on the black family since 1940, the first year that the Census included national information on family structure. But judging from the huge 1981–1983 increase after coding procedures were changed, the magnitude of undercounting must have been considerable. Consequently, figures showing that female headship was only 10 percent among whites and 18 percent among blacks in 1940 are totally suspect; the actual figures could have been half again as high, or more.

Still, even before coding procedures were revised, the official statistics show that black female headship in particular rose rapidly in the 1960s, especially toward the end of the decade when the AFDC explosion occurred. It could therefore be argued that coding procedures, while leading to gross underestimates of the actual proportions of female headship at any given point in time, nevertheless did not distort the trendline, which moved sharply upward in the 1960s. But that conclusion is wrong for another reason.

The AFDC explosion did in fact produce an explosion in the number of families headed by females, but not at all in the sense that it provided incentives for such families to form. What it did instead was to make *visible* hundreds of thousands of families that had previously not been counted because they were subunits of larger families. The liberalization of AFDC in the late 1960s—especially the raising of grant levels in northern states—made it financially possible for these single mothers and their children to establish independent households. And that is exactly what a great many of them did.

It has been estimated that more than one-third of the officially recorded growth of female-headed families between 1940 and 1970 resulted from an increase in independent living arrangements (Cutright 1974; see also Ross and Sawhill 1976). Recent studies show that this tendency accelerated rapidly in the 1970s. Of black children born into single-parent families during the 1969–1973 period, 60 percent lived in households headed mainly by a grandparent or grandparents, as did 56 percent of white children born into single-parent families; in the 1974–1979 period, however, those proportions fell to 37 percent of black children and 24 percent of white children. And the process is continuing (Ellwood and Bane 1986; see also Smith and Cutright 1985).

Indeed, for all the considerable research that is now available on the question whether AFDC causes changes in family structure—including more illegitimacy, separation, and divorce and less frequent remarriage—AFDC has been shown to have had only one definitive effect. In states with higher benefit levels, AFDC provided female family heads with the resources to live separately from their parent or parents. And once they established independent living arrangements, *the Census identified them,* thus making it appear that the rate of formation of these families was far greater beginning in the late sixties than in earlier periods. In this sense, the expansion of the AFDC rolls created the "facts" that made it possible for critics such as Murray to claim that the black family system in particular had collapsed all of a sudden, and that AFDC was responsible.

To sum up, migration and urban unemployment and subemployment put the black family under intense stress after 1940, and the proportion of single-parent families began to climb. The full extent of this growth was not recorded officially, however, until a pattern of independent living was set in motion by mass protest and the rise in the welfare rolls that followed in the late 1960s. In other words, *single-parent families were much less likely to be counted before the AFDC rolls expanded, and they were much more likely to be counted thereafter.* Consequently, the correlation between the growth of the AFDC rolls and black female headship is spurious; it is an artifact of official recording procedures.[8]

---

[8] If it is determined that past undercounting of single-parent subunits has been substantial, such data could bear importantly on the long-standing academic debate about the impact of slavery, and of the semifeudal plantation system that replaced it, on black family structure. The classic exposition of the view that the southern system promoted families headed by women—E. Franklin Frazier's book *The Negro Family in the United States* (1939)—was challenged in the 1970s by a revisionist literature attempting to demonstrate that the two-parent nuclear family prevailed among blacks in

---

SINCE THE CORRELATION between the growth of black female headship and the AFDC explosion is spurious, it follows that the liberalization of AFDC should not have influenced the processes that lead to female headship: illegitimacy, separation, and divorce. Recent studies employing various advanced methodologies show that these causal relationships do not in fact exist.

First, the birth of a child to an unwed mother appears to precede as many as one in three episodes of AFDC use (Bane and Ellwood 1983: 18), thus seeming to suggest that the availability of AFDC causes illegitimacy. Again, the main increases in rates of illegitimacy occurred among blacks. In 1940, as we noted, the overall illegitimacy rate among black women between the ages of fifteen and forty-four was 3.6 percent, and it reached 9.8 percent in 1960. After social spending increased, however, the rate fell steadily, reaching 7.7 percent in 1980. The lack of correspondence between these trends, in short, is inconsistent with the charge.

Other data also help defeat the charge that AFDC promotes illegitimacy. If the charge is true, the rate of illegitimacy ought to be greater in locales where incentives are greater—that is, in locales with higher benefit levels. Studies of interstate variations in the relationship between benefit levels and illegitimacy, both at given times and over time, do not reveal such a relationship (Cutright 1973; Fechter and Greenfield 1973; Winegarden 1974; Moore and Cauldwell 1977; MacDonald and Sawhill 1978; Ellwood and Bane 1986). To give one illustration, although AFDC benefits in the North are twice those in the South, black illegitimacy in the North is only slightly higher (Vining 1983; see also Wilson and Neckerman 1986).

Or consider this finding: "The fraction of all children living in a female-headed household started rising much faster in the late 1960s, at precisely the time when the number of children on AFDC rose sharply. But then the trends diverge—dramatically so. Since 1972 the fraction of all children living in a female-headed house-

---

the nineteenth century and well into the twentieth century (Pleck 1972; Lammermeir 1973; Furstenberg, Hershberg, and Modell 1975; Shifflet 1975; and Gutman 1976).

hold rose from 14 percent to almost 20 percent [in 1980]." During the same period, however, "the fraction of all [AFDC children] held almost constant, at 12 percent." For blacks, the figures are even more dramatic: "Between 1972 and 1980 the number of black children in female-headed households rose nearly 20 percent [although] the number of black children on AFDC *fell* by 5 percent" (Ellwood and Summers 1986: 93). As Greenstein (1985) remarks, "How can welfare be encouraging more single women to have children if many of these same women do not collect welfare when the children are born?"

Murray's response to these results has been to argue that variations in welfare payment levels are not the crucial factor causing illegitimacy. Instead, he says, the welfare package, including food stamps and other benefits, is now sufficiently high in *all* states to encourage single women to have and keep their babies (1985: 441–2). Since AFDC exists in every state, there is no way of establishing a control group to test this kind of assertion. However, Ellwood and Bane developed an ingenious substitute method. As part of a series of different comparisons, they compared unmarried women who would probably be eligible for AFDC if they had an illegitimate child with a group of unmarried women who probably would not be eligible because of other likely sources of income. And they made these comparisons in high-payment states, where incentives to illegitimacy would presumably be greater. When they examined the rates of illegitimacy, they found no differences between these groups of unmarried women (1986: 139 and table 1).

D I V O R C E   A N D   S E P A R A T I O N are also a common antecedent of AFDC use. Ellwood and Bane estimate that almost half of all periods of AFDC use are preceded by such family events; by contrast, only 15 percent are preceded by a decline in family income (1983: 18). But to say that family disruptions are an important determinant of welfare use does not mean welfare causes them.

The findings on this question are somewhat ambiguous and contradictory. Some studies do show that higher benefits are related to higher marital disruption (e.g., Honig 1974, although the effects disappeared by 1970); others show a minor negative effect (e.g., Minarik and Goldfarb 1976); some find that higher benefits produce more marital disruption among nonwhites but not whites (e.g., Ross and Sawhill 1975); and most studies reveal no significant effects (e.g., Cutright and Madras 1974). A recent and influential study, employing several different advanced methods, generally demonstrates that the effects of benefit levels on family structure are slight (Ellwood and Bane 1986). Summing up the results of this body of research overall, Ellwood and Summers conclude that "more sophisticated regression techniques which control for differing socioeconomic characteristics across states typically also show little or no relationship [between benefit levels and marital disruption]. Our conclusion is that AFDC has far less to do with changes in family structure than has been alleged" (1986: 95).

Studies over time of the relationship between variations in AFDC benefits and marital disruption are similarly contradictory and inconclusive. One of the most useful sources of data on this and related questions is a study by the University of Michigan's Institute for Social Research called the Panel Study of Income Dynamics (PSID). The panel consists of 5,000 families drawn nationally in 1969, but with low-income people oversampled. A second panel, called the National Longitudinal Surveys (NSL), was begun at the same time, but it focused more on labor-market behavior. The families in these samples were reinterviewed at intervals, thus permitting changes in such matters as marital status to be studied in detail. Here again, there were inconsistent results. For example, Hoffman and Holmes (1976) found that low-income families living in high-benefit states were slightly more likely to dissolve their marriages and those in low-benefit states slightly less so, but an analysis of the same data by Ross and Sawhill (1975) failed to confirm the effect. Summing up the results of these longitudinal studies, Lane concludes that the "findings of this research have not shown convincingly that the availability of *more* rather than *some* AFDC makes much if any difference in rates of divorce-separation [or] remarriage (1981: 31, emphasis in original; see also Bishop 1980). However, Wilson and Neckerman reach a slightly less definitive conclusion. After reviewing studies using either cross-sectional or longitudinal methods, they conclude that AFDC has had "no effect on the incidence of out-of-wedlock births," but a "modest impact on separation and divorce" (1986: 251).

On the face of it, the overall results of this research are reasonable. It does not seem plausible that a relatively small welfare package, taken alone, has had so large an impact on sex and family behavior, nor is it plausible that these effects would be felt among blacks so much more than among other groups. We also note that James Q. Wilson, no friend of AFDC himself, finds that these studies, taken as a whole, undermine the charges against AFDC. In particular, he says that Murray has not proved his case: "He cannot show that young, poor men and women in fact responded to AFDC as he assumes they did, nor can he explain the racial differences in rates or the rise in caseloads at a time of declining benefits" (1985: 9). More generally, Wilson sums up some of the major reasons why allegations that AFDC produces family composition changes are questionable:

> If the system of payments under the program for AFDC was to blame for the rise in single-parent families, why did the rise occur so dramatically among blacks but not to nearly the same extent among whites? If AFDC provided an incentive for men to beget children without assuming responsibility for them, why was the illegitimacy rate rising even in states that did not require the father to be absent from the home for the family to obtain assistance? If AFDC created so perverse a set of incentives, why did these incentives have so large an effect in the 1960s and 1970s (when single-parent families were increasing by leaps and bounds) and so little, if any, such effect in the 1940s and 1950s (when such families scarcely increased at all)? And if AFDC were the culprit, how is it that poor, single-parent families rose in number during a decade (the 1970s) when the value of AFDC benefits in real dollars was declining? (1985: 8)

Finally, as this book went to press, the General Accounting Office released a report (March 22, 1987) concluding that "research does not support the view that welfare encourages two-parent family break-up," that the availability of welfare "has little impact on the child-bearing rates of unmarried women," and that the availability of welfare does not significantly reduce the incentive to work. The GAO reached its conclusions after reviewing more than 100 studies completed since 1975, studying case files of more than 1,200 welfare families in four states, and interviewing federal, state, and local officials.

AFDC AND POVERTY

The growth of families headed by women is a main source of the rapidly rising poverty among women and children. Without male wages or higher welfare grants, their economic condition is likely to persist or worsen. Even if these mothers could obtain child care, problems of job discrimination, poor education and skills, and declining wages would keep most of them in poverty. Nor is it likely that workfare will alter their poverty, judging from past experience with these programs.

The impoverished condition of many families headed by females is not in dispute. What is in dispute is the contention that AFDC produces their poverty. In this section, we take up a common charge—that AFDC induces poverty by disabling recipients for labor-force participation, particularly long-term recipients. Supposedly, the various social and psychological factors which go into the making of "work habits" atrophy, so that recipients come, over time, to compose a class enmeshed in a "culture of dependency."

We first note that there are fewer persistent users of relief than is commonly believed, which weakens the evidence in support of this theory of poverty. The long-term use of relief has been exaggerated because of the way data on recipients are typically gathered: by studying successive cross-sections of caseloads. If the recipients in these cross-sections have similar characteristics, it is presumed that they are the same people. To be sure, that could be so: the composition of caseloads from one time to another could conceivably consist mainly or entirely of the same people. But they could also be different people with similar characteristics, which would mean there is considerable turnover on the rolls. In other words, successive cross-sections do not reveal the extent to which relief use is persistent or transitory (Duncan 1984: 1–2). Recall the nineteenth-century study of poorhouse residents mentioned in chapter 1: the investigator underestimated the number of transients and concluded that most poorhouse inmates were long-term residents, which seemed to justify the claim that relief debilitates people and causes poverty.

The recent application of the panel method to the study of relief caseloads overcomes this potential bias. Using the longitudinal data developed at the University of Michigan, movements on and off the AFDC rolls by panel recipients have been analyzed by, among others, Rein and Rainwater (1978), Coe (1981), Bane and Ellwood (1983), O'Neill et al. (1984), Duncan (1984), and Ellwood (1986). In a summary of this overall body of evidence, Duncan and Hoffman (1986, table 3) first show that 48 percent of all women beginning a "spell" of AFDC use will remain on the rolls for only 1 to 2 years, and 17 percent for 8 or more years. The significance of this finding is that there are a great many more short-term episodes of AFDC use than is commonly assumed.

However, a different picture is revealed when we ask how many people on the AFDC rolls *at a particular point in time* are in the midst of a long or a short spell. Only 15 percent are undergoing a short spell, but 49 percent are undergoing one that will last eight or more years. In other words, looking at the rolls over a period of time shows a high degree of transiency, but looking at them at a point in time emphasizes persistent use. Bane and Ellwood (1983) use a hospital analogy to clarify this difference. On any given day, the majority of beds will be filled with long-term patients; over a week or two, however, the remaining beds turn over rapidly because they are filled with people who remain only for brief stays.

Multiple spells are also common, producing cumulative use. Of those first beginning a welfare spell, 30 percent will accumulate a total of 1 to 2 years of use (whether as a result of one or multiple spells), 40 percent will accumulate 3 to 7 years, and another 30 percent will accumulate 8 or more years. What can thus be said, overall, is that the temporary use of welfare is clearly the predominant pattern, but a good share of this temporary use is nevertheless by women who turn to welfare more than once. At any one time, about two-thirds of the mothers on AFDC are either continuous or multiple users (Bane and Ellwood 1983). Nevertheless, considering the total universe of those who turn to AFDC over a period of years, welfare spells are much more temporary than the "hard-core" imagery implies.

Who, then, are the longer-term users of welfare, and what reason is there to believe that they are disabled for subsequent labor market performance? The best predictors of accumulated time on welfare are age and previous marital status: older and previously married women remain on welfare less time, and younger unmarried women remain longer (Ellwood 1986; Murray 1986). For this younger group, welfare provides the financial means to rear children in the absence of male wages and realistic opportunities to work, at least while their children are very young.

No one thinks raising children as such disables these women for subsequent work. Rather, the contention is that relying on welfare for income while raising children produces a psychology of dependence, in contrast to relying on male wages, alimony, child support, or other unearned income. For that contention, there is no evidence, one way or the other.

Evidence is available, however, bearing on other variants of the argument that ascribes poverty to the persistent use of welfare. One line of argument is that without an adult wage earner in the family, children are not socialized in the work ethic, or there is inadequate information communicated to the young about the nature of work, or about ways to enter specific occupations. This is the familiar view that persistent welfare use results in the inter-generational transmission of dependency.

Available data do not seem to support this theory. In the 1968 PSID sample, among daughters from "highly welfare dependent" black families (defined as receiving at least 25 percent of family income from cash-assistance programs) who had reached ages 24 to 30 by 1982, only 19 percent were similarly highly dependent (Hill and Ponza 1984). Commenting on these findings, Duncan and

Hoffman remark that "regression models showed no statistically significant effects among blacks of parents' welfare dependence on their children's likelihood of welfare dependence" (1986: 15). This finding should be treated with some caution, since welfare use might increase as these daughters grow older. Still, it is remarkable, in the light of the stereotype, that relatively few daughters of recipients turn to cash-assistance programs as they enter adulthood.

Another presumed intergenerational effect is on male youth unemployment. The rising rate of youth unemployment, especially among black males, has become one of the main briefs against AFDC. The allegation is that many young men, having been reared in families where work is presumably not valued, do not enter the labor force upon reaching maturity. However, the study of this issue has mainly yielded contradictory and ambiguous results, and most analysts claim not to know how to explain the tangled data.

For the period between 1950 and 1970, Cogan (1982) attributes virtually all of the rising black youth unemployment to agricultural modernization in the South. In 1950, half of all black teenagers were employed as farm laborers, 90 percent of them in the South. But the agricultural revolution all but swept these jobs away during the next two decades. By the 1960s, with the black exodus from agriculture winding down, roughly a quarter of black youth were unemployed. Accepting this, as analysts on both sides of the debate generally do, the question remains why the black youth unemployment rate continued to rise relative to the white rate in the late sixties and seventies. By 1983, according to one estimate, "a bare 45 percent of black men who were aged 16 to 21 and out of school were employed, whereas 73 percent of their white counterparts were employed. . . . In many respects, the urban unemployment characteristics of Third World countries appear to have taken root among black youths in the United States" (Freeman and Holzer 1986: 1).[9]

---

[9] A few researchers do not agree that there is a wide gap in black-white youth unemployment. Cain (August 1985) argues that researchers overstate the numbers unemployed because they understate

In 1979 and 1980, the National Bureau for Economic Research arranged for what may be the most extensive in-depth survey so far available of black youth unemployment. They interviewed more than 2,000 black males in Boston, Chicago, and Philadelphia who lived on blocks identified in the 1970 Census as having at least 70 percent blacks and 30 percent of families below the poverty line. About one in three of the respondents lived in public housing; half lived in welfare families, and only 28 percent lived in families with an adult male present (Freeman and Holzer 1986: 8).

The main finding is that no single factor is "*the* cause of black male unemployment" (*ibid.*, 6, emphasis in original). Some of the many factors were these: tight labor markets produced less black male unemployment, but a high proportion of older women in the labor market produced more; black youth still face discrimination from employers, and are paid less than comparable white youth; black youth were more likely to hold jobs if either the male or female family head worked; those with "strong long-term career desires" fared better, as did those with a record of church attendance; and so on.

More to the point of our discussion, black male youth unemployment also appeared to be associated with family use of welfare and with residence in public housing. The unemployment rate among those 19 to 24 years of age who lived neither in a welfare or a public housing family was 28 percent. It rose to 43 percent for those in welfare families, and to 52 percent for those in both

---

the numbers in school. Thus, according to Cain, Murray looked at the reduction of labor-force participation contributed by schooling just in the period 1965–1970, and that does show little effect; but for the longer 1960–1979 period, Cain asserts that schooling was a major source of reduced labor participation rates by blacks. In addition, Murray used civilian labor-force statistics, which exclude military service; before 1972, a higher proportion of whites were found in the military, but proportionately more blacks were thereafter.

Mare and Winship (December 1979) attempted to correct for these alleged deficiencies by combining measures of participation in work, school, and military service in a "productively active index," and compared black and white youth for 1964 and 1978. Overall, racial differences in youth unemployment rates almost disappear. The largest difference, ten percentage points, occurred in 1978 in the 20–24 age group: 84.1 percent of blacks were productively active, and 94.1 percent of whites. Indeed, this measure shows that the overwhelming proportion of young people were productively active: for all ages between 16 and 24, and for both races, the lowest value on this measure was 84.1 percent. However, see Ellwood and Wise (1983) for findings that show a substantial residual black-white youth unemployment gap even when schooling and military service are factored in.

welfare and public-housing situations (Lerman 1986). However, this particular finding has been criticized on the ground that the methodology employed in the analysis of the data does not support the contention that there is a causal relationship running from welfare and public-housing experiences to unemployment: the "evidence is insufficiently persuasive to warrant acceptance of this simple unidirectional perspective" (Myers 1986: 44).

Furthermore, Ellwood and Summers (1986) report data that make it difficult to attribute black youth unemployment to AFDC use. One is that the "unemployment rates for young men living in two-parent families are not very different from those of youngsters living with one parent. . . . In 1975, some 23 percent of young black men living with two parents and 21 percent of young black men living with one parent had jobs. For whites, the figures are closer to 50 percent for both family types. . . ." Furthermore, "although unemployment does fall among blacks as family income rises, the differential among blacks and whites is largely unchanged." An additional puzzling finding reported by Ellwood and Summers is that in 1980 the rates of employment among out-of-school black youth were about the same for central cities (32 percent), suburbs (38 percent), and nonfarm rural areas (35 percent)—all of which vary widely from the overall employment figure for out-of-school white youth of 62 percent. Ellwood and Summers conclude: "The fact that black/white youth unemployment differentials seem to persist for all geographic locations, for all family types, and for all income groups clearly suggests something more fundamental is to blame than the growth of welfare programs."

THE THEORIES OF POVERTY we have just reviewed would, if true, contribute to pretransfer poverty (that is, poverty exclusive of government transfers). Murray rests his case on just this argument. Before the overall expansion of social spending on the poor in the late sixties, pretransfer poverty had been dropping steadily—from approximately one-third of the population in the fifties to 21 percent in 1965, and to 18 percent in 1968—which means that more and more people rose out of poverty without government assistance. "But this proved to be the limit of progress," he says (1984: 64–5). The pretransfer level moved up to 19 percent in 1972, to 20 percent in 1976, and to 22 percent in 1980. This "most damning statistic," as Murray interprets it, reveals that the poor were sustaining themselves less and less by work and more and more by relying on government assistance. They were, in short, "losing ground."

> The reason for calling this the most damning statistic is that economic independence—standing on one's own abilities and accomplishments—is of paramount importance in determining the quality of a family life. Hardly anyone, from whatever part of the political spectrum, will disagree. For this independence to have *decreased* would be an indictment of the American system whenever in our history it might have occurred. (Murray 1984: 65)

But it is a gross oversimplification to assume that pretransfer poverty is determined solely by whether people stand on their own "abilities and accomplishments." Pretransfer poverty has determinants that transcend individual motivation.

First, as we said in the previous chapter, it is true by definition that the *direct* consequence of welfare state programs is to increase pretransfer poverty. The express intent of major social programs is to permit certain groups to opt out of the work force, whether fully or partially, permanently or temporarily, such as the elderly, the disabled, the unemployed, and AFDC recipients. To say that social program recipients are no longer standing on their own abilities and accomplishments is redundant. Furthermore, the magnitude of this effect varies over time, depending on whether the social programs expand or contract. For example, the aging of the population means that many more elderly poor who would otherwise work are exempted from doing so; or, to take an opposite case, restricting access to unemployment benefits increases work effort and lowers pretransfer poverty.

Considering the huge work-reduction effects of the various social programs which we noted in chapter I, the alleged contribution to pretransfer poverty of the AFDC program alone—whether through family composition changes, personality changes, or intergenerational effects—is, by contrast, necessarily minor. Furthermore, pretransfer poverty is obviously affected by macroeconomic influences. Economic growth may reduce pretransfer poverty levels, just as unemployment and falling wages caused by severe recessions, deindustrialization, or farm bankruptcies will raise them. On the whole, critics of relief are not inclined to give such factors their due.

On this particular point, Murray's error is different. He does consider the effect of economic trends on pretransfer poverty, but his treatment of the subject is technically careless and misleading. He alleges that the seventies were a time of unparalleled economic growth: "Even after holding both population change and inflation constant, per capita GNP increased only a little less rapidly in the seventies than it had in the booming sixties, and much faster than during the fifties" (1984: 65). Consequently, he argues, the resulting expansion of opportunities ought to have enabled many people to do better for themselves. Instead, the level of pretransfer poverty rose during the seventies. "Growth did not stop," he says, "but for some reason, the benefits of economic growth stopped trickling down to the poor" (1984: 59). And it is because of this apparent contradiction between rising economic growth and rising pretransfer poverty that Murray feels justified in blaming social spending for having stripped people of their labor-force capacities.

There was economic growth in the seventies, to be sure, but its benefits were not evenly distributed throughout the class structure. It improved the position of the better off, but not of those at the bottom. As Greenstein (1985) points out, "Growth in the GNP does create jobs, but this growth was too slow in the 1970s to create *enough* jobs for the unusually large numbers of women and young people (from the baby-boom generation) who were entering the job market." As a result, unemployment doubled from 3.6 percent in 1968 to more than 7 percent in 1980. Blank and Blinder (1986) show that when unemployment rises by a percentage point, the poverty level rises by 1.1 points; by contrast, a point increase in inflation produces only a 0.15 increase. Consequently, the poverty rate would have been 4.5 points lower in 1983 if inflation and unemployment, but especially unemployment, had remained at the 1973 levels.[10]

In addition, real income fell in the seventies despite growth. In 1982 dollars, the median income earned by adult male workers rose to a high in 1973 of $18,360 for whites and $11,551 for blacks. But then it fell back in 1982 to $14,748 for whites and to $9,493 for blacks (Cain 1985, table 1). These were substantial declines, and they were greater for blacks than whites. The thrust of the evidence, then, is that pretransfer poverty rose in the seventies, despite growth in the GNP, because the economy produced more unemployment and less real income. Murray is right that the benefits of growth "stopped trickling down to the poor," but his reasons are wrong.[11]

Murray also misrepresents changes in social spending in such a way as to seriously distort his interpretation of changes in posttransfer poverty (a measure aggregating pretransfer income and income from government transfers which is generally referred to as the official poverty rate).[12] The posttransfer poverty rate dropped from 30 percent in 1950 to 18 percent in 1965, and to a low of 11 percent in 1973. At that juncture, however, the rate leveled off, and it actually rose toward the end of the decade, reaching 13 percent in 1980. The question, Murray asks, is why posttransfer poverty rose during the same years that Great Society social spending initiatives reached an all-time high? To be clear about this, posttransfer poverty rose in part because pretransfer poverty

[10] Blank and Blinder are referring to posttransfer poverty rates, but their point applies as well to pretransfer rates.

[11] Ellwood and Summers attribute the decline in real income during the seventies to a number of factors. One was the large increase in the number of households headed by women resulting from divorce, separation, and nonmarital births; the share of income going to single individuals also increased substantially. But they mainly attribute the decline to the drop in productivity growth to an annual rate of 0.8 percent in the seventies after nearly two and half decades of almost 3 percent annual growth (1986: 80). For a different interpretation of productivity changes, see Block's essay in this volume.

[12] Since we are interested in poverty trends rather than in the absolute level of poverty, we have adopted the "official" poverty measure as our measure of posttransfer poverty. It should be noted, however, that this measure does not include the cash equivalent of food stamps, or of certain other forms of government support. Comparisons of different ways of measuring poverty may be found in Smeedling (1977); Danziger and Gottschalk (1983); U.S. Bureau of the Census (1984); and Danziger and Plotnick (1986).

rose, for the reasons already given: rising unemployment and failing real income. But it also rose because of changes in the real value of transfer payments. Benefits for the elderly were indexed for inflation in 1972 and have increased steadily. In turn, their posttransfer poverty rate dropped rapidly, from 35 percent in 1959 to 25 percent in 1970 and to less than 16 percent in 1980. But the situation of AFDC recipients is vastly different. The real value of their benefits fell by 30 percent during the seventies, and by 20 percent if food stamps are included. The reason is that the states failed to raise benefit levels to keep pace with inflation. As Greenstein (1985) remarks:

> Indeed, no other group in American society experienced such a sharp decline in real income since 1970 as did AFDC mothers and their children Yet *Losing Ground* ignores this development. . . . [It is] *never mentioned*. . . . Murray tells his readers only that benefit increases "slowed" after 1970 and increased "little if at all" after the mid-1970s. No hint is provided that benefits actually fell.

In short, posttransfer poverty flattened out during the seventies and even turned up slightly toward the end of the decade because pretransfer poverty rose and because the real value of some transfer payments fell.

The validity of this analysis was confirmed by events in the early eighties. These years were disastrous for people at the bottom, particularly the recession years of 1980 and 1982–83, the latter of which saw unemployment levels reach 12 percent, the highest level since the Great Depression. The real value of the minimum wage also fell 25 percent after 1978, most of the decline occurring after 1981 when incremental increases were no longer legislated despite continuing inflation. Meanwhile, real wages fell because a major shift was taking place in the economy from relatively well-paid manufacturing jobs to low-wage service employment. Taken together, these trends are almost surely the reason that pretransfer poverty reached 24.2 percent in 1983, its highest point since 1965, the first year for which calculations are available (Danziger and

Plotnick 1986: 50, fn. 16). And with the real value of benefits continuing to fall as well, the posttransfer level jumped to 15.2 percent in 1983, a 38 percent increase over the low of 11 percent in 1973. These factors help explain why 35.3 million people were poor in 1983, or one in seven. And 31 million more would have been poor without government aid, for a total of 56 million, or one in four.

In 1984, as the economy recovered, unemployment fell to 7 percent, the erosion of the minimum wage slowed because inflation receded, and real income rose. All poverty measures showed improvement: pretransfer poverty fell back almost a point and a half to 22.9 percent, the posttransfer level dropped almost a point to 14.4 percent, and the numbers below the poverty line dropped by 1.5 million to 33.7 million. In conclusion, these data clearly undermine the main empirical foundation of the attack on AFDC.

SEVERING POVERTY FROM SOCIETY

Although the empirical findings do not lend much support to the welfare state critics, there is nevertheless an important sense in which the critics have won the day. It is their charges that have set the research agenda and dominated the ensuing public debate. Researchers who defend the welfare state are reduced to claiming that the charges are not true, that the receipt of welfare benefits does not produce most of the deleterious consequences attributed to it. The conclusion reached by Ellwood and Summers after reviewing this corpus of work exemplifies the weakness of such a defense:

> It is true that current transfer policies do relatively little to help the poor achieve self-sufficiency or to ameliorate some of the serious social problems attending poverty, but a review of the record does not support the view that they have caused them. (1986: 96)

That the main body of empirical evidence provides scant support for the critics is important, to be sure. But it is much more important that the charges have come to frame public discussion, since that fact of itself has the effect of giving salience and a measure of credibility to the classical view that the problems of poverty and the poor are somehow associated with relief-giving. As the debate focuses public attention on the effects of welfare, the larger social processes that underlie poverty and disorganization recede from view. The impact of welfare benefits on the lives of the poor is subject to intensive scrutiny, but not, for example, the impact of the displacement of millions of people from agriculture after World War II, or the present-day transforming impact of rapid "deindustrialization." In effect, a research agenda dominated by the charges helps to make the most basic societal processes that affect poverty and the poor seem peripheral. In these terms, the contraction of the scope of inquiry is a major victory for the opponents of the welfare state.

Before the escalation of the current campaign against the social welfare programs, the importance of large-scale institutional processes in generating and sustaining poverty, and a range of symptoms of social disorganization associated with poverty, was taken as the common wisdom. One of the most publicized examples of this kind of analysis was contained in Daniel Patrick Moynihan's 1965 report entitled *The Negro Family: The Case for National Action.* Like most conservative analysts today, Moynihan claimed that "the heart of the deterioration of the fabric of Negro society is the deterioration of the Negro family" and that "the family structure of lower-class Negroes is highly unstable and in many urban centers is approaching complete breakdown" (1965: 51). He also thought that the degree of disorganization was so serious, so complete, that the black family had become incapable of socializing its young for labor-force participation, with the apparent consequence that lower-class blacks were no longer able to take advantage even of improving employment opportunities. In support of this contention, Moynihan pointed to the fact that trends in applications for AFDC in the early 1960s no longer paralleled trends in black unemployment rates:

Our study has produced some clear indications that the situation may indeed have begun to feed on itself. It may be noted,

for example, that for most of the post-war period male Negro
unemployment and the number of new AFDC cases rose and
fell together as if connected by a chain from 1948 to 1962. The
correlation between the two series of data was an astonishing
.91. (This would mean that 83 percent of the rise and fall in
AFDC cases can be statistically ascribed to the rise and fall in
unemployment rates.) In 1960, however, for the first time,
unemployment declined, but the number of new AFDC cases
rose. In 1963 this happened a second time. In 1964 a third.
The possible implications of these and other data are
serious. . . . (1965: 93).

In the political climate of the middle and late 1960s, these asser-
tions aroused a storm of controversy. Moynihan was excoriated
because he seemed to imply that attention should be shifted away
from economic discrimination and focused instead on the pathology of the black family. But unlike contemporary polemicists
against the welfare state, Moynihan was emphatic in attributing
the problems he perceived in the black family to the larger social
structure and not to relief-giving. American slavery, Moynihan
began by saying, uniquely fostered matriarchy, and was the original cause of family breakdown. Uprooting and migration to the
cities were another source of strain for the family. Finally, the
breakdown of the traditional two-parent family had its roots in
"the fundamental, overwhelming fact . . . that *Negro unemployment,* with the exception of a few years during World War II
and the Korean War, *has continued at disaster levels"* (1965: 20,
emphasis in original). Given this combination of forces, the social fabric of the black community has disintegrated, especially
the family, producing "a tangle of pathology . . . that is capable of perpetuating itself without assistance from the white
world."
    In the present political and intellectual climate, the main thrust
of Moynihan's analysis, with its emphasis on exogenous economic
forces, has been largely forgotten. What is remembered, because
it matches the rhetoric of the classical assault against relief, is his

discussion of the pathology of the black family, and his hints that accelerating family breakdown was beginning to lead to increased reliance on relief.

Most of the current research does take *some* account of exogenous labor market trends, mainly by introducing into the analyses changes in unemployment rates or family income. These indicators do not, however, reveal the full impact of labor-market changes on particular groups. Unemployment levels tell little, for example, about the massive upheavals in people's lives which are set in motion as capital flows from one sector to another, and from one region to another. The resulting shifts in the availability of jobs in the post–World War II period meant that people searching for a livelihood were drawn or driven from rural areas to the big cities, from the Old South to the North and then back to the "New South," from central cities to outlying metropolitan centers, and so on, in a pattern of apparently perpetual flux. At best, unemployment rates and changes in pretransfer income deal only with the labor-market aspect of these dislocations. They tell nothing about the weakening and destruction of family ties and community infrastructure. And they tell nothing about the cultural disorientation and personal disturbance that follow in the wake of uprooting and resettlement.

Indeed, there is an important way in which the current debate over the effects of the welfare state on the contemporary poor turns on the question of the relative adaptations by different groups to uprooting and resettlement. The charges by the critics reflect the unstated assumption that blacks in particular are adapting less well than earlier immigrant groups, and that it is the welfare state which is impeding their progress. Except for the destructive effects of social spending, blacks would have the strong work ethic, stable two-parent family system, and cohesive community life which ostensibly facilitated the advance of other groups. As it is, the welfare state has presumably accelerated social disorganization and retarded black economic advance.

The disorganization associated with the rapid urbanization of blacks and Hispanics is the subject of endless reports and discussion. At the same time, there is a corresponding tendency to gloss over the trauma that accompanied the assimilation of earlier groups into American society. In a portrait that is more folklore than history, the Irish, the Italians, the Poles, and the Jews, for example, are depicted as rapidly reconstructing strong ethnically based social ties in the urban neighborhoods in which they settled. That happy view compresses into an instant the efforts of generations of new arrivals who in fact had to painfully construct a community fabric in the face of the disorganizing and disorienting impact of immigration and the continuing instabilities of the market economy, including massive shifts in the location and kinds of jobs, and periodic collapses in the market. As Albert Fried says of the experience of earlier immigrants, "For its victims, unregulated economic liberty—the pitiless laws of the market—could be as destructive as any natural calamity."[13]

The Irish provide an example. Like blacks, they also came from an impoverished rural background, and from all reports their encounter with the urban world was traumatic. Studies such as Asbury's *Gangs of New York* chronicle the pervasive thievery, murder, adult street-gang wars, mayhem, drunkenness, family disorganization, and political corruption that characterized the Irish adaptation during the nineteenth century. It was this history which prompted Moynihan to remark that the social disorganization following the mass exodus by blacks from the South was not worse:

> It was [a similarly abrupt] transition that produced the wild Irish slums of the 19th century Northeast. Drunkenness, crime, corruption, discrimination, family disorganization, juvenile delinquency were the routine of the era. In our own time, the same sudden transition has produced the Negro slum—different from, but hardly better than its predecessors, and fundamentally the result of the same process. (1965: 63)

[13] Albert Fried, "Let the Torch Cast True Light on the Immigrant Story," *New York Times*, July 4, 1986. On labor mobility generally in the late nineteenth century, see Thernstrom and Knights, 1970. For an excellent critique of the view that Irish social mobility was rather easily achieved see Erie (1978).

This parallel between the Irish slums of the nineteenth century and the black ghettos of the late twentieth century is underlined when it is remembered that it was not until World War II that large-scale black migration to the cities got under way, and it was not until the late sixties that it subsided. Given the brief time-span since, blacks may be adapting as well as other groups from similar backgrounds at the same stage of urbanization.

It is a sociological cliché to say that the eventual integration of earlier immigrants, however long it took, was made possible by the community-based ethnic social networks that eventually developed. Strong ethnic social ties based in the neighborhoods helped newcomers get jobs, sustain their families, and rear their young; facilitated the upward rise of an ethnic petty bourgeoisie; made possible the political organization of the newcomers and a share in political patronage that went with political organization; and created an infrastructure for the regulation of everyday life in the ethnic neighborhood, including the regulation of the amounts and types of permitted forms of criminal activity (see for example Bell, [1953] Whyte [1955], and Cloward and Ohlin [1960]). This, too, is more folklore than history. A cohesive community life may have helped people cope, but it did not make them prosperous. The penury endured by immigrant communities is all too easily forgotten, especially in the current flush of prosperity. From the beginning, it was economic expansion that recruited and integrated masses of the unskilled. Most immigrant groups did not make substantial economic advances until after both the labor union and social welfare gains of the 1930s and the unprecedented prosperity of the postwar years. Some blacks made progress too, largely through employment in the mass-production industries and government. According to a recent Rand Corporation study, the black middle class now outnumbers the black poor. At the same time, however, deindustrialization is dimming the economic prospects of the black poor.

There is also reason to think that, even as economic opportunity is shrinking, the construction of the kind of community infrastructure that helped other groups take advantage of opportunity as well as cope with adversity has become far more difficult. That

something is seriously different is argued by Wilson, who contrasts
the disorganization of contemporary urban black neighborhoods
with black communities of the 1930s and 1940s as described by
Drake and Cayton in *Black Metropolis.* Before World War II,
black communities apparently exhibited "features of social organization—including a sense of community, positive neighborhood
identification, and explicit norms and sanctions against aberrant
behavior" (Wilson 1986). The black poet June Jordan strikes the
same theme in her reminiscences of the Bedford-Stuyvesant community where she grew up in the 1940s:

> On our own block of Hancock Street, between Reid and
> Patchen Avenues, we had rice and peas and curried lamb or,
> upstairs in my aunt and uncle's apartment, pigs' feet and
> greens. On the piano in the parlor there was boogie woogie,
> blues and Chopin. Across the street there were cold-water flats.
> . . . There were "American Negroes," and "West Indians."
> Some rented their housing, and some were buying their homes.
> There were Baptists, Holy Rollers and Episcopalians, side by
> side. On that same block, Father Coleman, the minister of our
> church, lived and worked. . . . And a black policeman. And a
> mail carrier. And a doctor. . . . And Nat King Cole and calypso
> and boyfriends and Sunday school and confirmation and choir
> and stickball and roller skates and handmade wooden scooters
> and marbles and make-believe tea parties, and I cannot recall
> feeling underprivileged, or bored, in that "ghetto." (1986)

What distinctive circumstances, then, might have inhibited the
construction of community among post–World War II immigrants, and even destroyed existing communities? One difference
may have been the sheer scale and rapidity of the influx of displaced people from the American South, Puerto Rico, and Mexico
in the decades after 1945 (and more recently from Central and
South American and the Caribbean), so that established community structures were overwhelmed by newcomers. For example, in
1960 half of all blacks in each of the six cities with the largest black
populations (New York, Chicago, Philadelphia, Detroit, Los An-

geles, and Washington, D.C.) were born elsewhere, chiefly in the
South (Bureau of Labor Statistics 1968: 15). Another difference is
that poor urban neighborhoods, especially minority neighborhoods, fell victim to the bulldozer and the speculator in the massive demolition and redevelopment of the built environment of
American cities stimulated by the expansion of the American
economy that followed World War II.

The social organization of immigrant communities depended
on residential stability and proximity. It was in the neighborhoods
that earlier immigrants constructed the social networks that
helped them cope with life in a new environment. But the new
immigrants have not enjoyed much stability. The neighborhoods
that harbored them after World War II have been wracked by one
incursion after another. It was these neighborhoods that were
typically targeted when new highways were cut through from the
burgeoning white suburbs to the central city, or when land was
assembled for urban renewal projects to house the expanding white
middle class and to provide facilities for business. True, these areas
were labeled "blighted" in the language of federal oversight agencies, and the buildings were in fact often run-down. But the people
displaced—Herbert Gans (1982: 388) estimates that some 735,000
households were displaced between 1950 and 1980—typically were
forced into even worse housing elsewhere, often under more
crowded conditions and at higher rents.[14] This made people
poorer, and there is evidence that many of them turned to welfare
specifically as a way of coping with higher housing costs (see Piven
and Cloward 1971: 287–8). More to our point here, the process of
displacement weakened or destroyed whatever social attachments
and networks people had been able to form to orient and support
family and individual life.

Poor neighborhoods that escaped the bulldozer were often
targeted by real estate operators for quick speculative profits in
maneuvers that also resulted in displacement. Patching up deteri-

---

[14] The U.S. Advisory Committee on Intergovernmental Relations estimated that 177,000 families
and 66,000 individuals were displaced between 1943 and 1963 alone, and that most of them were
poor and black. See *Relocation: Unequal Treatment of People and Businesses Displaced by Government* (Washington, D.C.: U.S. Government Printing Office, 1965).

orating housing for sale to poor people who were eligible for low-cost federal mortgages was one way to make fast money. When the roof leaked, the boiler broke down, and the plumbing backed up, people who could not afford repairs and mortgage payments often simply abandoned the dwellings. Another way to make a fast buck was to buy buildings for the tax deductions they made possible, meanwhile "milking" the rent rolls and putting no money back into building maintenance or property taxes, with a view to eventually abandoning the structure, or even torching it for the insurance. Either way, huge stretches of poor residential areas that had once been neighborhoods soon lay empty and lifeless, except for the people who sought shelter in the blackened structures. And it was not just buildings that were destroyed, but the laboriously constructed matrix of relationships to place and others through which people live their particular lives.

In recent years, "gentrification" has overtaken the neighborhoods of the poor. Quick profits are being made through the renovation of entire areas which suddenly become fashionable to "upscale" markets. From the perspective of low-income tenants in these areas, the results are similar to urban renewal. They are displaced, either evicted as renovations are scheduled, or forced out eventually by higher rents.[15]

NOT ONLY HAVE community conditions been ignored in the research agenda dominated by the charges, but so have the conditions of work. Scarcely any attention has been directed to the effects on the poor of the changing conditions of employment, particularly the employment likely to be available to low-income people. From the perspective of the reasoning that underpins the attack on the welfare state, this oversight is entirely illogical. The very inconsistency of fastening on the "rewards" of welfare while

[15] Some estimates show that between 1970 and 1980, rents increased nearly twice as fast as tenant incomes, with the result that many of the very poor are displaced (Dolbeare 1983; Hopper and Hamberg 1986). And the combination of conversion, arson, abandonment and gentrification probably results in the loss each year of about half a million low-rent housing units (Hartman, Keating, and LeGates 1982).

ignoring the declining rewards of work hints at the political agenda of those who make the charges.

The argument underpinning the attack on the welfare state and the research questions stimulated by the attack flow from a model that explains human behavior as responses to economic incentives. Presumably, the availability and liberality of the "welfare-package," consisting of the several income, nutritional, health, and housing programs for which a family may be eligible, constitute an incentive that draws people away from stable labor-market participation and from marriage.

Although we think an economic-incentive model falls considerably short of explaining human behavior as a whole, we agree that it explains a good deal of what people do. It accounts, after all, for the historic opposition of employers to social provision; a labor force that is guaranteed a measure of income security will be less likely to work at jobs that do not offer something more or something better. But this is to say that it is the *relative* incentives of welfare and work that are at issue. To speak only of the work disincentives generated by welfare benefits implies that recipients simply cease making work efforts. A more reasoned way to state the incentive point is that it takes more favorable job opportunities to draw them into the market. This is surely the main meaning of the work-disincentive effects of the guaranteed-income experiments: the experimental income payments were relatively high, so that people did not have to take any job on any terms, and some reduced their work effort. But because the research agenda has been so closely limited by the charges against the welfare state, attention has been focused almost exclusively on the work-disincentive effects of welfare payments, without comparable attention to the question whether the incentives associated with work have been weakening.

A consistent use of the incentive model would explore the impact of the availability of welfare benefits on labor-market behavior in the context of changes in real wages, benefits, and working conditions. That requires directing attention both to the decline of the mass-production industries, such as auto, steel, and rubber, with their unionized and relatively well paid jobs even for

the unskilled, and to the expansion of the service sector with its
low-wage, nonunion jobs. Manufacturing employment declined
from 28.2 percent to 22.2 percent of the total labor force between
1960 and 1980. The largest relative decline occurred among production workers, and quickened as the years wore on so that, by 1980,
the manufacturing sector was shrinking in absolute terms (Rosenberg 1983: 80), and the largest losses were in the durable-goods
sector where the highest-paying manufacturing jobs are concentrated (Morehouse and Dembo 1986: 9). The contraction was more
than offset by service sector expansion, but these new jobs were
concentrated in the lowest-paid categories of the service sector
(ibid). The Bureau of Labor Statistics reported in May of 1986, for
example, that 30.5 percent of the jobs added since January 1980
were in retail trade, and nearly 60 percent were in the category of
miscellaneous services, such as hotel and motel jobs, business services (including temporary office jobs), and hospital jobs.

The dramatic shift from industrial to service-sector employment has been accompanied by comparably dramatic changes in
the terms of work. Annual wages in retailing average $9,036, or
about $2,000 less than the poverty level for a family of four, and
only 44.3 percent of average earnings in manufacturing, down
from 63.1 percent of manufacturing wages in 1962 (Morehouse and
Dembo 1986: 14). Annual wages in miscellaneous services of $13,-
647 did not much exceed the poverty line. But in fact, almost no
attention is paid to the impact on work patterns of declining real
wages in sectors of the economy in which potential or actual
welfare recipients are likely to be employed. Similarly, little is
made of the steady erosion of the real value of the minimum wage
at which so many jobs in the expanding service sector are pegged.
The National Council on Employment Policy reports that in 1984,
about 8 million workers received wages at or below the minimum
wage of $3.35 an hour, and according to Sar Levitan, another 6
million received wages just above the minimum.[16] Nor is there
attention to the spread of temporary and part-time work, or to the

---

[16] According to the *New York Times,* June 8, 1986.

revival of home work, or to the reduction or elimination of work-related benefits which occurs under these arrangements. In April 1986, according to the Bureau of Labor Statistics, nearly 20 percent of the work force was employed part-time. When added to those employed in temporary jobs, the numbers of such "contingent workers" have increased from 23.5 million in 1975 to 29.5 million in 1985.[17] In a nutshell, welfare benefits may have become more attractive simply because work has become less so.

WE COULD GO ON, and at length, to consider an array of important changes in American social institutions that ought reasonably to be investigated for their impact on the lives of the poor. Consider the ramifications of changing political attitudes. For example, it seems reasonable to surmise that the bitter discord of the 1960s changed the interpretations held by the minority poor of the institutional arrangements that had always subordinated and impoverished them. Conflict focused attention on these structures, and led people to question their legitimacy to a degree perhaps unprecedented in the American experience. Some gains were made, mainly by lowering barriers to the upward mobility of a stratum of better positioned blacks and Hispanics. There were, however, far larger numbers whose hopes were stirred but whose circumstances did not improve, and even worsened. Political conflict has made the arrangements that once enforced the subjection of blacks (and to a lesser extent, of other poor minorities) less legitimate and therefore less tolerable.

Under these circumstances, it may not be surprising that many people, especially young people, seem to be impatient and even rebellious, perhaps because they are unwilling to settle for the hard labor and mean life prescribed by the old terms of race and class subordination. The National Bureau of Economic Research study cited earlier reported that when asked, young black men from the inner city were willing to work at levels of pay only slightly lower

[17] According to Audrey Freedman, a Conference Board economist quoted in the *New York Times,* July 9, 1986.

($4.47 an hour) than the levels named by white youths ($4.59). But
those young black men who did work were in fact paid an average
of $4.00 an hour, compared to $4.75 for white youths. Perhaps it
is not surprising that one-third of the young black men surveyed
thought they could earn more "on the street" from criminal activity than from taking a job, and that they actually derived one-
quarter of their income from such activities (Freeman and Holzer
1986: 14). This alternative may well have become more viable as
legitimate economic arrangements for blacks were discredited. Eleanor Holmes Norton (1985) captures something of the change
when she mourns the passing of the old "values of the black
working poor and middle class—where husbands often work two
jobs, [and] wives return to work almost immediately after child-
birth."[18] What Norton is sentimentalizing is exploitation, the bit-
terly hard life which many young blacks may have come to think
after the 1960s was neither inevitable nor legitimate, even while
shifts in the American economy and polity were dashing any
practical hope for something better. This change in outlook, this
rebelliousness bred by political challenge, may be far more important than the receipt of welfare benefits in accounting for the
tendency among some of the young to spurn regular work and to
turn instead to the streets for income.

Our general point is obvious enough, and it does not depend
on the validity of any of these particular observations. The work
and family lives of the poor, particularly the minority poor, have
been affected by a broad range of changes in the American economy and society over the course of the last two decades, the period
when welfare utilization also increased. True, the effects of these
large changes, and their ramified and variable consequences on
particular groups, are difficult to measure empirically. But they are
not for that reason insignificant, and they are surely more significant than the availability of welfare benefits in shaping the work
and family lives of the poor.

---

[18] See "Restoring the Traditional Black Family," *New York Times Magazine,* June 2, 1985.

WELFARE AS A SYSTEM OF DETERRENCE

There is another glaring omission from the research agenda. On the one side, critics attack the programs for liberal benefits which generate perverse economic incentives. On the other side, defenders claim that evidence in support of these incentive effects is weak or nonexistent. What is ignored in a debate framed in this way are the *disincentives* to welfare utilization itself which have been built into the programs as the result of a history of employer opposition. Ignoring the deterrent features of welfare almost surely muddles research findings. Worse, it muddles our heads. Inundated with arguments about the perverse incentives generated by welfare programs, we forget that being a recipient of means-tested programs in the United States is a rotten existence.

To be fully cognizant of the *disincentives* built into welfare programs, we have to go beyond the model on which the critics rely—a model of economic actors responding to economic incentives. Such a model radically simplifies the options people confront, and radically simplifies the motives of the people who respond to these options. To be sure, the penurious level of benefits attached to the AFDC program is not much of an incentive. In 1984, benefits averaged about $5,500 for a family of four, or half the official poverty line, and in many states benefits were much lower. A life of the meanest poverty is part of what the New Poor Law Commissioners had in mind when they contrived ways to deter pauperism.

But that is not all of what they had in mind. They thought that people cared even more about their "free agency," which was why the workhouse requirement furnished an "unerring test of the necessity of applicants." In a similar if less brutal way, the degraded social status of the welfare recipient, a degradation rooted in welfare procedures and investigations, also deters utilization. So too do the circuitous, exhausting, and humiliating procedures associated with establishing eligibility for means-tested programs drive people away. That is why such evidence as we have—and this is not a question to which much research has been directed—

shows that there is chronic underutilization of means-tested programs by those eligible. In other words, the logic of the argument
that people choose welfare over work or marriage when welfare
yields higher dollar benefits is not wrong. What is wrong—and
Murray's discussion of Phyllis and Harold provides one example
of the error—is the assumption that the calculus of dollars is the
only calculus, for it turns our attention away from the features of
welfare programs which are intended to discourage utilization, at
the price of great human suffering.

The history of the AFDC program illustrates these deterrent
effects. Between 1950 and 1960, the AFDC rolls rose by only about
110,000 families, and this despite the fact mentioned earlier that
millions of destitute people were leaving southern agriculture and
huge pools of eligible but unaided people were building up in the
cities. Almost certainly many were kept from applying by the
shame of being on welfare. Lack of information and misinforma-
tion about eligibility were further reasons many did not apply;
welfare departments provide very little public information, and
certainly do not conduct outreach campaigns. Debasing and bur-
densome eligibility procedures kept still others from completing
the application process, and those who completed the process were
often denied assistance because of restrictive interpretations of
eligibility. Only the rise of the black movement in the 1960s over-
came these multiple deterrents. With the politicization of poverty,
the weakening of the stigma of welfare, and the wide circulation
of information about entitlements by the antipoverty programs
and by the welfare rights movement, annual application rates shot
up, from about half a million in 1960 to more than a million in 1968.
Because of these pressures, including successful litigation against
eligibility barriers, welfare departments were forced to make less
restrictive interpretations of eligibility rules in processing those
applications, so that acceptance rates rose from 50 percent in 1960
to more than 75 percent later in the decade. These are the reasons
for the great rise in the AFDC rolls which we noted earlier—from
800,000 families in 1960 to more than 3 million in the seventies
(Piven and Cloward 1971: chap. 6).

The more conservative political climate of the seventies and eighties, and the absence of an antipoverty movement, probably explain why participation rates in the newer programs have not reached the levels of AFDC. In the SSI program, participation is about 55 percent (Warlick 1982); it is less than half in the food-stamp program (Coe 1981). In 1976, poor respondents in the Panel Study of Income Dynamics were asked why they had not applied for food stamps. About 60 percent said they were not aware of their eligibility or thought they were ineligible (ibid.). To make matters worse, the Reagan administration has slashed the food-stamp public information budget. Moreover, the escalation of public attacks on the means-tested programs is almost surely having the effect of increasing the stigma of being "on the welfare." With the president castigating food stamp cheats, it becomes much harder to hand the stamps to a cashier while standing in a super-market check-out line.

A recent example illustrates the force of the multiple *disincentives* embedded in the means-tested programs. Shortly after Reagan took office in 1981, his administration proposed and the Congress enacted a series of changes in the AFDC program which terminated payments to 400,000 working mothers whose wages were so low as to entitle them to supplementary welfare payments. (An additional 300,000 families had their monthly benefits cut on average between $150 and $200 a month.) In most cases the cutoffs meant not only that these women would lose their supplementary benefits, but that they and their children would also lose their entitlement to Medicaid. Under these conditions, many women would have been financially better off if they had quit work and subsisted solely on welfare benefits. Indeed, critics of the administration warned that most recipients would do just that, thus making the cutoffs irrational. Here was, in a sense, the Great Experiment of 1981, a real-life test of the model which posits that welfare and work choices are the result of purely material calculations.

The predicted return to the welfare rolls of hundreds of thousands of women working at low-wage jobs apparently did not occur, or at least did not occur quickly. It seems a reasonable surmise that something besides the relative dollar advantages of work and welfare was responsible. Very likely these cutoffs were implemented in a way that made the exercise of any choice at all unlikely. Sarri's (1985) study of a Michigan sample shows that women received cutoff notices without warning, and for reasons they did not understand. Perhaps as people came to understand, they nevertheless shunned the increased stigma associated with subsisting solely on "the welfare." Or perhaps they were unwilling to give up the social respect yielded by work, or wanted the sociability that work often provides and that is usually denied to women who stay at home with their children. Or perhaps holding a job suggested to them that a better life might be possible someday. Or perhaps other powerful motives, or entirely different perceptions, account for what they did. It would be worth finding out. But studies that ignore the multiple deterrent features of welfare programs by assuming a human nature motivated solely by calculations of economic advantage are not likely to help us find out.

These observations may help explain the striking fact that the prodigious body of research on welfare has failed to yield definitive findings. It does, after all, seem reasonable to expect welfare state programs to have consequences in the lives of people. That the findings are so inconclusive is at least partly because the modeling of the relationship between welfare and social behavior has been far too simple. As Duncan and Hoffman (1985) point out, the effects of welfare benefits on people's decisions can only be understood in relation to the other institutional options they confront. Those options include the availability of work and the rewards of work. And both work and welfare are experienced and evaluated by people not only in terms of their relative rewards but also in terms of the penalties incurred. Finally, the rewards and penalties that actually motivate people cannot be reduced to dollar gains and losses, but include a range of other things that are valued by real people. Not least, people want and need to be granted a measure of social respect, and this the means-tested programs are designed to deny them.

EXPUNGING POLITICS

Still another major consequence of the narrowed research agenda is to direct attention away from the politics of the welfare state, and away from the deep political conflicts that underlie the current attack. As we said in the previous chapter, we think faltering profits in the 1970s led American business interests to try to reduce uncertainty and shore up profits through a series of changes in public policy. In part the business mobilization was simply an effort to shift the distributional effects of government taxation and spending by reducing business taxes, increasing spending on military contracts, and slashing programs that distribute income and services to the poor and working class. But because of the pervasive effects of income protection programs on labor market relations, the political stakes in the attack on welfare state programs may well be far larger than the direct distributional effects of changes in the public budget would suggest.

Our point here, however, is not to reiterate our interpretation of the politics of the welfare state. Rather, our point is that the bare fact that there is a politics underlying the effort to dismantle welfare state programs, that some groups stand to gain and others to lose, and that these gains and losses motivate political action has been deleted from the debate or relegated to the fringes of academic discourse.

Critics of social provision have always portrayed themselves as engaged in consensual efforts to help the poor. The contemporary opponents portray their mission similarly. The Manhattan Institute unabashedly illustrated the frontispiece of a pamphlet promoting *Losing Ground* with the somber and empathetic portrait of a poor black man. This insistent attempt to divorce the attack on welfare state programs from class politics is buttressed by the parallel denial that class politics had anything to do with the initiation and expansion of welfare state programs in the first place. It is said of the sixties, for example, that it was not poor or working people who demanded expanded social provision, but a

particular elite stratum variously labeled as liberals, the "intelligentsia," or the "new class."

One can scarcely blame the assailants for assuming a posture
of political disinterestedness in their effort to make a public case
against social welfare programs. But one can certainly blame the
erstwhile defenders of the welfare state for failing to examine or
challenge that posture, in effect going along with the argument
that there are no major class stakes in the politics of the welfare
state. This is the inevitable result, however, of concentrating on the
association between welfare and poverty and disorganization. By
agreeing that this is the main question, the researchers in effect
underline the critics' definition that the assault on the welfare state
emanates from essentially consensual and benign motives. Everyone is presumably exploring together which social policy options
work best to reduce poverty. If political questions emerge at all,
they tend to remain within the narrow and relatively neutral
sphere of bureaucratic implementation. Meanwhile, no one, at
least no one in the welfare state research establishment, investi-
gates the political interests of different groups and classes in the
welfare state, and the political strategies through which those
interests are or are not advanced. On these questions, the main
body of research is silent.

We hasten to add that welfare state researchers are not alone
in their inclination to develop an apolitical perspective on welfare
state issues. The main intellectual tradition that purports to explain the welfare state has always underplayed political conflict
in favor of a consensual and evolutionary interpretation of the development of social programs (Gronbjerg 1977; Lieby 1978; Trattner 1979; Wilensky 1975). That tradition was constructively
challenged, however, in the 1970s and 1980s by a range of
new work that placed political conflict, and especially class conflict, at the very center of their interpretations (Bowles and
Gintis 1982; Gough 1979; O'Connor 1973; Piven and Cloward
1971).

Now, however, perhaps influenced by the newly hostile political climate, as well as by the veritable torrent of discussion of the
perverse effects of welfare programs, intellectuals are once again

turning away from analysis of the deeply conflictual issues involved in social provision. In any case, there is not much analysis
of the stakes of different groups and classes in the welfare state,
or of the mobilization of business groups against the welfare state,
or of the large role played by struggles by groups of the poor and
working people in initiating and shaping the welfare state. A class-
conflict perspective has fallen out of fashion and out of favor, and
this at the very historical moment when the welfare state is embat-
tled by class forces.[19]

Not only have the interests of business disappeared from the
mainstream research agenda, but so have the popular movements
that helped shape social provision. Indeed, class politics from
below is virtually blotted out. There are few accounts of the political aspirations and efforts of the unemployed of the 1930s, of the
impact of their protests on local and national politics, and of how
that impact was translated into influence on the federal relief
initiatives that began in 1933.[20] Similarly, the black protestors who
marched, rallied, and rioted, and the complex pressures their protests exerted in local and national politics, are deleted from explanations of the expansion and liberalization of welfare state
programs in the 1960s and early 1970s.[21] The pride of political place

[19] Perhaps it is needless to add that this turning away from the politics of class has not been
complete. As we noted in chapter 1, some recent work on the emergence of the welfare state in the
1930s has begun to pay close attention to the role of business interests in crafting the programs
designed under the Social Security Act. And some accounts of the Reagan policy initiatives
characterize the effort to contract welfare state programs as part of a business political program
(see for example Ferguson and Rogers 1986; Edsall 1984; Lekachman 1982).

[20] Thus Heclo writes on the emergence of the categorical aid programs in the 1930s that the "key
political actors" were a few liberals and professional social workers (1986: 315).

[21] In fact, there is an enlarging body of empirical research confirming the role of black protest in
the expansion of the AFDC roles in the 1960s (see, for example, Jennings 1979; Isaac and Kelly 1981,
1982; Hicks and Swank 1983; Schram and Turbott 1983). Furthermore, the impact of the black
movement, when it is acknowledged at all, is usually confined to the expansion of the AFDC rolls.
But the disturbances generated by the movement had pervasive effects on other welfare state
programs. For example, the federal takeover in 1974 of the so-called adult categorical programs—
aid for the disabled, the blind, and the aged—was clearly a response to the clamorous lobbying for
federal aid by mayors and governors who had to deal with the fiscal strains generated by the
expansion of AFDC. Except for the fiscal crisis generated at the local level by the AFDC explosion,
there probably would not have been sufficient political pressure from local politicians to secure
enactment of SSI, which relieved localities of substantial costs for the so-called "adult" programs.
The establishment of the new Supplemental Security Income Program was thus, if only indirectly,
an achievement of the black movement. And almost everyone would agree that it is an achievement,

is given instead to a narrow group of "liberals" or "intellectuals" or to the "scarcely tested social theories" of a small circle of Kennedy people "committed to 'action' " (Heclo 1986: 322; see also Reider 1985). In just the same vein, Murray says that the domestic social welfare measures adopted in the 1960s did not reflect a change in American public opinion but a "shift in assumptions . . . among a small group relative to the population, but one of enormous influence . . . best labeled the intelligentsia" (1984: 41–2). In other words, the transformation of the institutional structure of the welfare state is attributed to a passing fashion among intellectuals. As Murray puts it, ideas are "in" or ideas are "out," depending on what is "au courant" (ibid., 42). So much for political analysis.

THE WELFARE STATE AND THE GOOD SOCIETY

We have yet to discuss what we consider the most serious intellectual constriction that results from ceding the research agenda to the critics. It is the ubiquitous acceptance of the premise that the impact of welfare on work and family patterns ought properly be the main criterion for evaluating the programs. If the availability of welfare benefits reduces work effort among recipients, and if the availability of benefits increases the rate of marital dissolution, then *ipso facto* the programs are to be condemned. With this assumption, the welfare state researchers are unwittingly lending support to a class and gender mobilization that can only worsen welfare state programs and worsen the condition of the poor, especially poor women.

The ideological basis of this premise is deeply rooted: it is the contemporary representation of the nineteenth-century idea that the giving of relief is a violation of natural law. Then and now, natural law did not actually refer to nature, but to a socially constructed system of economic relations called capitalism (and to

---

for it means there is now a national minimum standard for aid to these poor, and also that stigma is greatly reduced, since the new program is administered by the Social Security system.

a socially constructed system of family relations called patriarchy, which we will discuss in a moment). The argument is that welfare programs must not be allowed to interfere in any way with the operations of capitalist markets. The Commissioners who designed the New Poor Law of 1834 captured this understanding of the proper relation of social provision to the market in the principle of "less eligibility," which meant that those who receive relief must always be worse off than the lowest-paid worker.

> The first and most essential of all conditions, a principle which we find universally admitted, even by those whose practice is at variance with it, is, that his [the relief recipient's] situation on the whole shall not be made really or apparently so eligible [desirable] as the situation of the independent laborer of the lowest class. (See Piven and Cloward 1971: 35)

Undergirding the assumption that social provision must not be allowed to interfere with wage labor—an assumption which, if not "universally admitted," is surely shared by both critics and defenders of the American welfare state—is the deep and long-standing conviction that the "self-regulating" market is and should be the pre-eminent social institution. The market does and must organize society, dictating what government can and should do, and in this sense, it sets the limits of political possibility. The market does and should determine where people live and how their communities ought to be organized, and in this sense, it shapes our collective life. The market does and should mold us as individuals by inculcating the personality traits that lead us to work hard and consume even harder.

The idea that the self-regulating market must necessarily be pre-eminent in political, social, and individual life is capitalism's central myth. In the nineteenth century, this idea was so unquestioned that social commentators treated the inevitable hegemony of the market as a natural law. The myth gained its force, not because it accurately described reality—capitalist markets in fact always depended on state policies, and collective and individual life never was shaped solely by economic forces—but because it

captured the broad sweep of the historical process through which
the spread of markets smashed traditional economic arrangements
fixed by law and custom. In this sense, the myth served in the
construction of a new social order, and it served the interests of
the bourgeoisie that rose with the new social order.

In reality, of course, modern capitalism has become progres-
sively more deeply and intricately dependent on state policies: for
regulating and stabilizing the pace and direction of economic activity, and for providing necessary economic infrastructure; for the
conduct of foreign and defense policy on which overseas markets
depend; and for the huge military and aerospace contracts that
now sustain whole sectors of the economy. All of these policies can
be understood as at least partly the result of the political efforts
of businessmen to limit their exposure to the instability and insecurity of the self-regulating market. In this large sense, it is
capitalists themselves, by their demands for state intervention,
who have given the lie to the myth that powered their ascendancy.

The myth of the self-regulating market has outlived the conditions that gave rise to it. Nevertheless, the myth remains part of
our cultural repertoire, and is regularly hauled out in political
combat over the welfare state. The myth of the self-regulating
market thus continues to set the parameters of debate on social
welfare programs. Neither the antagonists nor the protagonists in
the current debate over welfare state programs challenge the premise of the inviolability of the market. If welfare state programs are
defended, it is presumably because they have few or no labor-
market effects.

The force of this assumption and the ideological conviction
that animates it are suggested by the unthinking use of the term
"dependency" to characterize the condition of people who receive
welfare benefits. The term is charged with connotations of psychological ineptitude associated with welfare receipt, connotations
embroidered by journalistic accounts of the lives of welfare recipients. By contrast, those who work for wages, no matter the kind
of work they do, or the conditions under which they work, or the
wages they receive, are presumably "independent," with the associated psychological traits of personal discipline and self-reli-

ance. This language and these connotations reflect the myth of the self-regulating market, which depicts the buying and selling of labor as the interplay of free actors, all vigorously pursuing their own advantage on more or less equal terms. But this language and its connotations do not match the reality of participation in the labor market for most people, and they certainly do not match the experience of wage workers at the bottom of the labor market. They do not describe labor-market participation in the fast-food industry, or in retailing, or in office-cleaning companies, or in hospitals. In these jobs, low wages and insecure employment make workers vulnerable and *dependent*—vulnerable to the vagaries of market conditions, and dependent on the whims and interests of particular employers.

If anything, given the realities of the labor market, and especially the nonunion and low-wage sectors of the labor market, it is the availability of welfare benefits that introduces a measure of independence into the circumstances of workers. Knowing they can turn to unemployment benefits or welfare benefits if they are fired probably makes workers a little more secure in their dealings with employers and therefore a little more "independent." The evidence reported earlier in this chapter suggests that many people do use welfare in just this way. Contrary to the stereotype of a large permanent underclass created by welfare usage, many people move on and off the welfare rolls, and a majority stay on rolls for relatively short periods of less than two years. Moreover, until legislation introduced by the Reagan administration terminated supplementary benefits to women who were working but whose earnings were low, many people used welfare income in combination with other sources of income, primarily wage income (Duncan and Hoffman 1986; Rein and Rainwater 1978; Harrison 1977). These facts suggest that, rather than miring them in dependency, welfare benefits help people cope with unsettled and difficult life circumstances, including unsettled and difficult employment circumstances. It is not farfetched to say that income-protection programs make many people a little more self-reliant.

Welfare state programs protect people from the vagaries of the labor market and the power of particular employers by providing income that is not conditional on market performance. That is their great accomplishment, for it not only eases the worst poverty but brings a small measure of security into the lives of people who are otherwise very insecure. But that accomplishment has its price. The income supports that reduce insecurity and make people more independent also blunt the force of market incentives and disincentives. After all, desperate people without any protections at all will work at any job, no matter how harsh the terms. This is the heart of what the conflict over the welfare state is about, and it is what conflicts over relief have always been about.

No contrivance of policy can break this tension between the welfare state and the market. To the extent that people are given some economic protection and are not stripped of social respect by the conditions attached to that protection, there must be some work-disincentive effects. More humane programs, which permit people to live in physical decency and do not stigmatize them, will have larger disincentive effects. Of course, these disincentives can always be outweighed by improvements in working conditions. But by the same reasoning, contracting welfare state benefits and making the treatment of beneficiaries more onerous allows employers to degrade working conditions further. Researchers who treat the avoidance of disincentive effects as a policy imperative rule out the possibility of a more humane welfare state, and even lend tacit support to efforts to make existing programs more restrictive. In the process, they smooth the way for further assaults on the conditions of work at the bottom of the American economy.

Discussions of welfare "dependency" and family life are just as much marked by inconsistency. Thus women raising their children by themselves who rely on welfare programs for income are considered dependent, and therefore they and their children are supposedly susceptible to all of the demoralizing consequences associated with "dependency." But women in traditional two-parent households who rely on men for their income are not labeled dependent, or at least no one worries that dependency disables them and makes them incapable of socializing their children adequately for future labor-force participation and marriage. Nor does anyone worry over the effects of dependency on women who rely on alimony or child-support payments or on other "unearned" assets.

In fact, just as the availability of income supports helps people (mainly women) cope with the vagaries of the labor market, so does it reduce the helplessness of women and children in the face of the weakening of the traditional family. Whatever the causes of rising rates of divorce and separation and out-of-wedlock births, these patterns are spreading in all sectors of American society, and indeed in all Western societies. This erosion of the traditional family form makes all women acutely vulnerable economically, including those still living with men and sharing in a family wage. For many women, marital breakup means that after contributing years of unpaid household labor in exchange for a share of the wages earned by men, they and their children confront the threat or the reality of being cut off, in most cases with only negligible alimony or child-support payments, if any at all. The NOW Legal Defense and Education Fund estimates that only one in four of the families with children headed by women receive child-support payments regularly. And as Weitzman (1985) documents, in California the average woman's standard of living drops by 73 percent in the first year of divorce, while the average man's improves by 42 percent. At the same time, women confront a labor market in which they are still largely segregated in low-wage occupations, an arrangement justified historically by the idea that women were only secondary earners. Welfare payments provide some security for women and their children in the face of the upheaval in traditional family arrangements. The data show that "family events" are even more important than unemployment in explaining why women turn to AFDC.

The availability of welfare benefits is almost surely not the fundamental cause of changing family patterns, just as welfare benefits are not an important cause of unemployment. Nevertheless, while it is clear that these changes in the family have roots in society-wide changes, it also seems reasonable to surmise that the availability of welfare has some influence on the way women (and the men with whom they are associated) respond to these changes. If income supports reduce the vulnerability of women, then the absence or reduction of such supports might well make them more fearful of the prospect of raising children without men, and more willing therefore to bend to the demands men make. In this sense, access to income independent of the whim or will of male breadwinners is similar in its effects to access to income independent of the whim or will of employers. By providing a measure of security to women and children, the social programs make women a little less vulnerable and a little more independent in the face of a male power that, at least in the short run, actually increases as traditional family norms that previously constrained the behavior of men weaken and the threat of breakup becomes more acute. In other words, it may well be that the availability of welfare weakens the element of economic compulsion in traditional family relations, and in that limited sense may contribute to marital breakup or to the failure of women to marry in the first place. But preserving traditional families by preserving the economic power of men is a policy objective which at the very least demands public scrutiny and discussion.[22]

In sum, very large choices about our institutional life, choices with profound moral consequences, are dictated by the assumption that welfare policies must not be allowed to intrude on the labor market or on the traditional family. These choices have not been examined in the debate over the welfare state. Instead, work and family are treated by all sides as inviolable. But since there is an inherent and ineradicable tension between the welfare state and the unfettered market, and between the welfare state and the patriarchal family, and because these tensions increase as the welfare state is liberalized, the effect of that assumption is to greatly weaken the defense of the welfare state.

Indeed, the only defense that remains possible is to acquiesce in efforts to mold social programs according to the old principle of "less eligibility." Welfare programs are in effect defended only insofar as the circumstances of recipients remain "less eligible" or

---

[22] Sarri (1985) says that in a sample of current and former AFDC recipients in Michigan, 45% reported their spouse had repeatedly been violent toward them or their children or both. "At some point in the cycle of violence, each of these women decided to leave home with their children and applied for AFDC" (8).

less desirable than even those of the lowest-paid worker, and less eligible than even the circumstances of women and children in the poorest two-parent family or in the most abusive male-headed households. Consistently, so long as the imperative of work on any terms is assumed, there is no persuasive basis for enjoining against measures to make welfare programs more restrictive, such as the coercive workfare programs that are spreading across the country under the Reagan administration's prodding, except perhaps to argue that these programs have been shown to be ineffective.

Just as the defense of the welfare state is weakened when the primacy of the market and the traditional family are treated as axiomatic, so is the contemplation of more generous and less punitive welfare state programs precluded. Even the imagination of authentic reforms is stifled because a more generous and humane welfare state would almost surely increase work-disincentive and family-disincentive effects. As a consequence, there is little public discussion of raising social welfare benefits to levels that would permit a living standard that does not mire people in poverty and marginalize them from the larger culture. There is little discussion of the consolidation of programs so that people are not shuffled among a rat's maze of different programs designed to specify exactly the various circumstances that do or do not entitle people to benefits, and to precisely what benefits, in a restrictive and work-conforming welfare state. Elaborate and arcane categories such as AFDC, SSI, and UI make it far more difficult for people to understand their entitlements, and also divide people whose circumstances are otherwise similar, thus weakening them as political constituencies. Similarly, so long as the imperatives of market and family are assumed, there can be no thought of the possibility of simplifying eligibility criteria so that people can effectively exercise *rights* in dealing with welfare state bureaucracies. And we cannot even imagine the possibilities for innovative forms of social provision that might encourage the development of a sense of community, a spirit of democracy, and an appreciation of diversity within the terrain of the welfare state. All of these possibilities are categorically eliminated by the assumption that the market and the traditional family must at all costs remain pre-eminent.

In other words, so long as work and family are assumed to be
inviolable, the central moral choices that we as a society in fact
make through our welfare policies remain concealed, the options
defined away by ideological fiat. These choices are enormous in
their scope. They include the relative power we think workers
and employers should have in labor market relations, and husbands and wives in family relations. Our welfare policies also
bear directly on the question whether the work women do in
rearing children and caring for families is to be regarded as a
legitimate contribution to our society. Current policies that are
contorted by mechanisms intended to force mothers into the
labor market obviously deny that contribution. Welfare policies
are also choices through which we create and recreate the culture of class and race in our society, both through the impoverishment and ritual degradation of recipients and as a result of the
material and social crippling of the children who will be tomorrow's adult poor. These policies are also choices about the question, so profoundly important to us collectively, of how much we
want to tolerate the widespread insecurities and inequalities considered necessary for the optimal functioning of labor markets.
And the scale and organization of our welfare state programs
also bears importantly on the great classical question of the appropriate relationship of government, markets, and families.
These are all moral choices of profound importance, and they
ought not to be buried in the unthinking assumption that wage
work and the traditional family must be considered sacred, no
matter the costs.

Finally, these moral dilemmas have become more acute, and
the political stakes in how they are resolved have grown, as a result
of the major transformations occurring in the American economy
and family. By invoking the myth of the pre-eminence of the
market during a period of economic transition and uncertainty, the
vulnerability of people at the bottom is increased. In the name of
"natural law" we take sides in a contemporary class conflict whose
repercussions could be awesome. The current efforts of employers
to reduce wages and increase work discipline are in part a response
to economic instability, and particularly to heightened interna-

tional competition and sagging profits. But the conditions that prompted this employer mobilization to force working people to absorb the costs of a restructured economic order have also become a weapon in the campaign. The threat of disinvestment or offshore production or roboticization is regularly used to beat down worker demands, for increased economic flux makes working people more fearful and quicker to concede to employer demands. Similarly, increased family instability makes women more fearful, and therefore heightens the power of men. It is because the protections provided by the welfare state bear on the power relations of the market and the traditional family that these policies have come under attack. But that is also the reason that the conflict over the welfare state is a conflict about the future shape of American society.

REFERENCES

Anderson, Martin. 1978. *Welfare: The Political Economy of Welfare Reform in the United States.* Stanford, Calif.: Hoover Institution.

Asbury, Herbert. 1928. *The Gangs of New York.* New York: Alfred A. Knopf.

AuClaire, Philip Arthur. 1984. "Public Attitudes Toward Social Welfare Expenditures." *Social Work* 29.

Auletta, Ken. 1982. *The Underclass.* New York: Random House.

Bane, Mary Jo, and David T. Ellwood. 1983. "The Dynamics of Dependence: The Routes to Self-Sufficiency." John F. Kennedy School of Government, Harvard University, Cambridge, Mass. Mimeo.

———. 1984. "Single Mothers and Their Living Arrangements." John F. Kennedy School of Government, Harvard University, Cambridge, Mass. Mimeo.

Banfield, Edward. *The Unheavenly City: The Nature and Future of Our Urban Crisis.* 1970. Boston: Little, Brown & Co.

Bell, Daniel. 1953. "Crime as an American Way of Life." *Antioch Review* 13: 146–51.

Bishop, John H. 1980. "Jobs, Cash Transfers, and Marital Instability: A Review and Synthesis of the Literature." *Journal of Human Resources* 15(3): 301–34.

Blank, Rebecca M., and Alan S. Blinder. 1986. "Macroeconomics, Income Distribution, and Poverty." Pp. 180–208 in Sheldon H. Danziger and Daniel H. Weinberg, eds., *Fighting Poverty: What Works and What Doesn't.* Cambridge, Mass.: Harvard University Press.

Bowles, Samuel, and Herbert Gintis. 1982. "The Crisis of Liberal Democratic Capitalism: The Case of the United States." *Politics and Society* 11(1): 51–94.

Burtless, Gary. 1986. "Public Spending for the Poor: Trends, Prospects, and Economic Limits." Pp. 18–49 in Sheldon H. Danziger and Daniel H. Weinberg, eds., *Fighting Poverty: What Works and What Doesn't*. Cambridge, Mass.: Harvard University Press.

Cain, Glen. 1985. "Comments on Murray's Analysis of the Impact of the War on Poverty on the Labor Market Behavior of the Poor." Pp. 9–35 in *Losing Ground: A Critique*, Special Report no. 38. Madison: Institute for Research and Poverty, University of Wisconsin.

Cloward, Richard A., and Lloyd E. Ohlin. 1960. *Delinquency and Opportunity*. Glencoe, Ill.: Free Press.

Coe, Richard D. 1979. "Participation in the Food Stamp Program Among the Poverty Population." In *Five Thousand American Families—Patterns of Economic Progress*. Vol. 7, edited by Greg Duncan and James N. Morgan. Ann Arbor: Institute for Social Research, University of Michigan.

————. 1981. "A Preliminary Examination of the Dynamics of Welfare Use." In *Five Thousand American Families—Patterns of Economic Progress*. Vol. 9, edited by Martha S. Hill and James N. Morgan. Ann Arbor: Institute for Social Research, University of Michigan.

Cogan, J. 1982. "The Decline in Black Teenage Employment: 1950–70." *American Economic Review* 72: 621–38.

Cutright, Phillips. 1971. "Income and Family Events: Marital Instability." *Journal of Marriage and the Family* 33: 291–306.

————. 1973. "Illegitimacy and Income Supplements." *Studies in Public Welfare*. Paper no. 12, prepared for use of the Subcommittee on Fiscal Policy of the Joint Economic Committee, Congress of the United States. Washington, D.C.: Government Printing Office.

————. 1974. "Components of Change in the Number of Female Family Heads Aged 15–44." *Journal of Marriage and the Family* 36: 714–21.

Cutright, Phillips, and P. Madras. 1974. "AFDC and the Marital and Family Status of Ever Married Women Aged 15–44: United States, 1950–1970." *Sociology and Social Research* 60: 314–27.

Danziger, Sheldon, H., and Peter Gottschalk. 1983. "The Measurement of Poverty." *American Behavioral Scientist* 26(6): 739–56.

Danziger, Sheldon H., Robert H. Haveman, and Robert D. Plotnick. 1981. "How Income Transfer Programs Affect Work, Savings, and the Income Distribution: A Critical Review." *Journal of Economic Literature* 19: 975–1028.

————. 1986. "Antipoverty Policy: Effects on the Poor and the Nonpoor." Pp. 50–77 in Sheldon H. Danziger and Daniel H. Weinberg, eds., *Fighting*

Poverty: What Works and What Doesn't. Cambridge, Mass.: Harvard University Press.

Danziger, Sheldon H., and Robert D. Plotnick. 1986. "Poverty and Policy: Lessons from the Last Two Decades." *Social Service Review* 60(1): 34–51.

Danziger, Sheldon H., and Daniel H. Weinberg. 1986. "Introduction." Pp. 1–17 in Sheldon H. Danziger and Daniel H. Weinberg, eds., *Fighting Poverty: What Works and What Doesn't.* Cambridge, Mass.: Harvard University Press.

Davis, Laura F. 1986. "Public Attitudes Toward Welfare Allocation." Department of Social Work, University of Wyoming, Laramie. Mimeo.

Dolbeare, Cushing. 1983. "The Low-income Housing Crisis." In Chester Hartman, ed., *America's Housing Crisis: What Is to Be Done?* Boston: Routledge & Kegan Paul.

Drake, St. Clair, and Horace R. Cayton. 1945. *Black Metropolis: A Study of Negro Life in a Northern City.* Vol. 2. New York: Harper & Row.

Duncan, Greg J., with Richard D. Coe, Mary E. Corcoran, Martha S. Hill, Saul D. Hoffman, and James N. Morgan. 1984. *Years of Poverty, Years of Plenty.* Ann Arbor: Institute for Social Research, University of Michigan.

Duncan, Greg J., and Saul D. Hoffman. 1986. "Welfare Dynamics and the Nature of Need." Institute for Social Research, University of Michigan, Ann Arbor. Mimeo.

Ellwood, David T. 1986. "Targeting 'Would-Be' Long-term Recipients of AFDC." Mathematica Policy Research, Princeton, N.J. Mimeo.

Ellwood, David T., and Mary Jo Bane. 1986. "The Impact of AFDC on Family Structure and Living Arrangements." *Research in Labor Economics* 7: 137–207.

Ellwood, David T., and Lawrence H. Summers. 1986. "Poverty in America: Is Welfare the Answer or the Problem?" Pp. 78–105 in Sheldon H. Danziger and Daniel H. Weinberg, eds., *Fighting Poverty: What Works and What Doesn't.* Cambridge, Mass.: Harvard University Press.

Ellwood, David T., and David A. Wise. 1983. "Youth Unemployment in the Seventies: The Changing Circumstances of Young Adults." Working Paper no. 1055, National Bureau of Economic Research, Washington, D.C.

Erie, Steven P. 1978. "Politics, the Public Sector, and Irish Social Mobility: San Francisco, 1870–1900." *Western Political Quarterly* 31: 274–89.

Fechter, A., and S. Greenfield. 1973. "Welfare and Illegitimacy: An Economic Model and Some Preliminary Results." Working Paper, Urban Institute, Washington, D.C.

Frazier, E. Franklin. 1939. *The Negro Family in the United States.* Chicago: University of Chicago Press.

Freeman, Richard B., and Harry J. Holzer. 1986. "The Black Youth Employment Crisis: Summary of Findings." Pp. 3–20 in Richard B. Freeman and

Harry J. Holzer, eds., *The Black Youth Employment Crisis.* Chicago: University of Chicago Press.

Furstenberg, F. F., T. Hershberg, and J. Modell. 1975. "The Origins of the Female-headed Family: The Impact of the Urban Experience." *Journal of Interdisciplinary History* 6: 211–33.

Gans, Herbert. 1962. *The Urban Villagers: Group and Class in the Life of Italian-Americans.* New York: Free Press.

Gilder, George. 1981. *Wealth and Poverty.* New York: Basic Books.

Glazer, Nathan. 1971. "The Limits of Social Policy." *Commentary* 52(3): 51–58.

Gough, Ian. 1979. *The Political Economy of the Welfare State.* London: Macmillan Press.

Greenstein, Robert. 1985. "Losing Faith in 'Losing Ground'." *New Republic,* March 25.

Gronbjerg, Kirsten. 1977. *Mass Society and the Extension of Welfare, 1960–1970.* Chicago: University of Chicago Press.

Gutman, Herbert G. 1976. *The Black Family in Slavery and Freedom, 1750–1925.* New York: Pantheon Books.

Harrison, Bennett. 1977. "Labor Market Structure and the Relationship Between Work and Welfare." Department of Urban Studies, Massachusetts Institute of Technology, Cambridge. Mimeo.

Hartman, C., D. Keating, and R. LeGates. 1982. *Displacement: How to Fight It.* Berkeley, Calif.: National Housing Law Project.

Haveman, Robert H. 1986. "Poverty Research and the Social Sciences." *Focus* (University of Wisconsin) 9.

Heclo, Hugh. 1986. "The Political Foundations of Antipoverty Policy." Pp. 312–40 in Sheldon H. Danziger and Daniel H. Weinberg, eds., *Fighting Poverty: What Works and What Doesn't.* Cambridge, Mass.: Harvard University Press.

Hicks, Alexander, and Duane H. Swank. 1983. "Civil Disorder, Relief Mobilization, and AFDC Caseloads: A Reexamination of the Piven and Cloward Thesis." *American Journal of Political Science* 27 (November): 695–716.

Hill, Martha S., and Michael Ponza. 1983. "Poverty Across Generations: Is Welfare Dependency a Pathology Passed on from One Generation to the Next?" Institute for Social Research, University of Michigan, Ann Arbor. Mimeo.

———. 1984. "Does Welfare Dependency Beget Dependency?" Institute for Social Research, University of Michigan, Ann Arbor. Mimeo.

Hochchild, Jennifer L. 1986. "Race, Class, and Power." Working Paper no. 10: *Democratic Values.* Project on the Federal Role. National Conference on Social Welfare, Washington, D.C.

Hoffman, Saul D., and John W. Holmes. 1976. "Husbands, Wives, and Divorce." In *Five Thousand American Families—Patterns of Economic Prog-*

ress. Vol. 4, edited by Greg J. Duncan and James N. Morgan. Ann Arbor: Institute for Social Research, University of Michigan.

Honig, M. 1974. "AFDC Income, Recipient Rates, and Family Dissolution." *Journal of Human Resources* 9: 303–22.

Hopper, Kim, and Jill Hamberg. 1986. "The Making of America's Homeless: From Skid Row to New Poor, 1945–1984." Pp. 12–40 in Rachel G. Bratt, Chester Hartman, and A. Meyerson, eds., *Critical Perspectives on Housing.* Philadelphia: Temple University Press.

Hutchens, Robert M. 1981. "Entry and Exit Transitions in a Government Transfer Program: The Case of Aid to Families with Dependent Children." *Journal of Human Resources* 16(2): 217–37.

Isaac, Larry, and William R. Kelly. 1981. "Racial Insurgency, the State, and Welfare Expansion." *American Journal of Sociology* 86 (6): 1348–86.

———. 1982. "Developmental/Modernization and Political Class Struggle Theories of Welfare State Expansion: The Case of the AFDC 'Explosion' in the States, 1960–70." *Journal of Political and Military Sociology* 10 (2).

Jennings, Edward T. 1979. "Civil Turmoil and the Growth of Welfare Rolls: A Comparative State Analysis." *Policy Studies Journal* 7 (Summer): 739–45.

Jordan, June. 1986. "Thank You, America!" *Newsday,* June 29.

Lammermeir, P. J. 1973. "The Urban Black Family of the Nineteenth Century: A Study of Black Family Structure in the Ohio Valley, 1850–1880." *Journal of Marriage and the Family* 35: 440–56.

Lane, Jonathan P. 1981. "The Findings of the Panel Study of Income Dynamics about the AFDC Program." Assistant Secretary for Planning and Evaluation, U.S. Department of Health and Human Services. Mimeo.

Lerman, Robert. 1986. "Do Welfare Programs Affect the Schooling and Work Patterns of Young Black Men?" Pp. 403–38 in Richard B. Freeman and Harry J. Holzer, eds., *The Black Youth Employment Crisis.* Chicago: University of Chicago Press.

Lieby, James. 1978. *A History of Social Welfare and Social Work in the United States.* New York: Columbia University Press.

Lipset, Seymour Martin. 1985. "The Elections, the Economy, and Public Opinion: 1984." *PS: The Journal of the American Political Science Association* 18(1): 28–38.

———. 1986. "Beyond 1984: The Anomalies of American Politics." *PS: Journal of the American Political Science Association* 19(2): 222–36.

Mare, Robert D., and Christopher Winship. 1979. "Changes in Race Differentials in Youth Unemployment and Labor Force Participation, 1950–1978: Preliminary Analysis." In *Expanding Employment Opportunities for Disadvantaged Youth.* Special Report no. 37, National Commission for Employment Policy. Washington, D.C.: Government Printing Office.

Matusow, Allen J. 1984. *The Unravelling of America: A History of Liberalism in the 1960s.* New York: Harper & Row.

Mead, Lawrence M. 1985. *Beyond Entitlement: The Social Obligations of Citizenship.* New York: Free Press.

Minarik, J. J., and R. S. Goldfarb. 1976. "AFDC Income, Recipient Rates, and Family Dissolution: A Comment." *Journal of Human Resources* 11: 243–50.

Moore, Kristin A., and S. B. Caldwell. 1976. "The Effect of Government Policies on Out-of-Wedlock Sex and Pregnancy." *Family Planning Perspectives* 9: 164–69.

Morehouse, Ward, and David Dembo. 1986. "The Underbelly of the U.S. Economy: Joblessness and Pauperization of Working America." Special Report no. 6, Council on International and Public Affairs, New York.

Moynihan, Daniel Patrick. 1965. *The Negro Family: The Case for National Action.* Washington, D.C.: U.S. Department of Labor, Office of Family Planning and Research.

Murray, Charles A. 1984. *Losing Ground: American Social Policy, 1950–1980.* New York: Basic Books.

———. 1986. "Have the Poor Been 'Losing Ground'?" *Political Science Quarterly* 100(3): 427–45.

Murray, Charles A., with Deborah Laren. 1986. *According to Age: Longitudinal Profiles of AFDC Recipients and the Poor by Age Group.* Prepared for the Working Seminar on the Family and American Welfare Policy.

Myers, Samuel L., Jr. 1986. "Comment." Pp. 438–41 in Richard B. Freeman and Harry J. Holzer, eds., *The Black Youth Employment Crisis.* Chicago: University of Chicago Press.

Navarro, Vincente. 1985. "The 1984 Election and the New Deal: An Alternative Interpretation." *Social Policy* 15(4): 3–10.

Norton, Eleanor Holmes. 1985. "Restoring the Traditional Black Family." *New York Times Magazine,* June 2.

O'Connor, James. 1973. *The Fiscal Crisis of the State.* New York: St. Martin's Press.

O'Neill, June A., Douglas A. Wolf, Laurie J. Bassi, and Michael T. Hannan. 1984. "An Analysis of Time on Welfare." Washington, D.C.: Urban Institute.

Parsons, Donald O. 1980. "The Decline of Male Labor Force Participation." *Journal of Political Economy* 88: 117–34.

Piven, Frances Fox, and Richard A. Cloward. 1971. *Regulating the Poor: The Functions of Public Welfare.* New York: Pantheon Books.

———. 1977. *Poor People's Movements: Why They Succeed, How They Fail.* New York: Pantheon Books.

———. 1982. Rev. and enl. ed. 1985. *The New Class War: Reagan's Attack on the Welfare State and Its Consequences.* New York: Pantheon Books.

Pleck, E. H. 1972. "The Two-Parent Household: Black Family Structure in Late Nineteenth-Century Boston." *Journal of Social History* 6: 3–31.

Plotnick, Robert. 1983. "Turnover in the AFDC Population: An Event History Analysis." *Journal of Human Resources* 18: 65–81.

Reider, Jonathan. 1985. " 'Middle American' Resistance to Liberal Reform." Paper prepared for colloquium, "The Changing Situation of Black Americans and Women: Roots and Reverberations in U.S. Social Policies Since the 1960s," sponsored by the Center for the Study of Industrial Societies, University of Chicago. Mimeo.

Rein, Martin, and Lee Rainwater. 1978. "Patterns of Welfare Use." *Social Service Review* 52: 511–34.

Rosenberg, Sam. 1983. "Reagan Social Policy and Labour Force Restructuring." *Cambridge Journal of Economics* 7: 179–96.

Ross, H. L., and Isabel Sawhill. 1975. *Time of Transition: The Growth of Families Headed by Women.* Washington, D.C.: Urban Institute Press.

Sarri, Rosemary C. 1985. "The Impact of Federal Policy Change on Low-Income Working Women." School of Social Work, University of Michigan, Ann Arbor. Mimeo.

Schram, Sanford F., and J. Patrick Turbott. 1983. "Civil Disorder and the Welfare Explosion." *American Sociological Review* 48: 408–14.

Shapiro, Robert Y., and Kelly D. Patterson. 1986. "The Dynamics of Public Opinion Toward Social Welfare Policy." Paper delivered at the annual meeting of the American Political Science Association, Washington, D.C.

Sheehan, Susan. 1976. *A Welfare Mother.* Boston: Houghton Mifflin Co.

Shifflett, C. A. 1975. "The Household Composition of Rural Black Families: Louisa County, Virginia, 1880." *Journal of Interdisciplinary History* 6: 235–60.

Smeedling, Timothy M. 1977. "The Antipoverty Effectiveness of In-Kind Transfers." *Journal of Human Resources* 12(3): 360–78.

———. 1982. "The Anti-Poverty Effects of In-Kind Transfers." *Policy Studies Journal* 10: 499–521.

Smeedling, Timothy M., and Marilyn Moon. 1979. "Valuing Government Expenditures: The Case of Medical Care Transfers and Poverty." Discussion Paper no. 568–79. Institute for Research on Poverty, University of Madison, Madison.

Smith, Wade A., and Phillips Cutright. 1985. "Components of Change in the Number of Female Family Heads Ages 15 to 44, An·Update and Reanalysis: United States, 1940 to 1983." *Social Science Research* 14(3): 226–50.

Thernstrom, Stephan, and Peter R. Knights. 1970. *Men in Motion: Some Data and Speculation About Urban Population Mobility in Nineteenth Century America.* Los Angeles: Institute of Government and Public Affairs, University of California.

Trattner, Walter I. 1979. *From Poor Law to Welfare State: A History of Social Welfare in America.* 2nd ed., rev. New York: Free Press.

U.S. Advisory Committee on Intergovernmental Relations. 1986. *Relocation: Unequal Treatment of People and Businesses Displaced by Government.* Washington, D.C.: Government Printing Office.

U.S. Bureau of the Census. 1984. *Estimates of Poverty Including the Value of Noncash Benefits: 1979 to 1982.* Technical Paper no. 51. Washington, D.C.: Government Printing Office.

U.S. Department of Labor. Bureau of Labor Statistics. 1967. *Social and Economic Conditions of Negroes in the United States, October 1967.* BLS Report no. 332. Washington, D.C.: Government Printing Office.

————. 1968. *The Negroes in the United States: Their Economic and Social Situation, June 1966.* BLS Report no. 1511. Washington, D.C.: Government Printing Office.

————. 1969. *Recent Trends in Social and Economic Conditions of Negroes in the United States, July 1968.* BLS Report No. 347. Washington, D.C.: Government Printing Office.

Vining, D. R. 1983. "Illegitimacy and Public Policy." *Population and Development Review* 9: 105–10.

Warlick, Jennifer. 1982. "Participation of the Aged in SSI." *Journal of Human Resources* 17: 236–60.

Weitzman, Lenore J. 1985. *The Divorce Revolution: The Unexpected Social and Economic Consequences for Women and Children in America.* New York: Free Press.

Whyte, William F. 1955. *Street Corner Society.* Enl. ed. Chicago: University of Chicago Press.

Wilensky, Harold I. 1975. *The Welfare State and Equality: Structural and Ideological Roots of Public Expenditures.* Berkeley: University of California Press.

Wilson, James Q. 1985. "The Rediscovery of Character: Private Virtue and Public Policy." *Public Interest* 81 (Fall): 3–16.

Wilson, William Julius. 1986. "The Crisis of the Ghetto Underclass and the Liberal Retreat." Department of Sociology, University of Chicago. Mimeo.

Wilson, William Julius, and Kathryn M. Neckerman. 1986. "Poverty and Family Structure: The Widening Gap Between Evidence and Public Policy Issues." In Sheldon H. Danziger and Daniel H. Weinberg, eds., *Fighting Poverty: What Works and What Doesn't.* Cambridge, Mass.: Harvard University Press.

Winegarden, C. R. 1974. "The Fertility of AFDC Women: An Econometric Analysis." *Journal of Economics and Business* 26: 159–66.

C H A P T E R 3

Rethinking the Political Economy of the Welfare State

Fred Block

IN THE CURRENT CLIMATE of American politics, anyone with the courage to argue in favor of an expansion of the welfare state will be immediately denounced as economically unrealistic by a chorus of voices. Across most of the political spectrum, politicians and policy analysts accept the "realist" view that American capitalism cannot afford even the existing level of civilian spending, much less any systematic efforts at expansion.[1] According to this "realist" argument, since welfare state expenditures reduce economic efficiency, they are a costly luxury that we cannot afford in a period of growing federal budget and foreign trade deficits.

The core of the "realist" argument is captured in Paul Samuelson's caricature of the beliefs that he attributes to most American businesspeople and college graduates:

> The Roosevelt New Deal brought in some needed reforms. But this last half century has witnessed an overshoot of government regulations, taxation, and deficit spending. The vigor of the market economy has thereby been sapped—just as it had been in so many of the mixed economies abroad. United States inflation, stagnation in productivity, class struggle, and popular unrest is the inevitable consequence of the cancerous

[1] On the convergence between conservative and leftist analyses, see Block (1986).

growth of the public sector engineered by powerseeking bureaucrats and politicians. (Samuelson 1980: 666)

Samuelson himself does not accept all of these arguments; like many other mainstream economists, he prides himself on having a more subtle and nuanced view of the relationship between the state and the economy.[2] Yet most academic economists have done little to challenge the "realist" position, and it has become the consensus view among American elites. It dominates policy discussions within the Reagan administration and holds sway over large sections of the Democratic party as well.

But despite the broad consensus, the "realist" position is simply wrong because its premises are shortsighted and antiquated. "Realists" are shortsighted because they continually confuse raising profit levels in the short term with strengthening the economy over the long term. "Realist" premises are antiquated because they hold on to nineteenth-century premises that have little relevance for an increasingly postindustrial economy. Their arguments continually rely on "the myth of the self-regulating market" (Piven and Cloward, pp. 93–94 above), which has little relevance to an advanced capitalist society that is profoundly shaped by state actions.

The shortsightedness is exemplified by the "realist" assumption that what is good for big business is good for the economy as a whole. Charles Wilson's famous line that what is good for General Motors is good for the country was wrong back in the 1950s and continues to be wrong precisely because individual interests do not automatically aggregate into a collective good. For example, businesses could all succeed in driving wage levels down in their search for greater profits only to find that their profits and income

---

[2] Nevertheless, economists bear a good deal of responsibility for the triumph of the "realist" position; the latter view pushes to the limits premises that underlie mainstream views. Hence, neoclassical economics is built around conceptions of the self-regulating market—the equilibrium price auction. While economists are aware of a variety of factors that might interfere with market self-regulation, "realists" simply take the additional step of assuming that markets can always operate effectively on their own.

collapse when the public's reduced purchasing power results in a depression.

It is also the case that profitability and the overall efficiency of the economy are two different things, and that it is easy to have more profits and less efficiency. The United States does have, for example, a highly profitable private health-care industry that manages to deliver health services with extraordinary inefficiency, driving up health-care costs throughout the economy. There are also data to show that unionized firms in the United States tend to have higher rates of productivity than nonunionized firms, but they are less profitable because workers get a larger share of the output (Freeman and Medoff 1984: chaps. 11, 12). That means that if conservatives had their dream and all labor unions were eliminated tomorrow, corporate profits would rise but productivity and economic efficiency would decline. By consistently failing to understand that what is good for corporate profitability is not necessarily good for the economy as a whole, the "realists" are able to advance mistaken and irrational policy prescriptions.

The "realist" argument is antiquated because it fails to take account of basic structural transformations in the economy that undermine long-established economic assumptions. Changes such as the growing importance and weight of services in the economy, the increased impact of advanced technologies on the production process, and dramatic increases in the percentage of people who are employed or looking for employment are beyond dispute, but there has been insufficient recognition that these changes necessitate a rethinking of much of our inherited economic wisdom. Arguments that were developed to make sense of an industrial economy must be fundamentally revised if we are to understand an increasingly postindustrial economy—that is, one organized around services and computer technologies (Hirschhorn 1984; Block 1985).

These crippling problems mean that much of the data and the analysis on which the "realist" position rests are mistaken. Their case against the welfare state is a collection of ideological prejudices, unexamined assumptions, and faulty economic arguments.[3] These false arguments have contributed to great human suffering as millions have been denied adequate support from the state. But it is also important to recognize that the triumph of these arguments has been a great diversion; it has kept the society from recognizing that the revitalization of the economy depends on an expansion of the welfare state. The irony is that when one analyzes the actual economy in which we live, it turns out that the "realists" have been profoundly unrealistic, and that their much-maligned opponents—those who advocate an expanded welfare state—are the true realists.

For example, when one submits the "realist" arguments to comparative analysis, the results are devastating. If the "realist" arguments were valid, one would expect that the more highly developed a society's welfare provisions, the poorer its overall level of economic performance would be. One would imagine that those countries of Western Europe whose rates of taxation and welfare expenditures are significantly higher than those in the United States would be showing even more dramatic signs of economic distress. But a whole series of comparative analyses (Kuttner 1984; Friedland and Sanders 1985; Katzenstein 1985; Cameron 1985; Goldthorpe 1984; Andrain 1985) have produced contrary evidence. Friedland and Sanders found that the countries with strongest rates of growth in transfer payments also had the strongest rates of economic growth, and Cameron's comparative analysis failed to find a link between the growth of government spending or deficits and inflation rates. All of these studies suggest that the connections that the "realists" make between welfare state spending and negative macroeconomic consequences such as slow growth and inflation are much too simple. The reality is that there are other institutional factors that are important in determining whether more welfare spending will or will not strengthen the economy.

---

[3] By far the best critique of the "realist" view is by the economic journalist Robert Kuttner in *The Economic Illusion* (1984).

THE "REALIST" VIEW OF THE WELFARE STATE

The "realist" view of the welfare state is primarily rooted in "free-market" arguments that have been elaborated by such conservative theorists as Milton Friedman, Arthur Laffer, and George Gilder.[4] Their arguments have been picked up and endlessly repeated by business propagandists and the media. And many political liberals have borrowed some of these same arguments. On the issue of economic growth, for example, formulations of Democratic party neoliberals are often indistinguishable from the views of Reaganites, despite their significant differences on other issues. While individual politicians, publicists, and theorists pick and choose amongst a range of different arguments, for the purposes of systematic critique it is valuable to present the opposition's argument as a coherent whole. The current version of the "realist" diagnosis is built up out of three key elements. The first stresses the disincentives to investment that are produced by a substantial government role in providing social welfare. The second emphasizes the disincentives to work effort that result from governmental social provision. The final set of arguments see welfare state expenditures as a luxury that the society cannot afford at a moment of huge federal budget deficits and foreign trade deficits.[5]

THE CASE THAT THE WELFARE STATE DISCOURAGES INVESTMENT

"Realists" argue that the growth of welfare state expenditures necessitates higher rates of taxation and these higher rates of taxa-

---

[4] These writers, in turn, have simply been elaborating the tradition of economic liberalism that goes back to Adam Smith and whose leading twentieth-century theorist has been Friedrich Hayek.

[5] There is another important strand of the "realist" argument: the critique of government regulation of economic activity. It is this argument that underlies Reagan administration efforts to weaken such agencies as OSHA, EPA, and EEOC. Considerations of space prevent my addressing this strand of argument here.

tion discourage productive investment. When the marginal rate of taxation is high, the rich will have little incentive to take the risks of investment, since a disproportionate share of the returns will be taxed away. They will choose instead to increase their consumption. As George Gilder (1981: 77) writes:

> The chief threat to this system is taxation with rates so progressive—graduated so steeply to capture increasing portions of larger incomes—that the rich refuse to risk their money. Wealth is withdrawn from productive uses, hoarded in gold or collectibles. . . .

Moreover, high rates of taxation will lead to a decline in the overall pool of after-tax profits available for reinvestment, so there will be problems both with the supply of investment resources and in the rate of return that could be expected from the productive use of those resources.

The resulting lower rates of investment create a vicious circle of difficulties. First, inadequate investment will mean slower rates of productivity growth (Norsworthy, Harper, and Kunze 1979). Second, since overall output grows at a slower rate and the state sector continues to expand to provide more welfare, then inflation will intensify (Gordon 1975). Third, inflation constitutes an additional tax on productive investment, so the likelihood is that the rich will increase nonproductive investments—gold, real estate, and collectibles—that are perceived as a hedge against inflation (Gilder 1982: 22). This further reduction in productive investment will intensify the productivity problem and increase the inflationary pressures.

In this argument, investment should be understood as encompassing both money and entrepreneurial effort. In supply-side theory particularly, entrepreneurial effort plays an absolutely central role (Wanniski 1978; Gilder 1982). The Reagan tax cuts were designed to unleash the entrepreneurial energy of individuals who might otherwise decide there would be insufficient gain from such efforts. But even in the more sober arguments of neoliberals, great stress is placed on the encouragement of entrepreneurial efforts through limiting taxation on high-income individuals.

In a word, "realists" insist that the distribution of income produced by the market is optimal and the government's interference with market allocation of income—through taxation and transfers—produces less than desirable economic outcomes. In recent years, inadequate rates of investment and mounting inflationary pressures have been the price we have paid for interfering with the logic of the market.[6]

THE CASE THAT THE WELFARE STATE DISCOURAGES WORK EFFORT

As Piven and Cloward show (chapter 1), contemporary "realists" echo the historic complaint of employers that the availability of forms of economic assistance for the poor, the unemployed, and the disabled encourages people to avoid work. In the Friedmans' pithy sentence: "Those on relief have little incentive to earn income" (1981: 98). While the psychological consequences of this dependence are perceived as damaging, the economic consequences are also substantial. When people have viable alternatives to employment, the effective working of the labor market is impaired. In theory, the optimal matching of people to jobs occurs when wages are free to rise and fall with the relative productivity of the firm or industry (Hayek 1980). But the existence of welfare programs, along with unions and minimum-wage legislation, increases the rigidity of wages (Gordon 1975: 835) and prevents effective working of the market mechanism. The consequence is lower than optimal levels of output and higher rates of inflation. If, on the other hand, all those who are capable of work but are currently receiving some form of welfare largesse were to enter the

---

[6] "Realists" also extend this argument by insisting that when governments use tax money to produce services, they do so inefficiently because they are not subject to the competitive discipline of the market. This inherent inefficiency of government means that even more taxes will be required to support a given level of governmental effort. The "realist" response is to advocate "privatization" as an alternative to public provision. Some of these arguments are addressed below.

labor market, wages would be bid down by the intense competition for jobs, with benign consequences for the rate of inflation. Moreover, when employed workers have options such as unemployment insurance, they are able to extract more substantial wage concessions than if they faced the alternative of acute hunger. This bidding up of wages operates to discourage investment and also contributes to inflationary pressures.

"Realists" also point to a decline in labor discipline that results from welfare measures. They frequently cite a decline in the work ethic that is a consequence of the too easy availability of transfer payments. George Gilder (1982: 87–8) is an example:

> The first principle is that in order to move up, the poor must not only work, they must work harder than the classes above them. Every previous generation of the lower class has made such efforts. But the current poor, white even more than black, are refusing to work hard.

He goes on to argue that "work effort is the crucial unmeasured variable in American productivity and income distribution and that current welfare and other subsidy programs substantially reduce work." According to Gilder, the corrosive effects of welfare extend into the workplace when employees come to believe that even if they are fired, welfare will protect them from economic disaster. The resulting lack of discipline at the workplace means that productivity across the whole economy suffers, dampening profits and adding additional inflationary pressures.

THE CASE THAT THE WELFARE STATE IS A LUXURY

Both of these arguments contribute to a final argument that the society simply cannot afford a costly welfare state at this moment in history. The two prohibitive factors are the growing competitiveness of international trade and the size of the federal budget deficit. For this argument, it is axiomatic that some of the previous mechanisms operate, so that welfare state expenditures *are* demonstrably a drag on the efficient use of resources. Under different circumstances that sacrifice of efficiency might be justified, but in the current context, the sacrifice of efficiency could have catastrophic consequences. In the context of intense international trade competition, expanded welfare state spending with higher rates of taxation would place American businesspeople at an international disadvantage (Scott 1982). If they pass those taxes through in the form of higher prices, their products will not be competitive, and if they attempt to absorb the taxes, they will not generate high enough levels of profit to remain viable. Moreover, to the extent that the United States is perceived as a high-tax country, capital will tend to relocate abroad where tax rates are lower. The result would be a further decline in productive investment domestically and a further exacerbation of problems of productivity and inflation.

As for the federal budget deficit, "realists" argue that in the absence of dramatic cuts in the military budget or higher taxes, even retaining current levels of welfare spending is highly problematic. The danger is spelled out in the report of the White House Conference on Productivity:

> Further increases in government borrowing relative to the supply of funds will add to the upward pressure on already high interest rates. Higher interest rates "crowd-out" private investments that would add to the productive capacity of the economy. (1984: 19)

Moreover, the high interest rates push up the value of the dollar and lead to a further deterioration in the U.S. trade balance (Lawrence 1984: 87). Since cuts in the military budget are politically impractical for the "realists," and higher taxes on the rich would also discourage new investment, there appears to be only one way out of the current impasse.[7] This is to rein in public-sector spending and encourage new investment in the hope that the economy

[7] The other alternative is to raise taxes on middle Americans, but this is seen as politically impractical, particularly if the taxes are to be raised to pay for welfare state expenditures.

can grow its way out of the deficit. In this scenario, at some point in the future, it might again be possible for the public sector to expand its provision of services.

T A K E N   T O G E T H E R , this set of arguments has made it impossible for any politician to support expanded social spending and be taken seriously beyond very limited constituencies. In the 1984 election, for example, Walter Mondale pledged that he would not initiate any significant new civilian programs, and Ronald Reagan was still able to tag him as a big spender. But while these arguments have great political potency, they are also wrong. As we examine each argument in detail, it becomes clear that in certain cases, the "realists" have identified a false problem, and then have blamed social welfare spending for that problem. In other cases, they are correct in identifying the problem, but the chain of reasoning that blames the problem on social welfare spending is severely flawed. The intention here is to show in these cases where "realist" thought identifies actual problems, a stronger case can be made that an *expansion* of the welfare state is the most rational policy option.

WHY THE "REALISTS" ARE WRONG: INVESTMENT AND PRODUCTIVITY

As we have seen, one of the core elements of the economic critique of the welfare state is the argument that investment levels have been insufficient because of the negative effects of welfare spending and tax rates. In many ways, the argument is a continuation of the claims by the business community in the 1970s that the United States faced a massive shortage of capital unless there was a serious reversal in public policy. While the capital-shortage hypothesis was discredited (Kuttner 1980: 230–71), similar arguments live on.

A number of recent studies have effectively critiqued the claim of a slowdown of investment in the 1970s (Bowles, Gordon, Weisskopf 1983: 53–61). Skepticism about an investment shortage is strong enough among mainstream economists that even the White House Conference on Productivity convened by Reagan in 1983 ended up equivocating on the issue; one published table in the final document shows that by several measures, investment rates were higher in the 1970s than in the golden age from 1951 to 1965 (1984: 18–19; Appendix H: 3–5).

Efforts to hold on to the investment-slowdown hypothesis depend on a glaring gap between current economic theory and the data published by the federal government. In the Commerce Department's data on National Product, the investment category is restricted to plant and equipment—buildings and capital goods. However, investment also includes a variety of intangibles such as expenditures for education and training—"human capital,"[8] research and development, and computer software, as most economists have come to recognize.[9] But economists have been slow to realize that as technology advances, intangible capital grows relative to tangible capital. Expenditures for research and development will be much higher in technologically sophisticated industries such as health care and computers than they were in autos and steel. Moreover, as computerization progresses, expenditures for software grow relative to purchases of hardware; when large banks or airlines buy a new central computer, the cost of the software is a very large proportion of the overall purchase, and the same thing is true of factory automation systems. *Business Week* (1984: 75) estimates that by 1989 software purchases will take up close to 40 percent of total expenditures for hardware and software, as compared with close to 20 percent in 1983. Finally, in technologically advanced settings, there are increased expenditures for employee training, management consultants, and other business services precisely because it is not at all obvious how the new technologies should be utilized. The result is a powerful tendency for intangible capital expenditures to rise.

While measuring the amount of intangible capital investment

---

[8] The phrase "human capital" is objectionable because it transforms human attributes into equivalence with machines. However, the phrase continues to be useful because it reflects the economists' grudging recognition that human attributes play a critical role in the production process.

[9] This is not an exhaustive list. I have argued elsewhere that many of the business services that have expanded in recent years—management consultants, industrial engineers, and specialists in organizational design—are also offering a form of intangible capital. See Block 1985.

is more difficult than measuring tangible capital, a number of serious attempts have been made to calculate recent trends for *all* investment. These studies (Kendrick 1976; Eisner 1985) show that total investment as a percentage of Gross National Product has been rising and that intangible capital has been growing relative to tangible capital. Such findings strongly suggest that there is no substance to the claims that the rate of investment in the U.S. economy has been inadequate in recent years. According to Eisner's data, investment as a percentage of GNP rose from 32.2 percent in 1950 to 43.9 percent in 1979, and intangible capital as a percentage of total investment rose across the same period from 37.3 percent to 43.9 percent (calculated from Eisner 1985:31).[10] Those who argue that investment rates are inadequate are aware of these studies; for example, George Gilder in *Wealth and Poverty* (1982:138) mentions Kendrick's study, but then goes on to emphasize that the proof of the pudding is in the performance of the economy and that the low level of productivity growth provides overwhelming evidence that investment levels have been inadequate.

But before turning to productivity growth, there is one additional point that needs to be made about investment levels. Even if one confines the analysis to tangible capital, one must contend with an additional measurement illusion. Capital-saving technologies are now common; this year's machine tools, for example, might be capable of producing twice the output of previous models, but may cost no more. Where capital saving is pervasive, the actual dollar amount of investment in tangible capital might decline, even though the economy's productive capacity is increasing significantly because the new machines are so much more productive than the old.[11] Since computer-based technologies such as robots, computer-controlled machine tools, and computers them-

---

[10] Eisner's estimates are the best available, but his procedures for calculating intangible capital are insufficient. He fails to measure some of its newer forms, and this leads to anomalous findings of high rates of intangible-capital investment in the late 1940s.

[11] This happens because the techniques used by the Bureau of Economic Analysis for computing total investment do not examine changes in the utility of products but focus on changes in price levels.

selves have been falling in price, this point is not simply academic.[12]

In fact, the federal government has recently made a revision in the way it measures computer output that has a direct bearing on this issue. For years, the government failed to develop a price index for computers when calculating the constant-dollar (adjusted for inflation) Gross National Product. Such price indexes are used to separate out purely inflationary price increases from actual increases in output. Similarly, they are needed to separate out the impact of simple price reductions from declining output. Since computer prices have dropped sharply over many years, the absence of a price index has understated the output of this sector. For example, the price of a standard IBM PC has fallen at about 20 percent a year, so if the same number of IBM PC's had been sold in both 1982 and 1983, the government's data would have shown a 20 percent decline in PC output. At the end of 1985, the Bureau of Economic Analysis announced that it had developed a price index for computers that showed prices falling at about 14 percent a year. The government found that when GNP was measured in 1972 dollars, the recalculation resulted in an increment to 1984 output of more than $100 billion (*Survey of Current Business,* December 1985, pp. 16–17; and Cartwright 1986).

With this recalculation, it turns out that expenditures for producers' durable equipment—capital goods—grew at a spectacular annual rate of 12.6 percent from 1972 to 1984 rather than the previously reported 5.6 percent (unpublished data made available by the Bureau of Economic Analysis). If a more accurate measure of computer output makes such an enormous difference, it is easy to imagine that improved measures for other capital goods would further undermine the claims of insufficient new investment.

Proponents of the inadequate-investment line of argument will ask why, if there is all this hidden growth in investment—both tangible and intangible—productivity has advanced so slowly in recent years. The "realist" argument always returns to the recent

---

[12] Some advocates of the investment-slowdown hypothesis have retreated to the argument that even though rates of investment have not fallen, the investment is less effective because of a slowdown in technological progress (White House Conference on Productivity 1984: app. H, p. 5). In light of the rapid advances in computer-based technologies during the 1970s, this claim is implausible.

productivity trends precisely because the evidence on the inadequacy of investment expenditures is unpersuasive. The sharp downturn in the rate of measured productivity growth during the 1970s is the major empirical foundation for the line of argument that holds the growth of welfare spending responsible for the decline of economic vitality.

The United States experienced a productivity panic during the 1970s. The previously obscure figures on aggregate productivity trends became the frequent topic of news stories and political speeches. While the *New York Times Index* averaged only 1.3 column inches for productivity-related entries in the late 1960s, the annual average jumped to 13.9 column inches in the 1970s—a rough indicator of the extraordinary growth in concern with productivity trends. This concern, fueled by the efforts of the business community, helped lay the basis for the election of Ronald Reagan and the pursuit of a conservative political agenda.

While some economists have expressed bafflement or skepticism about the productivity trends, other economists and the business community have seen the productivity decline as a symptom of deep economic problems, particularly inadequate rates of new investment (Federal Reserve Bank of Boston 1980; Kendrick 1984).[13] Yet the data on productivity slowdown are a weak foundation on which to build such an elaborate theoretical structure. There are two fundamental problems: the first is in the assumption that inadequate investment is necessarily *the* cause of slower productivity growth, and the second is in the assumption that current measures accurately reflect underlying trends in productivity. Both of these assumptions are worth close scrutiny.

EXAMINING THE RELATIONSHIP BETWEEN INVESTMENT AND PRODUCTIVITY

Conservatives are fond of accusing liberals of believing that social problems can be solved by throwing money at them, but the as-

---

[13] Other economists have stressed the burden of governmental regulation and the declining discipline of the labor force as critical causes of the productivity decline.

sumption that inadequate investment is the main cause of slow productivity growth is a version of the same magical thinking. With slow productivity growth, as with social problems, there are many other factors that mediate between the amount of money being spent and the effectiveness of the outcomes. As we will discuss below, one possibility is that slow productivity growth is an illusion that results from problems of measurement. But even if one assumes that the measurement bias is small, there are several other important mediating factors. For one thing, the market could be misallocating resources so that too many investment dollars were being spent on building new suburban shopping malls or new nuclear power plants that had only a marginal impact on expanding overall output. It could also be that firms were using their investment dollars to buy stretch limousines for their executives. In such cases, the appropriate policy response would not be to increase investment, but to shift investment flows into more productive channels.

Another possibility is that investment goods are not being adequately utilized. In the case of tangible goods, it is common for firms to buy sophisticated high-technology capital goods for factory or office and then not be able to get them to work properly. A typical *Wall Street Journal* (April II, 1983) report reads:

> Experts agree that high-tech manufacturing equipment often is underused or misused. "Companies are buying equipment hel- ter skelter, without thinking about how they want to use it," says Stephen Rosenthal, a Boston University business-school professor who has surveyed more than 50 factory automation projects. . . .

Part of the problem is that businesses, like individuals, are often mesmerized by the hottest new gadgets regardless of their utility. But there is also evidence that some of the new production tech- nologies work best when the firm's labor relations and organiza- tional structure are transformed.[14] Seymour Melman (1984) has

---

[14] See Larry Hirschhorn (1984).

shown, for example, that when a Flexible Manufacturing System—a highly automated group of interlocking computer-controlled machine tools—is used with a labor force that is deskilled and closely supervised by management, the results are disappointing, particularly because downtime—the periods when the System is waiting for repairs—is so high (see also Shaiken 1984 and Jaikumar 1986). In contrast, when the same technology is run by a highly skilled labor force that is given considerable control over the production process, the amount of downtime is considerably lower and production levels are much higher. Firms that fail to reorganize the pattern of work relations accordingly could well find that increased investment in tangible capital produces disappointingly slow productivity growth.[15]

The problem with throwing money at productivity problems is also indicated by statistical evidence for a negative correlation between investment in physical equipment and rates of productivity advance in recent years for certain specific industries (Boucher 1981). There are certainly some traditional U.S. manufacturing industries which have been slow to keep pace with foreign competition, but their productivity problems probably have more to do with the institutional arrangements for bringing together people and technology than with insufficient aggregate investment.[16] One critical factor has been the investment priorities of giant corporations that prefer corporate takeovers to the production of goods. Perhaps the clearest example is the USX Corporation, formerly U.S. Steel, whose ample financial resources have been used to purchase oil companies rather than to improve its steel-making capacities. (For discussions of "paper entrepreneurialism," see Reich 1983: 140–72 and Melman 1983.)

---

[15] Similar points can be made about intangible investments. A firm might invest a great deal in retraining its labor force, but then not be able to motivate these employees because of defects in its organizational design. There is no guarantee that investments, whether tangible or intangible, will actually produce results.

[16] This argument is also supported by Edward Denison's (1979) effort to account for the recent slowdown in productivity growth. He found that changes in either capital inputs or labor inputs played little part in explaining the productivity decline. He found instead that what he terms the residual—a category that includes scientific advances, innovations in organization, improvements in communication—had switched from a positive role before the 1970s to a negative role.

How Reliable Are the Productivity Data?

Those who rushed to proclaim the existence of a productivity crisis rarely bothered to examine the numbers closely, but the measurement of changes in aggregate productivity is an extremely delicate matter. While it sounds like a simple process to calculate output per hour of labor input, the need to adjust the figures for inflation and the problem of measuring output in certain sectors create a tangle of problems.

One indication of the importance of these problems is the evidence already cited that introducing a price index for computers had a significant impact on measured output and hence on the rate of productivity growth. But the measurement problems are not confined to computers. For example, there continues to be no price index for various types of communications equipment that account for an even larger share of GNP than the computer industry, and some of the most important pieces of communications equipment are special-purpose computers. Even if the decline in price for these items has not been quite as rapid as for computers themselves, the underestimation of output would still be considerable.

In addition, output is an extremely shaky concept throughout the service sectors of the economy, and the techniques used to estimate output are unsatisfactory. For banking services to individuals, for example, the growth in output is estimated to be proportional to growth in total banking employment, so that productivity is assumed to be the same as it was in 1948.[17] This means that every year the data find that there was zero productivity growth in banking services to individuals, but other studies show that commercial banking productivity rose at a 6 percent annual rate during the 1970s (Brand and Duke 1983). The result is that the substantial investments that banks made in new facili-

---

[17] This procedure is used because of the difficulty of finding any direct way to measure the constant-dollar output of banks. A previous technique—the liquidity measure—had "indicated a persistent and substantial decline in output per worker" (*Survey of Current Business* 1976: 22).

ties and in computerization are shown by the published data to
have depressed the rate of productivity advance in the whole
economy. Similar methods are used to measure output for legal
services, medical services, and the nonprofit sector of the economy, and in all of these cases the assumption of zero or very low
productivity growth is built into the method of measurement. In
medical services, for example, total consumer expenditures for
doctors are deflated with a price index for medical fees. However, this procedure fails to distinguish increases in fees that are
purely inflationary from those that result from increased productivity. If, for example, the fee for a comprehensive physical exam
increases by 20 percent, but new technologies make it possible
for the physician to obtain twice as much information about the
patient's health, the price rise should be seen as resulting from
increased productivity. If one used this same procedure and
deflated manufacturing output with an index based on manufacturing wages, rates of productivity growth in that sector would
also be substantially lower. Since these poorly measured service
industries have been growing as a proportion of the whole economy, the measurement problems loom larger with every passing
year. Were the Bureau of Economic Analysis to continue the
process of revision that it began with the new data for the computer industry with a complete overhaul of measures of service
productivity, the size of the recent productivity decline would
continue to shrink.[18] The answer to the puzzle as to why output
has failed to grow faster despite increases in intangible capital

---

[18] But even if one limits the analysis to manufacturing and ignores the issue of unmeasured quality
changes, another change in the economy distorts the data. In recent years, there has been tremen-
dous growth in the purchase by manufacturing firms of business services, including such diverse
items as management consulting, software for factory automation, employee training, security
guards, and health insurance for employees. But when the government calculates the net output
of the manufacturing sector, it subtracts the cost of these purchased business services, thus lowering
the total of manufacturing output and manufacturing productivity. But the reality is that the dollar
value of the steel produced per worker should not really change just because management hired
some fancy consultants or paid more for employee health insurance. Hence, if one measures
manufacturing productivity without subtracting business services, the record in the 1970s is much
stronger than the standard data suggest. This problem alone accounts for close to a third of the
productivity slowdown in manufacturing when 1960–1966 is compared to 1973–1979 (Block and
Burns 1986).

and capital cheapening is that our standard measures of output are deeply flawed.[19]

Finally, theorists of inadequate investment levels must deal with the inconvenient fact that productivity gains are strongest when output is rising fastest. This relationship—known as Verdoorn's Law (McCombie and De Ridder 1984)—makes sense, since a firm that is expanding its output quickly is able to realize economies of scale and to develop more effective production methods. (Expansion also creates more opportunities and more security for workers, with obvious positive effects on morale.) If demand is relatively slack so that output levels are not rising, then one can expect productivity to rise more slowly than in the case of vigorous demand and rapidly rising output. This provides another explanation for the observed slowdown in productivity growth in the 1973–1979 period when compared to 1960–1966. Annual average growth in private Gross Domestic Product fell from 5.6 percent in 1960–1966 to 3.0 percent in 1973–1979. This 46 percent drop in the rate of growth seems substantial enough to explain much of the measured decline in manufacturing productivity (Szymanski 1984; Matthews 1982). But the deeper point is that if productivity is one's main concern, the most direct policy response is to strengthen demand. Instead of the "realist" remedy of limiting government spending in the hope that private investment would increase, an expansion of social welfare spending would strengthen purchasing power among working people and the poor, which could contribute to faster growth and more rapid gains in measured productivity growth.

To be sure, strengthening demand is not a sufficient policy by itself; institutional reforms are necessary to bring together people and technology more effectively. But the "realists" have misunderstood the nature of the productivity problem because they have ignored the distortions in the official data and the impact of slower growth in the 1973–1979 period. Most important, there is no foundation for the claim that faster productivity growth depends on higher rates of aggregate investment.

---

[19] The argument is that so much of the economy's output is poorly measured that the problems of accounting become cumulative rather than self-correcting. See Block (1985).

WHY THE "REALISTS" ARE WRONG:
DISINCENTIVES TO WORK

Piven and Cloward have already made the case that welfare state measures do have work-disincentive effects; they give people an alternative to taking the worst kind of work on the worst terms. But the "realist" argument rests on two additional premises that are rarely stated. First, that if these disincentive effects are too strong, then either the size of the overall labor force will be too small to get the society's work done, or a shortage of labor will push wages too high. Second, that the society's economic well-being depends directly on the willingness of people to take the worst kinds of work—the low-wage work where the disincentive effects are strongest. While these premises might have had great relevance in the early nineteenth century, they do not make much sense today.

Fears that there will not be enough workers to get the jobs done are contradicted by the fact that labor-force participation rates have been rising dramatically in the United States. During the same historical period in which various forms of income support for different categories of the nonemployed have become more readily available, the percentage of all adults who are in the labor force has been increasing. By 1986, more than 65 percent of people aged 16 and over were in the labor force, as compared to rates below 60 percent in the early 1960s. (While an increase of 5 percentage points might not seem that large, it represents more than 9 million additional people in the labor force.)[20] Even with dramatic spurts of new job creation in the 1970s and during the 1982–1984 recovery, close to 7 percent of the labor force are still counted as unemployed in the official statistics, and there are

---

[20] Data are from the *Handbook of Labor Statistics* and the *Survey of Current Business.* Participation rates are the percentage of the civilian noninstitutional population who are in the civilian labor force—either employed or officially unemployed. Both numerator and denominator exclude the military.

The rising rates of participation occur in both the 1970s and the 1980s, so they cannot be explained by the recent Reagan cutbacks in welfare spending.

millions of others who would join the labor force if they had a reasonable prospect of finding work. In 1977, Eli Ginsberg estimated the size of the "labor market overhang"—the people who are not currently in the labor force but who might enter if jobs were available—at 17 million people, and the figure is probably even larger today.

Much of the confusion that surrounds issues of aggregate labor supply derives from the assumption that when everything else is equal, people will generally choose leisure over work. Yet this assumption vastly exaggerates the seductiveness of idleness; both historically and currently, work has a powerful attractiveness that is independent of any monetary reward. This attractiveness is rooted in the social meaning and social rewards that derive from participation in the world of work. Some indication of the strength of these feelings is indicated by a 1977 survey showing that 84 percent of men and 77 percent of women reported that they would continue working even if they did not need the money (Veroff, Douban, and Kulka 1981: 295).

It would seem that in recent years, this attractiveness of work has been increased by growing status rewards that come from working. The recent increases in labor-force participation rates result from the massive entrance of married women into the labor force, growing participation rates among young people,[21] and a decided slowing in the exit of older people from the labor force.[22] While many specific factors have been cited to explain why married women, young people, and some older people seem more likely to seek paid employment than in the past, the strength of the trend suggests a general cultural shift. There is an enhancement of social status that comes from being a member of the paid labor

[21] Labor-force participation rates are about ten points higher now for people aged 16–19 than they were twenty years ago (*Handbook of Labor Statistics*). Moreover, these teenagers are working longer hours than previously (Steinberg and Greensberger 1980).

[22] Among workers aged 55 and over, there has been a marked slowing in the 1980s in the measured rates of withdrawal from the labor force (*Handbook of Labor Statistics: Employment and Earnings*). Moreover, some of the labor-force participation of older workers is hidden because of the complex rules surrounding the administration of the Social Security system (Rones 1983). This has created growing measurement problems, since we know that a significant percentage of "retired" people re-enter the labor force (Parnes 1981: 168).

force—from being perceived as a productive individual who receives monetary compensation—and this status gain has increased in magnitude in recent years. Perceptions of the social status of work are internalized by individuals, and they in turn feel better about themselves when they are working rather than being merely a "housewife," a "student," or a "retired person."

Others might argue that it is simply the need for more income that has driven these people into the work force. However, there has *always* been a gain in income from having more family members in the labor force. (While average real wages have failed to increase since 1973, the increasing participation rates began well before wage stagnation.) Historically, there were significant status gains that came to families—or at least to the male heads of families—from being able to keep their women and children out of the labor force. These status considerations are still visible in the now rare case of the husband who refuses to allow his wife to work because it will reflect badly on his talents as a breadwinner. What needs to be explained is why these historic status considerations are no longer compelling. Clearly, the explanation has much to do with the triumph of a consumer culture that makes what one buys the most important aspect of one's identity and social standing: the more one works, the more new consumer needs one can satisfy (see Ehrenreich, chapter 4). But whatever the reasons, the relative status of working and nonworking activities has shifted dramatically in favor of work, and this makes it possible for individuals to get both more status and more income.[23]

But the resulting increases in labor-force participation threaten to have an impact on the labor market that is precisely the opposite

---

[23] It also appears there are increased status gains connected to working longer. The number of hours that individuals work rises with education and income. Well before there was media concern with the new "Yuppie" work ethic, Shirley Smith (1983) found that in 1979, men who had attended any kind of postbaccalaureate graduate school worked an average of 8.3% more hours each year than men with only a high school diploma. Men who were managers in manufacturing worked 19.4 % more hours than the average auto worker.

Instead of trading off their much higher hourly incomes for more leisure, these professional and managerial employees tend to work substantially longer than a forty-hour week. I would suggest that part of the reason is that it enhances their sense of social importance to have so much work to do.

of the fears of chronic labor shortage. We have more and more people demanding access to paid employment at the same time that technological advances are actually contracting employment in certain key sectors of the economy. Manufacturing employment is not expected ever to regain its 1979 level as robotization and automation make it possible for a smaller labor force to turn out a larger supply of goods. In late 1986, after several years of economic recovery, total manufacturing hours were still 8 percent below the peak reached in 1979 (*Business Statistics* 1984, and *Survey of Current Business,* November 1986). And there is evidence that certain types of clerical, service, and middle-managerial employment will be hard hit by office automation (Leontief and Duchin 1986: 63–91). These developments continue an established pattern since through much of the twentieth century, the exploitation of new technologies has made it possible to produce an expanded supply of goods and services while significantly reducing the amount of paid labor time per capital (Kuznets 1971; Block 1984). In other words, technological change tends to increase the availability of leisure time.

But what happens when people choose not to increase their leisure and more people compete for a supply of jobs that is growing only slowly? The result is more unemployment, more involuntary part-time employment, and lower wages as increasing competition for available jobs gives employers the upper hand. In short, even without the dramatic cutbacks in welfare spending that the most extreme "realists" favor, we face a dangerously overcrowded labor market.

Before examining the consequences of an overcrowded labor market, it is necessary to look at the second implicit "realist" assumption: the desirability of a large pool of people available for low-wage work. It is indisputable that those who are in the market for people to clean their houses or to pick crops in harvest season benefit directly from such a pool of people desperate for employment. However, while employers might benefit from cheap labor, it is not so clear that the macroeconomic effects of an overcrowded labor market are beneficial.

It is widely agreed that the core of economic prosperity comes from high-value-added employment in which the combination of sophisticated technology, innovative management, and a skilled work force produces large quantities of quality output. Even the misguided arguments about the inadequacy of capital investment in the U.S. economy rest on an understanding that new technologies and capital are critical for these high levels of productivity to be achieved. However, it is also well known that when the price of labor is low, it can become attractive for employers to substitute labor for capital—to produce more by hiring more hands instead of upgrading the productive apparatus (Hicks 1966: 114–20). This strategy is particularly attractive when uncertainty is high because added employees can simply be laid off, whereas funds that have been committed to idle machines cannot be recovered.

An economy with an overcrowded labor market has both these characteristics: cheap labor and high uncertainty. The uncertainty comes from problems of demand because the downward pressure on wages resulting from more intense competition for jobs places a damper on aggregate consumer purchasing power.[24] Overcrowding can encourage entrepreneurs to find new ways to exploit the cheap labor available, but most of this will consist of low-value-added employment. At the same time, other employers will substitute labor for capital and attempt to increase output by sweating the labor force instead of investing in more efficient ways to organize the production process. In short, an increase in employment might occur, but it will be at the expense of significant productivity advance since labor is being substituted for capital.

If one thinks in terms of international competition, it is possible to see concretely where this development leads. Entrepreneurs soon discover that it is possible to produce certain goods—clothing, shoes, or some types of furniture—in poorly capitalized factories at prices low enough to compete effectively against cheap foreign imports. This results in some savings on the import side,

---

[24] This problem is already apparent. An article noting the likelihood that 1986 would be the fifth consecutive year that American workers receive smaller pay increases than in the previous year goes on to say: "But instead of celebrating, many economists are alarmed by the moderate wage growth. To them, shrinking pay increases are a sign that an already weak economic expansion is becoming weaker" (*New York Times*, October 21, 1985).

but the magnitude is small precisely because these are cheap products. At the same time, the country's ability to compete in the production of more sophisticated goods is impaired because manufacturers who should be investing in sophisticated new technologies succumb to the temptation of using cheap labor instead. This may temporarily bolster the profit levels of the firms, but it gradually diminishes their capacity to make the technological advances necessary to stay competitive. The cost is a worsening trade balance for expensive, high-value-added products.

The point is that the amount of value added per employee hour for industries such as computers ($71.39), semiconductors ($54.12), or automobiles ($42.43) is many times higher than the output of workers in wood furniture ($13.77) or men's and boys' shirts ($13.43).[25] We no longer get richer as a nation by putting more people to work in sweatshops sewing shirts, but by raising the proportion of the labor force in high-value-added activities. Yet this task is in no way facilitated by cheapening the price of labor; it is no accident that when value added per employee is high, so too are wages.[26]

Other nations have understood this dynamic and have developed policies designed to overcome the problems associated with cheap labor. In Sweden, the Social Democrats deliberately pushed a "solidaristic wage policy" that raised wages in both high-value-added and low-value-added industries. The idea was that the low-value-added industries would be forced to invest in new technologies that would make them more competitive in the world market. Evidence of the success of this strategy is provided by the omnipresence of Swedish-made furniture in U.S. stores that market to consumers looking for style at moderate prices.

In sum, the argument that we can punish the poor while also increasing efficiency is based on a Dickensian image of the economy that has little relevance in the late twentieth century. Those who want to punish the poor either for reasons rooted in religion

[25] Data are for production workers in 1982 dollars, and are from *1982 Census of Manufacturers, Subject Series: General Summary.*
[26] To be sure, simply raising wages is no shortcut to high value added. But it is also obvious that pushing wage levels down is not the way to get there either.

or because they want to make it easier to find good household help should realize that their own concerns cannot be justified in terms of the economy's international competitiveness.

On the contrary, we have succeeded so well in attaching status to work that the need now is for correctives in the opposite direction to prevent overcrowding in the labor market with all of its negative human and economic consequences. We need social policies that induce people to choose other activities over paid work or to limit the number of their working hours. This has already become a major concern of social policy in Western Europe, where governments have sought to reduce problems of youth unemployment by facilitating early retirement among older workers. (Organization for Economic Cooperation and Development 1979: 53–7). This particular strategy seems unlikely to be successful in the United States, since older workers are unlikely to remain satisfied with the status loss associated with complete separation from the labor force. But whether the policy response is to encourage early retirement or more creative initiatives, it will have the character of making it economically attractive for people to do something other than be full-time workers. The point is that we need more disincentives to work, not fewer.

WHY THE "REALISTS" ARE WRONG: THE WELFARE STATE IS NOT A LUXURY

If inadequate investment has not been the source of slower measured productivity growth and if it does not make good sense to drive more of the dependent poor into the labor market, then the claim that the growth of the welfare state has been the source of our major economic problems no longer seems quite so compelling. But it is still possible to argue that even if the negative consequences of welfare spending have been exaggerated, we can no longer afford even existing levels of welfare state expenditures. In this view, the two great deficits—the federal budget deficit and the balance-of-trade deficit—provide a compelling case for severely restricting government welfare expenditures.

Is the Federal Budget Deficit an Economic Problem?

Like the issue of welfare and idleness, the question of the federal budget deficit taps deep cultural themes. Even during the peak of popularity of Keynesian economics, politicians were able to gain support by upholding the sanctity of balanced budgets. They could always argue the unfairness of a situation in which individuals and firms must live within their means but governments are able to spend more than they take in. Yet these everyday formulations are part of a system of ideas that serves particular class interests.

The point is that individuals and firms do not live within their means either; they borrow in order to accomplish their objectives. American families routinely carry home mortgages and car loans as well as billions of dollars of consumer debt to finance appliances, vacations, college education, and all kinds of other expenses. Businesses routinely issue stocks or bonds even for the purpose of buying other businesses. If families or firms were held to an accounting convention that prohibited them from separating current from capital expenditures, their accounts would show them in a state of chronic deficit.

Yet this is precisely what happens with the federal government. Billions of dollars of its outlays clearly fall in the category of capital expenditures that are designed to contribute to expanded output of the private economy and thus raise the flow of government revenues. Financing these expenditures by means of debt is every bit as rational as individuals borrowing to buy a house or firms selling bonds to finance productive investment. However, by convention, the federal budget is not disaggregated between current and capital expenditures. The result is that the size of the federal deficit is greatly exaggerated.

Robert Eisner (1986: 31) cites an effort by the Office of Management and Budget to distinguish between current and capital expenditures, which includes among "federal investment-type outlays" . . . $34 billion for construction, $67 billion for equipment, and $7 billion for inventory investment, $41 billion for research and development and $22 billion for education and training. Total federal investment (excluding loans and financial investment) thus came to $171 billion in fiscal 1984, almost identical, we might point out, to the fiscal year national income account deficit of $170 billion.[27]

Another key part of the ideology is the frequent emphasis on the astronomical size of the accumulated federal debt, but here again standard accounting conventions are ignored. In assessing a firm, one compares total debt to total accumulated assets. When one carries out the same assessment for the U.S. government, it turns out that the value of the government's assets—land, buildings, equipment, and mineral reserves—have been appreciating rapidly. Even with the accumulated Reagan deficits, the total federal debt is still smaller than the total value of the government's nonfinancial assets (Eisner 1986: 28–9).

Furthermore, Robert Heilbroner (1984) has persuasively argued that the traditional Keynesian arguments in favor of federal budget deficits when there is slack in the economy remain valid. In short, even if the accounts were done correctly and a federal budget deficit persisted, this would be the correct policy measure given the continuing high levels of unemployment. Eisner (1986: 146) concurs that the Reagan administration's deficits were extremely effective in pulling the economy out of the 1981–1982 recession.

With these insights, it is interesting to ask why the conventions for analyzing federal spending have remained unchanged; why, despite economic knowledge to the contrary, the federal budget accounting is still so archaic. The answer is that the balanced-budget ideology constrains the government's capacity to deliver

[27] Eisner (1986) goes on to argue that there are other critical distortions in the government's accounting of its debts, particularly the failure to adjust for the impact of inflation. He shows that in the Carter years, despite federal budget deficits, the real value of the federal debt declined (22).

services, particularly to working people and the poor. The *Wall Street Journal* (February 3, 1986) reports that when David Stockman was asked about changing the convention, he "responded that a capital budget would simply give big spenders in Congress an opportunity 'to rebuild every bridge in America.' " In a word, while masquerading as an objective economic constraint, the balanced-budget ideology serves as a powerful political constraint on the government.

This is only one example of the ways in which the Reagan administration has been able to manipulate the ideological arguments about budget deficits. As David Stockman has acknowledged, the original Reagan tax cuts were a Trojan horse designed to facilitate the cutting of civilian programs by creating a huge shortfall of revenues. With this mounting deficit, it would then be possible to insist that civilian spending at current levels was simply no longer feasible. But if one were simply talking about an economic dynamic at work, the obvious solution would have been to cut back dramatically on the administration's defense buildup. However, the strength of the Reaganites has been their continuing awareness that the real issues are political. They proceeded to construct a political rhetoric within which the defense buildup was unassailable because it was absolutely vital to national security. Hence, they were in a position to argue that the Trojan horse deficit could be eased only by slashing away at civilian programs they have always opposed on ideological grounds.

This political rhetoric has also effectively closed off the option of increasing tax rates on corporations and upper-income households—the most direct means to raise additional revenues. The "tax reform" legislation of 1986 does close some of the tax shelters that the rich have used, but it does this in exchange for a reduction in tax rates on upper-income families.[28] The idea of progressive taxation has given way to the supply-side claim that the rich will not bother to work and invest if their marginal tax

---

[28] Calculations in Aaron (1986: 97–9) make it clear that substantial amounts of revenue could be raised by relatively small increases in tax rates. In light of the broadening of the tax base in the current reform proposals, tax rates for the highest brackets could still be below pre-reform levels and produce greater revenue.

rates are too high. But the evidence against this proposition is overwhelming; many European nations have prospered with much higher tax rates, and even Japan has a far more progressive tax system than the United States (Kuttner 1984: chap. 5).

The federal budget deficit is fundamentally a political problem, not an economic problem. It is the result of four critical factors: an accounting scheme that fails to differentiate between current and capital expenses; a failure to recognize the validity of deficit spending as a policy response to insufficient aggregate demand; a set of tax reforms that dramatically lowered tax rates on upper-income families and on corporations in the mistaken belief that inadequate investment was a key problem; and a defense buildup that is wildly wasteful and extraordinarily dangerous. If the political will existed to solve these four problems, the resources would be available for the expansion of the federal government's social welfare expenditures.

Understanding the Foreign Trade Deficit

Growing awareness of the dynamics of international economic competition has led scholars of both the right and the left to insist that the United States is now being subjected to the discipline of the world market. One version of this argument discusses the Latin Americanization of the U.S. economy. The idea is that when faced with intense competition from Japan and from a wide variety of low-wage countries, the United States has little choice but to accept a reduction in living standards—in the form of lower wages and reduced social benefits—in order to be able to compete effectively (Barnet and Muller 1974: 213–53; Scott 1982).[29] Of all the arguments against the welfare state, this one is probably the most potent precisely because the evidence for it seems so obvious. Americans daily encounter the influx of foreign-produced goods and they hear regularly about plant closings made necessary by the

[29] To be sure, left analysts that make this argument see the necessity of a direct challenge to capitalism to defend the existing standard of living (Bluestone and Harrison 1982; Miller and Tomaskovic-Devey 1983). This challenge would include generalized protectionist measures to insulate the U.S. economy from international trade pressures.

impact of foreign competition. Yet in this case as well, there is a need to probe more deeply to understand what is going on.

The terms of the debate over international competition have changed remarkably little in the century and a half since Britain debated the Corn Laws. The categories of free trade and protectionism and the arguments about comparative advantage all date to the early nineteenth century, which was also the founding period of modern economics. At that time, advocates of free trade insisted that if Great Britain removed its tariffs on wheat, the cost of basic foodstuffs would decline. This decline would reduce the cost of labor and make British goods even more attractive on the world market. In a word, that debate took place in a context in which it was easy to imagine that the price of basic foodstuffs was the single major determinant of the price of labor and that the price of labor was the major determinant of the cost of the manufactured products.

While contemporary analysts are quick to acknowledge that the world has grown more complex, they cling to some of these same simplifying assumptions. The debate about international trade is still carried on as though goods production were the entire economy and as though *the* major determinant of the international competitiveness of a country's goods were the direct (wages) and indirect (government social programs) costs of labor. The presumption is widely shared that those countries that do best in lowering wages and public provision will do best in international trade. Neither of these assumptions has much to do with reality. First, success in international trade has very little to do with the price of labor; second, the growing centrality of services in modern economies renders much of the goods-based analysis obsolete.

If wage rates were the single most important determinant of international competitiveness, one would expect that Third World countries would be the dominant force in manufacturing trade. Such a view corresponds to academic and popular images of the developed nations being flooded by imports from low-wage countries. Much attention has been focused on the multinational corporations that have set up manufacturing platforms in various parts of the Third World to re-export parts and finished goods to the

developed world. But while this attention has been useful in expos-
ing the often horrible labor practices of multinational corporations, it has led to a distorted perception of international trade.

The reality continues to be that *most* of the manufactured
goods imported by the developed capitalist countries come from
other developed capitalist countries. Third World countries—with
only a handful of exceptions—still play a minor and marginal role
in international manufacturing trade. In fact, the major exceptions—South Korea and Taiwan—are so different from most other
Third World countries that it is best to treat them separately.[30] It
is largely in the production of relatively simple manufactured
goods such as garments and shoes that Third World countries have
had an impact on international trade.[31]

One can see the trends clearly by looking at data on U.S.
imports for 1985. Table 1 compares imports from all developing
countries with total U.S. imports of manufactured goods of different levels of complexity. It is only with the simplest goods—the
nondurable manufactures including garments and shoes—that
Third World imports have a dominant role. In the category of
durable manufactured goods, which includes items such as steel,
the Third World share is only 27 percent of the total. And in the
most complex category—machinery and transport equipment—
which is also by far the largest, the Third World role shrinks to
17.1 percent. Moreover, if the exceptional cases of Taiwan and
South Korea are left out of this accounting, as in column 2, the
figures for every category are far less impressive.

The category of machinery includes parts made for the automobile and electronics industries in various Third World export

[30] The exceptionality of South Korea and Taiwan suggests that the United States could deal with
these special cases without departing from its general commitment to open international trade. It
is difficult to understand why the United States needs to run a huge trade deficit with these two
client states that are notorious for their denial of democratic rights. At the very least, a policy that
insisted on full trade-union rights as a precondition for continued access to U.S. markets would
eliminate some of their current trade advantages by raising wages to more realistic levels.
[31] Further support for this argument is provided by Gordon (1985) that presents data showing that
nonoil imports from less developed countries represented a larger percentage of total imports to the
advanced capitalist countries in 1959 than in 1981. He also shows that the less developed countries'
share of international trade was higher in 1937 than in 1979.

TABLE I

Third World Imports as a Percentage of Total U.S.
Manufactured Imports—1985
(in millions of dollars)

	All Third World	Third World without S. Korea and Taiwan
1. Machinery and Transport Equipment		
Dollar value	$24,192	$15,639
% of global imports	17.1%	11.0%
2. Durable Manufactured Goods		
Dollar value	$13,362	$8,499
% of global imports	27.0%	17.2%
3. Nondurable Manufactured Goods		
Dollar value	$27,302	$13,526
% of global imports	52.8%	26.2%

Source: *1985 U.S. Foreign Trade Highlights.*

platforms. However, automation has reduced the electronics industry's dependence on Third World women to do such tasks as the delicate work of connecting wires to silicon chips. Many of the major American electronics producers are now performing more of their assembly operations at highly automated plants in the United States.

To be sure, the figures reported in table I represent a significant change from twenty years ago; Third World manufacturing looms substantially larger than in the past. Yet it is also sobering to see that U.S. imports of petroleum-related products from the Third World—valued at $36.9 billion in 1985 when oil prices tumbled—continued to be much larger than any of the manufacturing categories. The bulk of manufacturing trade continues to take place among the developed countries where living standards and wage rates are quite comparable. Moreover, this trade is dominated by machinery and transport equipment—items where wage costs are often a minor element in the total costs of production. In the automobile industry, for example, where the

U.S. loss of competitive advantage to the Japanese has had a major impact on the trade deficit, wage differences are a relatively minor part of the story. The key advantage of the Japanese is that they have reduced the number of employee hours required to produce a car through organizational innovations and the use of new technologies, while simultaneously maintaining high standards of product quality. It is estimated that "in the early 1980s the Japanese producers needed only about 65 percent of the labor required in the American industry to produce a comparable product" (Altshuler 1984: 159). Moreover, this huge difference in hours cannot be explained away by the greater dedication and work discipline of the Japanese labor force. On the contrary, the Japanese have invested heavily in automobile factories in the United States because they are confident that their organizational superiority will make such production profitable despite higher U.S. wage rates (Stavro 1985).

The importance of the Japanese edge in organization and in the utilization of new technologies has led two analysts of international trade to write:

> Comparative advantage in modern mass-production sectors will hinge not on wage rates but on the operational control of complex systems that reduce per-unit labor costs substantially. In this regard, comparing Japanese labor requirements with U.S. labor requirements for production in a wide range of sectors is quite sobering (Tyson and Zysman 1983: 33).

This argument suggests, in turn, the importance of a range of institutional variables in explaining trade differences. For example, one explanation for the Japanese advantage in using new technologies is that many Japanese workers in the major manufacturing firms are assured lifetime employment (Doz 1985: 201). The knowledge that the firm will redeploy workers who become redundant with technological change reduces the incentive for those workers to resist technological advances. On the contrary, workers might even perceive that the elimination of their present job will open up the possibility of more interesting work elsewhere in the firm. This stands in marked contrast to many U.S. firms where employees have a strong interest in resisting technological change for fear that it will result in significant reductions in staffing (Fadem 1984: 673–4).

But employment guarantees are simply one example of how institutional variables can be far more important than the price of labor or the intensity of work effort in explaining international competitive differences. A succession of management best-sellers have drawn attention to another such variable: the skill with which firms are managed. Numerous analysts have argued that American firms have suffered in international competition because of managerial rigidities that discourage innovation and because of incentive systems that encourage managers to emphasize short-term over long-term goals. Another critical institutional variable is the role of the public sector in providing some of the institutional supports for the development of new high-technology industries, such as funding for research efforts. As is well known, this kind of "industrial policy" worked in the United States to produce the computer industry, but only as an offshoot of military and space efforts. It seems obvious that were such efforts concentrated on civilian goals, as they have been in Japan (Tsurumi 1985: 56–8), the positive impact on the trade balance would be even stronger.

In sum, the U.S. foreign trade problem is not the flood of cheap manufactured goods from the Third World but a failure to compete adequately in the production of complex, high-value-added goods. There is little reason to imagine that this situation can be remedied by slashing industrial wages, intimidating the labor force, and reducing the role of the public sector. Conservative slogans are a poor substitute for the far more complex institutional reforms that are needed to strengthen American manufacturing.

THE CENTRALITY OF SERVICES

This latter point will become even clearer when the discussion is broadened to services. The attention to international trade creates the impression that most of what people consume are things that can easily be traded internationally. But this simply is not the case. Table 2 provides figures from the Department of Commerce on the personal-consumption expenditures of all Americans in 1984. The datable show that almost 60 percent of what Americans purchased in that year can be classified as services. To be sure, the distinction between services and goods is not a hard-and-fast one; the inclusion of housing as a service, for example, is problematic. It is categorized that way because people consume the services of an existing housing stock; only a very small portion of that housing stock is purchased new each year. Moreover, it is clear that capital goods and raw materials are used in the production of many services. Yet the converse is also true: there is a very large service component in the final cost of all of the goods that are itemized in table 2. Markups for shipping, for advertising, and for wholesaling and retailing represent probably half the cost of most consumer goods.

But despite these difficulties, the figures are illuminating, particularly for purposes of thinking about foreign trade. Virtually all of the items in the service category are relatively insulated from international trade; it would be difficult to import housing or medical care. In other words, a very substantial share of our total consumption is made up of services that are almost by nature homegrown. And in several respects, the 59.1 percent figure is an understatement. First, it excludes the services that people receive from government at all levels, including education, highways, public safety, and other social services. It also excludes the contribution to our standard of living of the unpaid labor in the home, particularly of women, in cleaning, cooking, child care, and care of the elderly.[32]

This dominant role of services in consumer purchases is a comparatively recent development. When the same calculation is made for 1960, services constituted only 46 percent of consumer purchases. It is also striking to contrast the 59.1 percent figure in

[32] In fact, the figures in table 2 probably also understate the size of purchased domestic services. The detailed data report these services at only $8 billion. This low figure might reflect the fact that much household help is likely to work "off the books."

TABLE 2

Services and Goods as a Percentage of Total Consumer
Purchases—1984
Total Purchases = $2,341.8 million

GOODS	Dollar Value	Percentage of Total
Food	$349.6	14.9%
Furniture, appliances, and consumer electronics	179.9	7.7
Clothing and related goods	157.5	6.7
Automobiles and related goods	149.8	6.4
Other	119.8	5.1
Total for Goods	*956.6*	*40.8*
SERVICES		
Housing	376.7	16.1
Medical care	227.4	9.7
Transport	169.7	7.2
Utilities	161.2	6.9
Personal business	139.5	6.0
Restaurant meals	124.8	5.3
Recreation	78.1	3.3
Other	107.8	4.6
Total for Services	*1,385.2*	*59.1*

Source: *Survey of Current Business.*

table 2 with the corresponding figure of 14.1 percent, which represents the sum of consumer durables—the cars, appliances, and consumer electronics—that loom so large in discussions of international trade. The contrast helps us to understand that a part of the reason for the extraordinary intensity of current international trade competition is that these international corporations are fighting over a relatively small share of consumer purchasing power. The shift of consumption toward services means that consumer durables are, in relative terms, a shrinking market, and this accounts for a good deal of the intensity of the competition.

But allowing this competitive battle over goods to dominate economic policy-making is to let the proverbial tail wag the dog. Most of the economic debate concentrates on the small area of

consumer durables, while the production of services that constitute the dominant component of people's standard of living is
treated as a residual matter that is relevant only for purposes of
cutting costs. This approach is doubly misguided because the services are not only the major element of consumption but are also
increasingly critical elements in production itself. The economists'
notion of "human capital" recognizes that expenditures for health,
education, and training are actually investments in maintaining
and improving the capacities of the labor force that can have a
demonstrable effect in improving the productiveness of the economy.

The positive relationship between spending on human services and economic efficiency has generally been ignored in the
public debates about the welfare state. Yet the existence of these
linkages make it far easier to understand such apparent anomalies as Sweden's success in world markets during much of the
period following World War II. By the conventional account,
Sweden should have a huge trade deficit because the high rates of
taxation required to finance the extensive welfare state would
make it impossible for Swedish firms to compete in the world
market. Yet the reality is that while Sweden is heavily dependent
on imports—since there are many items, particularly capital
goods, where the small size of the Swedish domestic market
makes it difficult to sustain a competitive industry (Katzenstein
1985: 82)—the Swedes have been able to pay for these imports
with a strong export trade. Swedish firms such as Volvo and Er-
icsson (electronics and communications equipment) have been
remarkably successful in capturing market niches for various
high-value-added products. Sweden's extensive investments in
human capital gave its labor force a comparative advantage in
the production of these goods.

Yet it is also important to emphasize that the success of Sweden and other small European social-democratic states in improving their citizen's standards of living in a highly competitive world
market rests on their policies for the production of consumer
services. The large public-sector role in the production of services
such as health care, housing, and child care has not only expanded

the availability of these services but has also increased the efficiency of their production. Since services constitute such a large part of consumer purchases, those countries that find ways to deliver services more efficiently will be able to offer their citizens a higher standard of living.

A number of analysts (Cameron 1978; Katzenstein 1985) have noticed that the small European nations that are heavily dependent on foreign trade also tend to have very large government budgets relative to their size. One way to explain this pattern is that these nations are seeking to improve their relative position in international commodity trade by gaining efficiency in the production of services through a substantial state role. Countries that can produce the service component of consumer income more efficiently will be able to sell their goods in international trade more cheaply.

Hence, a concern with the U.S. international trade position does not lead logically to proposals for starving the public sector. Rather, it leads to more intense efforts to improve and expand public provision of a range of services. These efforts are necessary to make production in the service sector more efficient and to enhance the society's human capital so as to strengthen the American competitive position in high-value-added goods.

ALTERNATIVE DIAGNOSES AND ALTERNATIVE POLICIES

The point is that many of the common assumptions about the American economy are simply wrong. An examination of the data does not sustain the claims of a catastrophic productivity slowdown or a crippling federal budget deficit or a dramatic loss of competitive position to low-wage producers in the Third World. Yet it cannot be denied that there are extremely serious structural problems in the American economy; the point is rather that the commonly accepted diagnoses of these problems are misguided.

One aspect of the inadequacy of the prevailing diagnoses is that they tend to fall back on fairly simple quantitative arguments. It is usually concluded that the economy needs higher rates of productive investment or a reduced federal budget deficit or lower rates of taxation or lower real wages—as though manipulation of one or the other of these variables will magically resolve the problems. The reality is that most of our economic problems are qualitative; they have to do not with manipulating one variable but with the fit between different economic elements. For example, more investment in high-technology capital goods or in raising the skill level of the work force will not automatically produce better economic results. First, the effectiveness of the investments depends very much on the sectors of the economy to which they are directed; more resources for physical and human capital for resort complexes for the rich will have little payoff. Second, even if the investments occur where they are needed, there is nothing automatic about the economy's ability to make use of better capital goods or a more skilled work force; both can be wasted in a wide variety of ways. Often, major changes in the way a firm is run will be required before it is able to effectively utilize the new tools and the new labor force.

Arguments about institutional fit are much more complex than purely quantitative arguments because they involve disaggregating the economy and looking in detail at particular economic sectors. While this makes it impossible to elaborate a complete diagnosis here, it is possible to focus briefly on two critical areas of institutional failure: the production of services and the structure of employment. In these two interconnected areas, the expansion of the welfare state can be a critical factor in improving economic performance.

PRODUCING SERVICES EFFICIENTLY

It has been argued above that services are an increasingly central part of the economy from the point of view of both consumption and production. But this centrality creates a problem for a market-oriented society because many of the services are not amenable to pure market arrangements. In cases such as medical care, education, and housing, reliance on the market alone would mean that many were forced to do without. Furthermore, services often have a public-goods component—like clean air, they cannot be produced by the market alone because of the obstacles to an effective and equitable system of pricing and revenue collection; this is clearest in the case of education and the production of new knowledge. However, even health care has a public-goods quality because our health is related to the health of the people around us. Finally, with some services such as communications networks and public utilities, the logic of having a single provider for a geographical area is overwhelming, so that pure markets give way to monopoly arrangments.

On occasion, this society has responded to the inadequacy of pure markets in these cases through public provision of the service. But the dominant response has been the development of hybrid arrangements that combine substantial governmental involvement with opportunities for private profit. Hybrid arrangements include government-regulated private monopolies and contracting out to profit-making firms to provide the service. These hybrids tend to combine the worst of both worlds: insulation from market discipline and strong incentives for the running up of costs. Nowhere is this more clear-cut than in the health sector, where Medicare has facilitated the bidding up of costs by doctors, private hospitals, and nursing homes. As a consequence of these hybrid arrangements, these important services are produced far less efficiently than they could be under a well-managed system of public provision.

It is relevant here that much of the inflation of the 1970s could be traced to just four sectors of the economy: health care, housing, energy, and food (Nulty, cited in Alperowitz and Faux 1980). While the difficulties of the farm sector are well beyond the scope of this essay, the other sectors fit directly into this framework. In the case of housing, a more extensive public-sector role in providing lower- and middle-income housing would have had a number of desirable effects. It could have reduced the inflationary pressures in the housing market, encouraged cost-saving innovations in construction technologies and energy-conserving technologies, reduced the problems of urban blight and urban sprawl through better planning, and averted the current crisis of homelessness. In the case of energy, a more active role of the public sector in providing mass transit and in directly producing electricity could have facilitated energy conservation, which would have dramatically diminished the impact of the energy shocks and significantly reduced the weight of oil imports on the balance of payments.

Similar problems with our hybrid arrangements are already developing on the cutting edge of information technologies. In France, for example, public-sector control over the telephone company has facilitated rapid advances in home computerization and the development of videotext services (*Business Week*, January 20, 1986). In the United States, in contrast, these developments are stalled by conflicts between telephone companies, cable companies, and computer companies. The basic reality is that the costs of hardware and networking are too high for any particular part of the private sector to afford, so development is blocked. In a word, the society's full utilization of the new information technologies will be stalemated unless the public sector plays a more active role in providing the necessary infrastructure.

The point, quite simply, is that services are too important to allow the preference for profit-making to constrain the society's choice of modes of service delivery. Efficiency criteria alone dictate the replacement of many of our hybrid forms with a much more direct public-sector role in provision. To be sure, an expanded public-sector role is not a panacea that will automatically produce desirable results. Public provision can mean the growth of technocratic bureaucracies that are unresponsive to public opinion, or the delivery of second-rate services by indifferent employees.

But while conservatives insist that these negative results are inevitable, the reality is that the character of public services depends on factors such as the responsiveness of government institutions and the political assertiveness of consumer groups.[33] It is well known, for example, that in Western Europe, public-sector provision of services such as transportation is often efficient and of high

---

[33] Hirschman (1970) shows the flaws in most standard arguments about public versus private provision of services.

quality. This has much to do with the fact that such services are used by both the middle class and the poor, so that both groups are united in demanding that quality be maintained. In the United States, in contrast, our tendency is to make the poor the only recipients of certain forms of public provision, and since such services are generally inadequately financed, the quality leaves much to be desired. Conservatives then point to the poor quality of these services as proof that public provision is inherently inefficient and ineffective.

It is possible to have both quality and efficiency in such services as health, education, communications, transportation, housing, and utilities, but we need to invent public institutions to deliver these services that are well funded, responsive, and willing to serve both the poor and the nonpoor. This might involve using local government or even nonprofit organizations to deliver the actual services, but a substantial share of the financing to make this work will have to come from the federal level. Without federal funding, lower levels of government will constantly face the pressure to lower tax rates and reduce services in order to prevent the flight of large employers.

REFORMING THE STRUCTURE OF EMPLOYMENT

The other major institutional problem that must be resolved to strengthen economic performance is the retention of obsolete forms of work organization. Postindustrial developments undermine the viability of old assumptions about how work should be organized. One aspect of the problem has already been discussed: the assumption that the threat of unemployment is a sound mechanism for maximizing work effort. The reality is that economic insecurity reinforces employees' tendencies to restrict output and increases their resistance to the introduction of new technologies. Facilitating more productive work requires, on the contrary, finding ways to give employees greater security of employment and income. Even President Reagan's White House Conference on Productivity reached such a conclusion:

There is a close connection between productivity improvement and employee security. Employment security is an important reward for individuals and in the absence of employment security it is hard for employees to improve their own performance and to suggest how to improve the performance of others. (White House Conference on Productivity 1984, app. K:40)

The traditional assumptions about labor discipline are closely linked to a second set of issues: the retention of authoritarian models for organizing the workplace. When work tasks are basically routine, it is logical that the key organizational imperative is to construct a system of penalties that will force people to do what they are told to do. But there is a growing body of evidence that for large sections of the economy such as manufacturing, human services, and business services, work is becoming less routine. In some cases, problem-solving becomes an increasingly important component, as when blue-collar workers must debug complex automated systems (Shaiken 1984; Butera and Thurman 1984; Hirschhorn 1984). In others, computerization requires that high levels of worker attention be mobilized in order to reduce error rates, as when bank tellers introduce information directly into the central computer (Adler 1983; Howard 1985; Albin and Applebaum 1986). Yet authoritarian structures are hardly effective in forcing employees to be good problem-solvers or in inducing higher levels of attention. This is much of the reason why a significant number of American firms have begun to experiment with alternative forms of work organization that are more democratic (Kochan, Katz, and Mower 1984; Hirschhorn 1984). Yet such experiments will continue to exist only on the margins so long as the insecurity of employment reinforces management's authority over employees and employees' distrust of management.

The issue of authoritarianism is also closely linked to the question of training. As the importance of problem-solving in the workplace increases, so too does the level of skill and knowledge that employees must have to do their jobs. Characteristically, the need is for employees who have learned how to learn—who have the ability to master the specific knowledge requirements of a changing array of particular tasks. But it is also well known that firms are reluctant to invest in training their work forces for fear the employees will go elsewhere with their newfound knowledge. This means that when in-house training is done, it tends to be biased toward quick and narrow forms of instruction; instead of learning how to learn, workers are offered only rote learning. At the same time, many individuals lack either the time or the resources to invest in further education once they have begun their working lives. Furthermore, the insecurity of employment reduces the incentive for both employers and employees to invest in training. The result is a systematic bias against the upgrading of employee skill levels that a changing economy needs.[34]

A final set of issues has to do with the relation between paid and unpaid work. The old model of the family wage meant that one family member's energies could be completely exhausted by work since the wife would be available to fulfill family and community obligations such as caring for children, caring for aging relatives, and maintaining neighborhood and community ties. While this arrangement was costly for women, it assured that someone was there to perform the unpaid labor that was vital for the society. But with the entrance of most wives into the labor force, little social adjustment has been made to assure that this unpaid labor is done. There has been no reduction in men's hours of labor and relatively little growth of community services to take up the slack. Many of these tasks are still done by women, who often find themselves stressed beyond endurance by the multiple demands of work and family. And in balancing work and family, community-related tasks are often abandoned. The elaborate structure of voluntary activity that women historically performed is in a decline as women do paid work instead. In a word, the movement of women into the labor force has created new problems concerning how family and community life are to be structured, questions that have important implications both for the quality of daily life and

---

[34] This is another case where Sweden has been highly successful in increasing its economic adaptability through an extensive program of state-funded employment training (Katzenstein 1985: 119–20).

for the level of economic output. There is evidence, for example, that the lack of adequate provision for child care impairs the productivity of employees (Fernandez 1986). Overcoming these problems requires both the development of a richer network of publicly provided family and community services and much greater flexibility in the organization of working time (Sirianni and Eayrs, forthcoming). The latter step, including a reduction in the full-time workweek, could restore time for family and community involvement while also making it easier for employed individuals to pursue educational options.

Greater employment and income security, more democracy at the workplace, greater options for adult education and training, more extensive family and community services, and more flexible working time are all aspects of a postindustrial transformation of work that would make the economy more efficient. Some of these elements—the increased emphasis on training, employment security, and participation at the workplace—have already been incorporated into the "Japanese model" of industrial organization. But despite its successes, the Japanese model has limited applications for the United States because of the importance it places on the paternalistic links between the individual and the firm. Such links have little appeal in the United States with its more individualistic culture and high rates of geographical and occupational mobility. The implicit Japanese bargain in which individuals surrender their autonomy in exchange for employment security and training opportunities from a firm simply would not work here.

The alternative that makes sense in this society is for the public sector to play a much greater role in providing income security and training opportunities for individuals. This would involve an expansion of government transfer programs to those who are not working and the elimination of the stigma and stinginess of current programs. The removal of stigma is absolutely central because the whole idea is for income and training supports to become a completely routine aspect of the economy. The existence of such a system of supports would effectively erode some of management's coercive authority over its employees. Without the easy resort to coercion, firms would be forced to change their internal practices to place more emphasis on employment security, training, and democratization to secure the cooperation of employees. Firms would be induced to transform work relations because they would face a new labor-market situation in which employees would have alternatives to the acceptance of authoritarian work conditions.[35] In spite of itself, American business would be forced to take advantage of the full potential of the new technologies and of new work relations in which employee problem-solving capacities became the key productive force.[36]

CONCLUSION

For some years now, many advocates of an expanded welfare state have suspected that the kinds of social reforms they believe in would diminish the efficiency of a market economy. In a time of affluence, they were willing to argue that the society could afford some reduced efficiency as a means to greater justice. As the economy became increasingly troubled, this argument was no longer viable. But no new argument emerged to fill the gap; many on the political left continued to advocate social justice, but they did so with the usually silent concern that the reforms they advocated would probably deepen the society's economic difficulties. The consequence was a certain lack of self-confidence and a loss of persuasiveness. When the left could not make a convincing case for the economic viability of certain reforms, it lost the support of earlier liberal allies. The result was the loss of initiative to the political right, which had no hesitation in claiming that its reforms would solve all economic problems.

What has been argued here is that the pursuit of social justice and the pursuit of economic efficiency are compatible. Once one clears away the mystifications of self-described realists, it is appar-

---

[35] These changes could also be facilitated by reforms in labor law and the laws on corporate governance.

[36] The obvious historical analogy for employers being forced to accept reforms that increase efficiency is the role of industrial unions. While management fiercely resisted the rise of the industrial unions in the 1930s, it is now generally agreed that the unions played a critical role in institutionalizing a highly productive system of work relations that functioned effectively in the 1950s and 1960s.

ent that we are again in a situation, like the 1930s, in which major institutional reforms can promote equality, democracy, and a stronger economy. The essential point is the recognition that the political preferences of the business community and the pursuit of economic efficiency are not the same thing. The vitality of the American political economy can be restored, but it will have to be done, once again, against the resistance of those whom Franklin Roosevelt called "the malefactors of great wealth"—the big businesspeople who confuse their narrow self-interest with the needs of society.

REFERENCES

Aaron, Henry, et al. 1986. *Economic Choices 1987.* Washington, D.C.: Brookings Institution.

Adler, Paul. 1983. "Rethinking the Skill Requirements of New Technologies." Working Paper no. 84-27, Harvard Business School, Cambridge, Mass.

Albin, Peter, and Eileen Applebaum. 1986. "The Computer Rationalization of Work: Implications for Women Workers." Unpublished paper.

Alperowitz, Gar, and Jeff Faux. 1980. "Controls and the Basic Necessities." *Challenge,* May–June, pp. 21–29.

Altshuler, Alan, et al. 1984. *The Future of the Automobile.* Cambridge, Mass.: MIT Press.

Andrain, Charles F. 1985. *Social Policies in Western Industrial Societies.* Berkeley, Calif.: Institute of International Studies.

Barnet, Richard J., and Ronald E. Muller. 1974. *Global Reach: The Power of the Multinational Corporations.* New York: Simon & Schuster.

Block, Fred. 1984. "Technological Change and Employment: New Perspectives on an Old Controversy." *Economia and Lavoro* 18 (3): 3–21.

———. 1985. "Postindustrial Development and the Obsolescence of Economic Categories." *Politics and Society* 14(1): 71–104.

———. 1986. "Social Choice and the Multiple 'Logics' of Capital." *Theory and Society* 15 (1–2): 175–92.

Block, Fred, and Gene A. Burns. 1986. "Productivity as a Social Problem: The Uses and Misuses of Social Indicators." *American Sociological Review* 51 (6): 767–80.

Bluestone, Barry, and Bennett Harrison. 1982. *The Deindustrialization of America.* New York. Basic Books.

Boucher, Tom. 1981. "Technical Change, Capital Investment, and Productivity in U.S. Metalworking Industries." Pp. 93–121 in Ali Dogramaci and

Nabil R. Adams, eds., *Aggregate and Industry-Level Productivity Analyses.* Boston: Martinus Nijhoff.

Bowles, Samuel, David M. Gordon, and Thomas E. Weisskopf. 1983. *Beyond the Wasteland: A Democratic Alternative to Economic Decline.* Garden City, N.Y.: Doubleday.

Brand, Horst, and John Duke. 1983. "Productivity in Commercial Banking: Computers Spur the Advance." Pp. 58–66 in U.S. Bureau of Labor Statistics, *A BLS Reader on Productivity.* Washington, D.C.: Government Printing Office.

Business Week. 1984. "Software: The New Driving Force." February 27, pp. 74–84.

———. 1986. "Why the French Are in Love with Videotex." January 20, p. 84.

Butera, Federico, and Joseph E. Thurman, eds. 1984. *Automation and Work Design.* Amsterdam: North Holland.

Cameron, David R. 1978. "The Expansion of the Public Economy: A Comparative Analysis." *American Political Science Review* 72 (December): 1243–61.

———. 1985. "Does Government Cause Inflation? Taxes, Spending, and Deficits." Pp. 224–79 in Leon N. Lindberg and Charles S. Maier, eds., *The Politics of Inflation and Economic Stagnation.* Washington, D.C.: Brookings Institution.

Cartwright, David W. 1986. "Improved Deflation of Purchases of Computers." *Survey of Current Business,* March, pp. 7–10.

Denison, Edward F. 1979. *Accounting for Slower Growth.* Washington, D.C.: Brookings Institution.

Doz, Yves. 1985. "Automobiles." Pp. 189–212 in Milton Hochmuth and William Davidson, eds., *Revitalizing American Industry.* Cambridge, Mass.: Ballinger Publishing Co.

Eisner, Robert. 1985. "The Total Income System of Accounts." *Survey of Current Business,* January, pp. 27–28.

———. 1986. *How Real Is the Federal Deficit?* New York: Free Press.

Fadem, Joel. 1984. "Automation and Work Design in the United States." Pp. 648–96 in Federico Butera and Joseph E. Thurman, eds., *Automation and Work Design.* Amsterdam: North Holland.

Federal Reserve Bank of Boston. 1980. *The Decline in Productivity Growth.* Boston: Federal Reserve Bank.

Fernandez, John P. 1986. *Child Care and Corporate Productivity.* Lexington, Mass.: D. C. Heath.

Freeman, Richard B., and James L. Medoff. 1984. *What Do Unions Do?* New York: Basic Books.

Friedland, Roger, and Jimy Sanders. 1985. "The Public Economy and Economic Growth in Western Market Economies." *American Sociological Review* 50(4): 421–37.

Friedman, Milton, and Rose Friedman. 1981. *Free to Choose: A Personal Statement.* New York: Avon Books.

Gilder, George. 1982. *Wealth and Poverty.* New York: Bantam Books.

Ginsberg, Eli. 1977. "The Job Problem." *Scientific American,* November, pp. 43–51.

Goldthorpe, John, ed. 1984. *Order and Conflict in Contemporary Capitalism.* Oxford: Clarendon Press.

Gordon, David M. 1985. "Globalization or Decay? Alternative Perspectives on Recent Transformations in the World Economy." Unpublished paper.

Gordon, Robert J. 1975. "The Demand for and Supply of Inflation." *Journal of Law and Economics* 18 (3): 807–36.

Hayek, Friedrich August. 1980. *1980s Unemployment and the Unions.* London: Institute of Economic Affairs.

Heilbroner, Robert. 1984. "The Deficit." *New Yorker,* July 30.

Hicks, John. 1966. *The Theory of Wages.* New York: St. Martin's Press.

Hirschhorn, Larry. 1984. *Beyond Mechanization.* Cambridge, Mass.: MIT Press.

Hirschman, Albert O. 1970. *Exit, Voice, and Loyalty: Responses to Decline in Firms, Organizations, and States.* Cambridge, Mass.: Harvard University Press.

Howard, Robert. 1985. *Brave New Workplace.* New York: Viking Press.

Jaikumar, Ramchandran. 1986. "Postindustrial Manufacturing." *Harvard Business Review*, November–December, pp. 69–76.

Katzenstein, Peter J. 1985. *Small States in World Markets.* Ithaca, N.Y.: Cornell University Press.

Kendrick, John W. 1976. *The Formation and Stocks of Total Capital.* New York: National Bureau of Economic Research.

———, ed. 1984. *International Comparisons of Productivity and Causes of the Slowdown.* Cambridge, Mass.: Ballinger Publishing Co.

Kochan, Thomas A., Harry C. Katz, and Nancy R. Mower. 1984. *Worker Participation and American Unions.* Kalamazoo, Mich.: Upjohn Institute for Employment Research.

Kuttner, Robert. 1980. *Revolt of the Haves: Tax Rebellions and Hard Times.* New York: Simon & Schuster.

———. 1984. *The Economic Illusion: False Choices Between Prosperity and Social Justice.* Boston: Houghton Mifflin Co.

Kuznets, Simon. 1971. *Economic Growth of Nations: Total Output and Production Structure.* Cambridge, Mass.: Harvard University Press.

Lawrence, Robert Z. 1984. *Can America Compete?* Washington, D.C.: Brookings Institution.

Leontief, Wassily, and Faye Duchin. 1986. *The Future Impact of Automation on Workers.* New York: Oxford University Press.

Matthews, R. C. O. 1982. "Introduction." Pp. 1–16 in R. C. O. Matthews, ed., *Slower Growth in the Western World.* London: William Heinemann.

McCombie, J. S. L., and J. R. De Ridder. 1984. " 'The Verdoorn Law Controversy': Some New Empirical Evidence Using U.S. State Data." *Oxford Economic Papers* 36: 268–84.

Melman, Seymour. 1983. *Profits Without Production.* New York: Alfred A. Knopf.

————. 1984. "Alternatives for the Organization of Work in Computer-Assisted Manufacturing." *Annals of the New York Academy of Science* 426 (November): 83–90.

Miller, S. M., and Donald Tomaskovic-Devey. 1983. *Recapitalizing America: Alternatives to the Corporate Distortion of National Policy.* Boston: Routledge & Kegan Paul.

Murray, Alan. 1986. "Government's System of Accounting Comes Under Rising Criticism." *Wall Street Journal,* February 3, p. 1.

Murray, Charles A. 1984. *Losing Ground: American Social Policy 1950–1980.* New York: Basic Books.

Norsworthy, J. R., Michael J. Harper, and Kent Kunze. 1979. "The Slowdown in Productivity Growth: Analysis of Some Contributing Factors." *Brookings Papers on Economic Activity* 2: 387–421.

Organization for Economic Cooperation and Development. 1979. *Socio-Economic Policies for the Elderly.* Paris: OECD.

Parnes, Herbert S., et al. *Work and Retirement: A Longitudinal Study of Men.* Cambridge, Mass.: MIT Press.

Prokesch, Steven. 1985. "Another Decline in Wage Increases Expected in 1986." *New York Times,* October 21, p. 1.

Reich, Robert. 1983. *The Next American Frontier.* New York: Times Books.

Rones, Philip L. 1983. "The Labor Market Problems of Older Workers." *Monthly Labor Review,* May, pp. 3–12.

Samuelson, Paul. 1980. "The Public Role in the Modern American Economy." Pp. 665–71 in Martin Feldstein, ed., *The American Economy in Transition.* Chicago: University of Chicago Press.

Scott, Bruce R. 1982. "Can Industry Survive the Welfare State?" *Harvard Business Review,* September–October, pp. 71–84.

Shaiken, Harley. 1984. *Work Transformed: Automation and Labor in the Computer Age.* New York: Holt, Rinehart & Winston.

Sirianni, Carmen, and Michele Eayrs. "Time, Work and Equality." *Theory and Society,* forthcoming.

Smith, Shirley J. 1983. "Estimating Annual Hours of Labor Force Activity." *Monthly Labor Review,* February, pp. 13–22.

Stavro, Barry. 1985. "Made in the U.S.A." *Forbes,* April 22, pp. 50–54.

Steinberg, Lawrence D., and Ellen Greensberger. 1980. "The Part-Time Employment of High School Students: A Research Agenda." *Children and Youth Services Review* 2: 159–83.

Szymanski, Al. 1984. "Productivity Growth and Capitalist Stagnation." *Science and Society* 48(3): 295–322.

Tsurumi, Yoshi. 1985. "Japan's Challenge to the United States." Pp. 39–79 in Milton Hochmuth and William Davidson, eds., *Revitalizing American Industry: Lessons from Our Competitors.* Cambridge, Mass.: Ballinger Publishing Co.

Tyson, Laura, and John Zysman. 1983. "American Industry in International Competition." Pp. 15–59 in John Zysman and Laura Tyson, eds., *American Industry in International Competition: Government Policies and Corporate Strategies.* Ithaca, N.Y.: Cornell University Press.

Veroff, Joseph, Elizabeth Douban, and Richard A. Kulka. 1981. *The Inner American: A Self-Portrait from 1957–1976.* New York: Basic Books.

Wall Street Journal. 1983. "Manufacturers Press Automating to Survive, But Results are Mixed." April 11, p. 1.

Wanniski, Jude. 1978. *The Way the World Works: How Economies Fail—and Succeed.* New York: Basic Books.

White House Conference on Productivity. 1984. *Report on Productivity Growth.*

C H A P T E R 4

The New Right Attack on Social Welfare

Barbara Ehrenreich

WITH THE EMERGENCE of the New Right in America in the mid-1970s, the character of the conservative arguments against social welfare changed dramatically. The underlying moral and economic bases of right-wing opposition to social welfare remain much as they were decades or even centuries ago, but in the rhetoric of the New Right, social welfare has joined a cluster of issues that had formerly not even been seen as "political"—issues like abortion, school prayer, and pornography. At the same time, the arguments against social welfare have become, even when dressed up with statistics and charts, more florid and emotionally evocative.

The New Right differs from the old conservatism in two major ways. First, it is determinedly populist in its appeal. Conservatism has traditionally been elitist, the ideology of dominant groups and entrenched interests, associated in America with images of "fat cats" and tuxedoed plutocrats. The opening for a more populist right-wing politics emerged with the backlash that extended from the late 1960s to the mid-1970s, when lower-middle-class and blue-collar constituencies mobilized to protest school busing (in Boston, for example), to eliminate textbooks deemed overly liberal (as in West Virginia), and to reverse the gains of the civil rights movement in a number of localities. Among the first on the right to articulate the resentments that inspired the backlash and incorporate them into a larger right-wing ideological framework were

George Wallace and Spiro Agnew, with their attacks on the "effete snobs" and "pointy-headed intellectuals" supposedly responsible for liberal reforms, including the gains of the civil rights movement. Anticipating the New Right by almost a decade, Wallace and Agnew pioneered one of its central themes: that liberalism is the ideological property of an elite that has contempt for the values and concerns of ordinary citizens.

Secondly, the New Right differs from the old in its emphasis on the so-called social issues, such as abortion and school prayer, which the right identifies as part of its "profamily" focus (Crawford 1980). What we might call the Old Right, represented, for example, by Barry Goldwater's 1964 campaign, focused on the more traditional conservative themes: a strong defense, belligerence in the face of international communism, limited domestic government, and market-oriented economic policies. Not until the early seventies did the leaders of the emergent New Right see the promise of the social issues, many of which, such as abortion and the Equal Rights Amendment, had been brought to the fore by the women's movement. To the architects of the New Right, these issues offered a way to mobilize the anxieties aroused by insurgent social groups such as women, minorities, and students. In the words of Richard Viguerie, one of the four men who framed the network of institutions and single-issue causes that defines the New Right, "We talk about issues that people care about, like gun control, abortion, taxes and crime. Yes, they're emotional issues, but that's better than talking about capital formation" (quoted in Paige 1983: 135).

The social issues are the key to the New Right's populist appeal; its economic outlook remains elitist, or at least, probusiness and antilabor. It is through the social issues that the New Right has made significant headway among religious constituencies such as southern fundamentalists, who are deeply conservative on "moral" issues but were traditionally Democratic in their political allegiance. Opposition to equal rights for women, to "humanism" in school textbooks, and to abortion have been among the most visible hallmarks of the New Right; and while it does not command majority support on these issues, it has proved its ability to mobilize a dedicated constituency. Efforts to control deficit spending, on the other hand, which are closer to the traditional core of conservative politics, elicit little mass enthusiasm—as Viguerie recognized years ago.

Thus the New Right presents an odd and even self-contradictory blend of themes and issues. On the one hand, it upholds the economic interests of the wealthy; on the other hand, it champions the "little man" against forces that would destroy his way of life. On the one hand, it advocates the unfettered free-market capitalism associated with classical liberalism; on the other hand, it represents a kind of moral authoritarianism that is reminiscent of European fascism.

Inconsistency has never yet stopped a political movement, but the New Right has developed a mythic view of society in which the contradictions are, if not resolved, at least less obvious. In this view, society is on the verge of moral breakdown—a common starting point for insurgent ideologies. Crime and corruption are everywhere; the young defy the old; the family is in peril. But the source of this disruption is not the obvious traditional enemy of would-be populist movements, the "bosses" and the decadent upper classes of the traditional populist stereotype. Rather, we have been led astray by another group, variously referred to as the "educated elite," the "liberal elite," or the "intelligentsia," and defined as a "new class" by the neoconservatives (who are themselves the educated elite of the New Right). It is this "new class" which, in the ideology of the contemporary right, created the feminist movement, drove religion out of the public schools, abetted the civil rights movement, allowed our national defenses to weaken, and launched the war on poverty.

By hypothesizing a corrupt and powerful new class, the right has been able to resolve the contradictions inherent in an ideology that is both populist in tone and aggressively procapitalist in spirit. In the New Right's synthesis, nothing is wrong with the free market except that it has been hampered by regulations and policies imposed by the liberal new class. Thus the moral breakdown perceived everywhere by the New Right is not a product of *laissez-faire* capitalism and the amoral individualism it inevitably fosters, but of the new class's attempts to abridge *laissez-faire* through various forms of government intervention in the economy. It follows that the appropriate target for resentment is not big business but big government, and not the corporate elite but the "educated elite." Capitalism itself is moral, even "Christian," and works in the interest of the average "middle American." It is the attempts to interfere with it—from affirmative action to social welfare programs—which lead to trouble.

Contradictions remain, of course, and lead to persistent tension between the New Right moralists and the more libertarian conservative traditionalists. Why, for example, proclaim *laissez-faire* in the marketplace while seeking to impose authoritarian restrictions (against abortion, gay rights, etc.) in private life? The resolution must lie in the assumption that the market, left to itself, engenders self-discipline and moral purity, chiefly by acquainting us with privation and the necessity for hard work. The moral laxity that leads to abortion, say, is an artifact of overly liberal "permissiveness" in public policy, and will presumably be cured when the discipline of the market is restored. Thus, in the view of the New Right, it would be misguided and perverse to recognize "rights" to certain practices or life-styles which are not only morally repugnant but have been arbitrarily imposed by new-class policies.

Unlike abortion, school prayer, or the ERA, social welfare has never been a major outreach issue of the New Right, and it is chiefly a concern of the expanding right-wing intelligentsia based in corporate-funded think tanks and, increasingly, in the academic world. Nevertheless, social welfare, or at least welfare, plays a key role in the rhetoric of the populist right, where it represents yet another proof of moral breakdown (as well, of course, as a coded way of invoking racist resentment). At the same time, New Right ideology has come to play a key role in the more intellectual conservative assessments of social welfare. Once focused more narrowly on the economic costs of social welfare, the conservative critique has come to emphasize its moral impact and to see that impact as part of a larger societal problem of "permissiveness."

But if social welfare is not one of the high-profile issues of New

Right populists, it is in many ways the linchpin issue of contemporary right-wing ideology, connecting the economic concerns of the old right with the social and moral concerns of the new. First, it provides the right with a clear-cut example of how attempts to interfere with the market contribute to general moral decline. Second, it provides a stark case study in the objectives and methods of the "new class," which the New Right identifies not only as the major source of moral laxity in American society but as the sole architect of the welfare state. Thus, in the worldview of the New Right, social welfare is no longer a public expenditure whose costs and benefits can be subjected to rational analysis and debate. Rather, it has become the subject of a cautionary tale illustrating the schemes of the new class, the debasement of its victims, and the stolid resistance of the ordinary "middle Americans" to whom the right's populist appeal is pitched.

In this chapter we will examine the way the New Right has come to see social welfare as a product of new-class policies and as a part of the larger moral breakdown engendered by permissive social policies. We will attempt to understand the actual social conditions that give plausibility—or at least emotional resonance—to the right's theories and critiques of social welfare, focusing in particular upon the role of the consumer culture in fostering the anxieties the right seeks to mobilize against social welfare. As we shall see, the contradiction between the imperatives of the market and the kind of morality upheld by the right is an inescapable one, but it is one that need not be fatal to the ambitions of the New Right. For if the right dissembles on fundamental issues of power and morality, liberalism, unfortunately, does not raise them at all.

THE "ELITISM" OF SOCIAL WELFARE

In *Losing Ground,* his influential 1984 attack on the welfare state, Charles Murray entitled a chapter on the origins of the Great Society programs "Implementing the Elite Wisdom." In his view, the impetus for those programs did not come from the civil rights movement or the larger black upsurge of the sixties, but from a thoroughly comfortable, apparently white "elite," which he defines as follows:

> The group is, with no pejorative connotations, best labeled the intelligentsia. . . . It includes the upper echelons of (in no particular order of importance) academia, journalism, publishing, and the vast network of foundations, institutes, and research centers that has been woven into partnership with government during the last thirty years. . . . Politicians and members of the judiciary (Senator J. William Fulbright and Justice William O. Douglas are examples from the sixties) and bankers and businessmen and lawyers and doctors may be members of the intelligentsia as well, though not all are. (Murray 1984: 42)

Murray's "intelligentsia" is the "new class" which the neoconservative writers of the seventies identified as the architect and, to a large extent, beneficiary of the expanded social programs of the sixties. Daniel Patrick Moynihan was perhaps the first of the neoconservatives to use the term, writing in 1972:

> The social legislation of the middle third of the century created "social space" for a new class whose privilege (or obligation) it is to dispense services to populations that are in various ways wards of the state. (Bruce-Briggs 1979)

In Moynihan's view at the time, this was a benign development, since "the self-interest of the new class is merged with a manifestly sincere view of the public interest." Writing in the same year, though, Norman Podhoretz attacked the "new class" of mindworkers, professors, bureaucrats, and so forth as the source of an "adversary culture" which was challenging the status quo in order to advance its own interests (Podhoretz 1979). The intellectual attack on the new class initiated by Podhoretz echoed—and reinforced—the populist attack on the "liberal elite" and "elite snobs" launched by Spiro Agnew and George Wallace in the 1968 and 1972 presidential campaigns.

In the analysis offered by the neoconservative intellectuals in the seventies, the new class was an elite of educated professional people who advocated sweeping social reforms in order to promote their own interests as a class. New-class self-interest was particularly evident, according to the conservative critics, in the liberal social welfare agenda. Though social programs might have been designed to help the poor, they actually enriched and empowered the "social engineers" who designed them and the army of bureaucrats and professionals who staffed them. Reflecting the mainstream right-wing view, the *National Review* editorialized that the poor themselves had very little to do with social welfare policy, other than to serve as pawns of new-class strategists.

> The "poor" must be understood in a special sense, as potential clients for the redistributive ministrations of the New Class, the middlemen of social justice. Analytically, "the poor," as a concept, legitimizes the power-grab of the New Class middlemen in the same sense as "the proletariat" legitimates the power-grab of the Leninists. (Rusher 1984: 322)

In right-wing writings, the new class is often described as "nonproductive" or even defined as "nonproductive elements," since, according to the theory, it does little other than promote its own interests in jobs and power. Through social welfare, moreover, the new class has succeeded in making significant other segments of the population equally useless. As right-wing essayist R. Emmett Tyrrell, Jr., puts it, somewhat flamboyantly:

> The chloroform of egalitarianism was spread everywhere in the 1970s. Prior American values of self-reliance, personal liberty, and competence were heaved overboard. . . . Along with this abandonment of older American values came a new class of busybodies to elucidate the new hokum and to harass the productive elements of the Republic. The welfare state had turned many theretofore toiling Americans into parasites, and this new class of busybodies lived as superparasites, deriving nour-

ishment from the dependence of the welfare clients. (Tyrell 1984: 36)

The left, too, has had a well-developed critique of the role of the "elite" in shaping social welfare programs. At the crudest level, New Left leaders rejected the welfare state entirely as a mechanism of social control, designed to pacify the poor and ultimately serving the interests of the business elite. In the more refined analysis growing out of New Left experience with Great Society programs, radicals criticized the professional domination of many of these programs and the use, by social welfare professionals, of professional expertise as a rationale for more general decision-making power. Too often, programs designed to serve and empower the poor turned into battlegrounds between the low-income client community and the overly technocratic professionals hired to staff them. For example, in Great Society–inspired health programs in New York City in the sixties and early seventies, low-income black and Hispanic communities frequently clashed with professionals and administrators over the issue of how much emphasis to place on preventive, community-based services as compared with high-technology, professionally dominated services (Ehrenreich and Ehrenreich 1970; Gross and Osterman 1972). In general, the struggle over "community control" highlighted the conflicting interests of low-income service consumers and the usually middle-class, college-educated providers of services.[1]

[1] Some on the left—David Bazelon, myself and John Ehrenreich, Alvin Gouldner—went so far as to identify a "new class"—relative to Marx's classic dyad of the bourgeoisie and the proletariat—of professional and managerial workers. Like a number of other theorists before us, we were attempting to understand the emergence, in industrialized capitalist societies, of a mass grouping of educated white-collar workers and their dependents. Many on the left, following the French theorist Serge Mallet, described the new group as a "new working class," distinguished from the "old," blue-collar working class only by the more "mental" nature of its work. Others, in the tradition of Veblen, saw the new, technocratic middle class as already winning crucial decision-making power in society and potentially replacing the business elite, or capitalist class.

In our analysis (1979), John Ehrenreich and I emphasized the ambiguous social position of the professional and managerial class, as we called it. Its members are, on the one hand, mere employees of the business elite, but on the other hand, they are people who may exercise considerable autonomy and power over others. The teacher, the social worker, the lawyer, and the plant manager may all be salaried employees, but they also enjoy a degree of authority inherent in their occupations—and are often resented by the poor and working-class people among their students,

It is one thing to analyze conflicts in terms of class differences, and another thing to use the notion of class solely to defame ideological opponents—and this is what the right has done. Murray's attempt to define the "intelligentsia" illustrates the overwhelmingly ideological motivation behind the right's conception of a "new class," for what he is defining is not a class or a coherent social grouping of any kind but a rather arbitrary group: namely, people who are middle class (or wealthier) and who are also in some sense liberal. Hence the two liberal examples—Fulbright and Douglas—picked out from the larger category of public officials, and hence the humorously redundant explanation that not all bankers are members of this "intelligentsia." Only liberals, apparently, can be members of the "intelligentsia" Murray wishes to castigate, leading us to wonder whether, in his scheme, it is possible to be both a conservative and an intellectual (or at least a "mind-worker") such as Murray himself and other residents of conservative think tanks. But liberals are not a class, any more than conservatives are, or any category of people defined by a particular view of things. And the fact that some bankers are more liberal than others, or more intellectual than others, or whatever, does not put them in a class by themselves, socially and economically distinct from all other bankers.

Furthermore, even if we were to agree on the existence of a new, professional-managerial class in American society, we would have to differ with the right as to how much power it wields. Any "new" middle class, no matter how it is defined, must occupy a subordinate position to the dominant business elite, or capitalist class. Most professional and managerial jobs are, after all, in the service of private capital, and while new-class members may resent their lack of autonomy, they have hardly become an insurgent class on a par with the economically deprived.[2] In conservative

---

clients, or subordinates. We saw the political interests of this new professional and managerial class as being equally ambiguous and not usefully pigeonholed as left or right, conservative or liberal.

[2] In most cases, conservatives identify as "new class" only those occupations or work settings that provide a modicum of autonomy from corporate imperatives, e.g., the university, government, and the media. Conveniently, the "captive" majority of the new class—the lawyers, engineers, managers, etc.—who are private-sector, corporate employees never even figure in the analysis. Yet obviously

theory, however, the new class has both pre-empted the role of less fortunate people in pressing for social change and, for all practical purposes, eclipsed the ruling business class. It has become the only interesting actor on the scene—a distortion which, one is tempted to suggest, may reflect a certain new-class parochialism among the conservative writers themselves.

THE WORKING CLASS IN THE NEW-RIGHT WORLDVIEW

In the constellation of classes invented by the right, the ruling elite, the business elite, is usually absent, and the poor are too weak to resist being dragged by the new class into "welfare dependence." Only one class has had the courage and conviction to defy the new class in its rise to power, and that is the working class, or, as they are sometimes called in the literature of the right, the "middle Americans."[3] To Murray and those who preceded him in the development of the right-wing attack on social welfare, the working class represents the "traditional values" of hard work and self-reliance, as opposed to the scheming new class and the passive poor. To New Right writer Samuel T. Francis, the "middle Americans" uphold a "Domestic Ethic," featuring "the necessity of sacrifice" and "the duty of work rather than the right of welfare" (Francis 1982: 79). It is the will of these blue-collarites or middle Americans to abolish the welfare state.

Historically, of course, it was the blue-collar working class that *created* the welfare state, or at least whose struggles led to the New Deal and whose unions have been loyal to the New Deal's unfinished agenda. But the right has never risen to power—peaceably, that is, and in this century—by advocating the interests of the

---

people do not change their class (however that term is defined) when they move from academic or government employment to a private firm or vice versa. However we look at it, the conservatives' new class is not a class at all but an ideological whipping boy.

[3] Though "blue-collar" and "middle American" are sometimes used interchangeably, "middle American" is often used as a broader category including small-town dwellers and small businessmen. Thus the term "middle American" is itself ideologically interesting in that it unites the blue-collar auto worker and the wealthy car dealer, the security guard and the bank manager.

wealthy and powerful. To be populist, the right needs a "little man" to speak for; and this has been the blue-collar worker, or the "middle American."

The opening for this unlikely rhetorical alliance was provided by George Wallace and his unexpected appeal to blue-collar voters in 1968, followed by the defection of many of them to the Republicans in 1968 and 1972. This blue-collar "backlash" reflected a variety of discontents: anger at the draft, which was notoriously biased to exclude the sons of the new class; resentment of black gains in jobs and education (limited as they were); and, no doubt, resentment of the new class itself, as represented by managers at work, condescending professionals, media "experts" (Carter 1979). But to the right-wing cadre who had been biding their time since Goldwater's defeat in 1964, the backlash provided an opportunity to reverse, at least rhetorically, all traditional class allegiances and to present social welfare as the nemesis of working people and the nefarious instrument of a social elite.

In reality, the backlash was both overstated and misrepresented. As Scammon and Wattenberg (1970: 62–3) concluded from their analysis of the crucial 1968 election:

> Despite all the recent comment about elitist Democratic intellectuals, the cold fact remains that the elite in America has a Republican majority. They are the doctors, bankers, and businessmen. . . . In the 1968 election the "professional and business" group went 56–34 percent for Nixon over Humphrey. The Democrats, despite the hoopla about the Democratic elitist establishment, are those "plain people who work with their hands." Manual workers went 50–35 percent for Humphrey over Nixon.

Furthermore, Scammon and Wattenberg's analysis of survey data showed that Wallace voters, who were more likely than Nixon voters to be blue-collar, were also more liberal on social welfare issues than Nixon voters, and that people who expressed the strongest identification with the working class were the most likely to vote Democratic. And these patterns have held up against even

Reagan's popularity: despite the right's repeated castigations of elite new-class "welfarism," it is the "little man" (and in even greater proportions, the "little woman") who is more likely to be liberal on economic and social welfare issues and the bankers and so on who are not (Edsall 1984).

But it should hardly be necessary to provide a detailed refutation of the idea that the advocates and beneficiaries of social welfare constitute an "elite." As Piven and Cloward mention in chapter 2, in any recent decade one out of four Americans has become sufficiently poor to require public assistance in the form of food stamps or Aid to Families with Dependent Children; and it is people in traditionally working-class occupations who are most vulnerable to economic dislocation and sudden poverty. As for employment, the numerically largest group of beneficiaries of social welfare jobs are women, disproportionately black women. In 1980, 70 percent of the 17.3 million social service jobs on all levels of government (including education) were held by women, and these jobs accounted for fully a quarter of all female employment (Peattie and Rein 1983).

Nor, on the other hand, is it possible to discern any consistent support for social welfare from key strongholds of the new class or intelligentsia such as the media, the think tanks, and the universities. Historically, people who might be described as middle-class intellectuals (or forerunners of the new class) have probably opposed social welfare more often than they have advocated it; at least, it was members of the educated middle class (or historically analogous groups) who developed the ideological rationale for social welfare cutbacks in the late nineteenth century (see chapter 1). It is true that in the 1960s the expansionary social agenda undertaken by Lyndon Johnson in response to black pressure attracted both talent and support from new-class liberals. Today, however, the views of the mass media and most prominent think tanks on social welfare are neoliberal to conservative, and in many respects closer to Charles Murray's views than to those of traditional liberalism.

Finally, for examples of unabashed elitism, one can hardly do better than the right itself, as in Tyrell's "chloroform of egalitarianism" or in the stunningly new-class statement by Spiro Agnew that he didn't campaign in ghettos because he didn't feel "there's any particular gain to be made by debating on streetcorners. . . . You don't learn from people suffering from poverty, but from experts who have studied the problem" (Witcover 1972: 265).

As a rhetorical device, though, the right-wing charge that social welfare is an instrument of the elite has a certain cynical force. What appears to be generosity is revealed as the self-seeking program of the already privileged; and what sounds like egalitarianism is actually an elite's scheme to shore up its own power. These themes found dramatic expression in Patrick Buchanan's well-publicized June 1985 attack on New York Governor Mario Cuomo. "Mario Cuomo's incessant invocations of the poor, the downtrodden, the ill," Buchanan wrote, "almost invariably turn up as preambles to budget requests that would augment the power of his own political class—the Welfare statists" (*New York Times* 1985a).

The political impact of the right's campaign to discredit social welfare as elitist is hard to judge. No doubt one effect has been to make it more risky for political leaders to be identified as advocates of an expanded welfare state, lest they invite the kind of invective illustrated by Buchanan's remark. Perhaps the most serious casualty, though, has been the very word "liberal." No doubt in part because of the right's campaign to link the words "liberal" and "elite," a campaign which extends from Wallace and Agnew in the late sixties to the New Right today, "liberal" has become one of Americans' least popular political designations, ranking far below "conservative," "moderate," and, oddly, even the quaint-sounding term "progressive" (*New York Times* 1985d).

"PERMISSIVENESS" AND SOCIAL WELFARE

The oldest conservative argument against social welfare is that it undermines the work ethic. The contemporary right has gone well beyond this, arguing that social welfare not only frees people from the discipline of the market but is an indulgence on a par with sexual libertinism, drug abuse, and uncontrolled consumerism. Most often the argument is made by a process of linguistic association, the key link being the notion of "permissiveness." To the right, permissiveness is the fundamental crime of liberalism, and is responsible for every perceived form of decadence and moral breakdown. Thus political analyst Kevin Phillips (a conservative but not a New Rightist) finds that liberalism is responsible for "permissiveness of various economic, diplomatic, sociological and sexual hues" (1982: 31), which turn out to include homosexuality and abortion, "judicial permissiveness" toward criminals, and "welfarism."

The effect, and no doubt the intent, of the right's emphasis on permissiveness and its moral consequences is to take social welfare out of the realm of economic issues and into the realm of what the New Right identifies as "social issues." The genius of the New Right has lain in recognizing that while middle Americans tend to be liberal on economic issues, many are conservative on social issues. By transmuting social welfare into a social or moral issue, an appeal could be made to people who were loyal to Democratic social welfare initiatives but disturbed about a perceived "moral breakdown" of American society.

"Permissiveness," like many contemporary right-wing notions, entered the political discourse in the 1960s, when it was used principally to castigate student radicals. In the argument popularized by Agnew and repeated by Nixon, the student left and the youthful counterculture were both products of permissive child-raising practices. In the seventies, neoconservatives expanded the notion of permissiveness to include the sexual revolution and sundry other manifestations of what they perceived as a breakdown of traditional sources of authority. Today the term has almost automatic connotations of sexual laxity and, at the same time, has become almost indispensable in conservative attacks on social welfare. In a recent short op-ed piece by conservative social scientist Lawrence Mead, for example, the word "permissive" appears four times, and is as tightly linked to the words "welfare programs" as the elements of a Homeric epithet (*New York Times* 1985c).

In conservative theory, permissiveness in social policy is an outgrowth of the personal permissiveness of the new class. Samuel T. Francis, for example, contrasts the middle-American values of "sacrifice and deferral of gratification" with the "cosmopolitan-managerial demand for immediate gratification, indulgence and consumption" (1982: 79). He does not explain how this class of technocrats, a group that is usually represented as supremely capable of disciplined, concerted action in order to advance its own aims, could be so given to personal hedonism. He simply insists that there is some mysterious link between the technocratic will to power and the propensity for self-indulgence.

> These [hedonistic] lifestyles, values, and ideals cannot be simply discarded by the old [liberal] elite; they represent the logical outgrowth of its own structural interests: large, social-engineering government in alliance with corporations, universities and foundations, the mass media, unions, and other bureaucracies. (Francis 1982: 81)

Surprisingly, to any sober liberal advocate of social welfare, the "perfect (though extreme)" exemplar of liberal values in Francis's analysis turns out to be the Rolling Stones's lead singer, Mick Jagger (p. 69).

An equally peculiar set of connections is offered by Kevin Phillips in a 1979 article on the new class. He lists as the targets of Spiro Agnew's invective "elitists, planners, the Eastern Media Establishment, Harvard and the Ivy League, nonprofit foundations like Brookings and Ford, campus activism, the drug culture, pornography, and the like" (Phillips 1979: 140). No doubt Agnew did attack everything on this list, but there is no obvious connection between the first few items (elitists, planners, etc.) and the last two (drugs and pornography)—certainly not enough to justify Phillips's phrase "and the like." What makes Harvard and pornography so alike? Only the unstated assumption that they are both manifestations of new-class power in society and, presumably, both sources of moral corruption.

Like conservative theories of social welfare, conservative theories of crime focus on the spread of permissiveness from an educated elite to the poor. In Elliott Currie's critical summary of the conservative view of the historic etiology of crime, "A pervasive . . . nineteenth-century effort to control 'self-indulgent impulses' was increasingly derided by the 'educated elite' as narrow-minded, fundamentalist, and provincial, and replaced by the 'self-expression ethic'" (Currie 1985: 36). According to conservative criminologist James Q. Wilson, the elite ethic of self-indulgence spread to the general public with particular rapidity in the 1960s, as a result of a "celebration of the youth culture in the marketplace, in the churches, and among adults," and led to an "institutionalization in all parts of society of the natural desire of youth for freedom" (cited in Currie 1985: 38).

In most conservative writings, permissive social welfare programs as well as judicial leniency played a key role in spreading the decadent life-style of the new class to the poor. The fact that American welfare and judicial policies are, if anything, excessively *nonpermissive,* miserly, and punitive[4] needs never be addressed, so compelling is the commonsense analogy to child-raising practices: Spoil a child, indulge someone in need, and this ("sex, drugs and crime," as New Right leader Paul Weyrich sums it up) is what you get.

"Permissiveness" is a complex metaphor and derives an insidious power from the wealth of associations it calls up. In the first place, if welfare programs are permissive and analogous to certain child-raising practices, then the poor are analogous to children. The image of the poor as childlike and undisciplined is a very old one; in the "culture of poverty" theories of the sixties, which many liberals subscribed to, the poor were described as intrinsically hedonistic, incapable of deferred gratification, and having little

---

[4] Contrary to conservative myth, the United States is excessively punitive in its response to crime, at least by international standards. As Elliott Currie points out, the rate of incarceration in the United States (217 per 100,000) is the highest of any industrialized nation except for the Soviet Union and South Africa. Sentencing is extremely strict in the United States: about 16 months served for the average crime, compared to about 5 months in Britain and 1.3 months in Holland. Nor can these differences be accounted for by differences in the seriousness of the crimes committed in the United States as opposed to comparable nations. For each type of offense, sentencing is heavier here. For example, the average maximum sentence for robbery was 150 months in the U.S. federal prisons and 68 months in the state prisons, compared to 19 months in the Dutch prisons (Currie 1985: 28–9).

sense of time. (In fact, it is interesting that the War on Poverty grew out of earlier programs focused on juvenile delinquency.) In the New Right's view, the childlike traits of the poor have been imposed from the outside, through the new class's indulgent social policies. Murray is insistent on this point. The poor did not change; they did not become more vicious, more dependent, on their own. Only "the rules changed" with the expansion of social welfare programs in the sixties. The poor did not participate in changing the rules—that was the work of the "intelligentsia"; they merely responded to the new, more indulgent expectations. They are a tabula rasa, awaiting the imprint of sterner, character-building policies. (In the *National Review* editorial quoted above, the ontological status of the poor is even more tenuous: they are only a "concept," presumably invented by the new class to justify its policies.)

To reject the image of the poor as children is not to deny that individuals in poverty are more likely to suffer from personal dislocation and a disordered life-style than are middle-class people. One of the goals of the War on Poverty, in fact, was to help overcome the disorganization of ghetto life by providing channels for leadership and decision-making in community-based services. But in the right-wing view that obliterates the poor as conscious participants in history, no such community involvement is possible, or perhaps even thinkable. Worse, if the poor are not innocents awaiting opportunities for citizenly involvement (as liberals, paternalistically, saw them), if they are already spoiled children, then the only course of action is to discipline them with punitive right-wing policies.

Implicit in the assumption that the poor are a temperamentally homogeneous group, and beyond that, that they bear the marks of a shared historical experience (having been spoiled by the briefly more generous social welfare programs of the sixties and early seventies), is the idea that the poor are a constant, self-reproducing subpopulation—the "underclass" of conservative theory. In reality, as Piven and Cloward argue in chapter 2, there is considerable turnover within the poverty population, which is likely to include, at any given time, many recent recruits from the middle class—

divorced mothers, laid-off industrial workers, dispossessed farmers. Such individuals surely bring with them into poverty the traditional values of hard work that conservatives find so admirable, and none of them could have been spoiled by prior shifts in social welfare policy. To imagine the poor as children, and particularly as a single cohort of children, is to deny the heterogeneity of the poverty population, and hence to deny the widespread vulnerability to poverty that so many Americans share.

The metaphor of social welfare permissiveness, like the notion that social welfare is the self-serving program of an elite, effectively undercuts the moral foundations of the welfare state. If social welfare programs are actually an avenue of contagion by which personal decadence spreads from liberal members of the middle class to the poor, then surely these programs should be abandoned in toto, as Charles Murray suggests. If, to state it less dramatically, social welfare programs are the means by which the poor have been misguided, exposed to the wrong "rules," and so forth, liberal social welfare advocates should at least feel remorse. And in some cases, they seem to do so. In a 1985 article presenting him as a "defender of 'the Welfare System,'" liberal social-policy analyst Sar Levitan is quoted as confessing, "We went too far. Permissiveness is the key word. We gave up on old-fashioned standards . . ." (*New York Times* 1985b).

THE SOURCES OF "PERMISSIVENESS"

The success of the metaphor of permissiveness has depended on a widespread sense that there has indeed been a moral breakdown within American society. Many factors have contributed to the perception that such a breakdown, or as the neoconservatives often put it, a "crisis of authority," occurred in the 1960s and 1970s. There was the emergence of a youth-oriented counterculture that did indeed uphold an ethic of self-indulgence and immediate gratification. There was a precipitous rise in the divorce rate, beginning in the early sixties and still under way. There were the various manifestations of a sexual revolution, including a proliferation of commercial pornography, increasingly explicit sexual references in the mass media, and the emergence of a visible gay-rights move-ment. Finally, there was the emergence of a feminist movement that explicitly challenged male authority within the family as well as in public life. All of these changes, magnified at times by the media and superimposed on a massive black insurgency, have been as threatening to some as they have been liberating to others.

But the "crisis of authority," as seen by the right, can hardly be blamed on elite "social engineering" or government permissive-ness. In some cases government did take liberal social initiatives (though often only to liberalize previously punitive and authoritar-ian laws): abortion was decriminalized, divorce laws liberalized, and the voting age lowered. However, the public sector played only a small role in encouraging the *demand* for such reforms. The right's ideological link between moral breakdown, as evidenced by pornography and greater sexual freedom, on the one hand, and government policies undertaken by a liberal "elite," on the other, is a highly imaginative construction.

To the extent that America has become in any way a permis-sive society, the source of permissiveness lies outside the public sector and the machinations of government bureaucrats: in the private sector, and particularly in the consumer culture. Take the problem of sexual laxity, which so alarms conservatives. No new-class elite decreed the various manifestations of sexual revolution (though individuals of different social classes, including what could be construed as the new class, worked to achieve a liberaliza-tion of American sexual mores). Rather, it is the media, including the advertising and entertainment industries, that have "sexual-ized" our culture with images intended to command attention and ultimately to sell products.

Or take the "youth rebellion" and the perceived youthful disre-spect for authority. Certainly social welfare policy had little to do with the emergence of the "youth culture" in the sixties (though the argument is often made that AFDC enables young women to flout parental authority and indulge their sexuality). In fact, the consumer culture played a major role in encouraging the sense of youth identity that underlay the emergence of a youth culture. Teenagers as teenagers became a major marketing target in the

1950s and 1960s; and marketing strategies that focused on teenagers recognized the importance of heightening young people's self-awareness as a legitimate social group, different from both children and young adults. Advertising to teenagers necessarily encourages the assertion of youthful needs in the face of parental restraint, while the emergence of distinctly teen products such as music and fashions creates an area of youth expertise impenetrable to many adults (Oakley 1986: 267–90). Whether these are positive or negative developments is open to debate, but there can be no question about the role of the consumer culture in promoting them.[5]

Or consider the "breakdown of the family," which is of so much concern to the New Right. The right uniformly attributes the rise of single-parent families among the poor to the disruptive effects of welfare. When they take into account similar trends among the middle class, they are likely to blame "women's liberation" or even male irresponsibility. Arguably, both of these factors have contributed to the rising divorce rate: women's increased work-force participation (which hardly represents "liberation," I might add) makes it easier for women to leave unhappy marriages, just as changed attitudes toward men's responsibility as breadwinners has made it easier for them to leave their families or never to marry in the first place. Both of these changes, however, can be related to the mounting demands of the consumer culture. As Barbara Bergmann and others have argued, women's influx into the work force represented not just the triumph of feminist ideology, or even the pressure of economic necessity (the great influx took place among women who were already middle class, not among the poor), but the need to keep up with a rising standard of living, as defined by the mass media and, to a certain extent, required by suburban living (Bergmann 1986: 28–31).

Similarly, the decline in male "responsibility," or long-term financial commitment to the family, can be linked, as I have argued

---

[5] A case can also be made that permissiveness in the original sense, as a philosophy of child-raising, arose in response to the developing consumer culture and took hold because it was consistent with the message from that culture. Permissiveness in child-raising should, ideally, inculcate the traits most desirable in consumers: self-indulgence and the inability to distinguish wants from needs (see Ehrenreich and English 1978: 212–14).

elsewhere, to the rise of a marketing strategy directed toward men as consumers in their own right. In general, there has been a shift since the 1950s away from a marketing focus on the family as the unit of consumption to a focus on the individual. Products for individual consumption by males have proliferated to include increasingly differentiated styles of clothing (not just for "work" and for "good" but for a range of leisure options), housewares (for the bachelor apartment), and most recently, cosmetics. At the same time, media vehicles responsible for targeting the male market, such as *Playboy* and *GQ* magazines, glamorize the single male and, sometimes explicitly, criticize traditionalist assumptions about men's responsibility as breadwinners (Ehrenreich 1983: 49–51).

In general, the consumer culture has little stake in the family as traditionally defined: working husband, homemaker wife, and children. For one thing, such a family does not earn or spend enough compared to a family with a wife who holds a job. For another thing, a family of any composition by its nature underconsumes key items like household appliances, at least relative to the amount that can be consumed by the same number of people occupying individual households. It is better for the consumer-goods market if the consumers (or at least the affluent ones) remain single or, if they marry, get divorced at some point and duplicate many of their possessions (see Ehrenreich and English 1978: 290; *Wall Street Journal* 1986).

But more generally, we know from everyday experience that the "ethic of self-indulgence" does not come from an overly generous government, but from a consumer culture that is endlessly inventive in producing new temptations and new rationales for yielding to them. Advertising's ubiquitous message is that every whim is a genuine need; every passing inclination, an imperative to consume. Nor is this message the adventitious result of a concentration of new-class operatives within the advertising and marketing industries. American capitalism, with its heavy reliance on individual consumer products, *requires* a mass disposition to self-indulgence, and would be severely threatened by a genuine resurgence of the traditional values of self-denial and deferred gratification attributed by the right to middle Americans. In a chapter on the development of the consumer culture in the 1950s, Douglas T. Miller and Marion Nowak quote from a motivational researcher's address to businessmen:

> We are now confronted with the problem of permitting the average American to feel moral . . . even when he is spending, even when he is not saving, even when he is taking two vacations a year and buying a second or third car. One of the basic problems of prosperity, then, is to demonstrate that the hedonistic approach to his life is a moral, not an immoral one. (Miller and Nowak 1977)

Just as the Protestant work ethic was appropriate to the earlier, accumulative stage of industrial capitalism, the "hedonistic approach" became an economic necessity as affluence created a vast domestic market for consumer goods. Actually, both are demanded of us: traditional values at the workplace and often in the family, and hedonism in the realm of consumption. As Daniel Bell has written, capitalist society is torn by a fundamental contradiction between the traditional values appropriate to stable community and family life and the hedonistic imperative of the consumer culture.

> American capitalism . . . has lost its traditional legitimacy, which was based on a moral system of reward rooted in the Protestant sanctification of work. It has substituted a hedonism which promises material ease and luxury, yet shies away from the historic implications of a "voluptuary system," with all its social permissiveness and libertinism. The culture has been dominated by a modernism that has been subversive of bourgeois life, and the middle-class life-styles by a hedonism that has undercut the Protestant ethic which provided the moral foundation for the society. (Bell 1976: 84)

It would hardly be in character for the right—old or new—to concur in pinpointing capitalism as a major source of permissiveness and moral breakdown. Shifting the blame to government, and particularly to social welfare programs, represents a remarkable, and on the face of it, almost nonsensical displacement. No government on earth is ideologically or practically permissive in the way that the capitalist consumer culture is; and those governments that are most intrusive and most controlling are also the least permissive. Yet the right continues to berate government for permissiveness and to uphold the free market as the natural inculcator of traditional values of discipline and self-denial.

There are hints that the leadership of the New Right may be ready to acknowledge the dominant role of capitalism in promoting moral breakdown. A recent column by Paul Weyrich (1986: 1), one of the four men credited with creating the New Right, points to "direct tension between cultural conservatives and some economic conservatives." If cultural conservatism, or an emphasis on the "social issues," was initially an opportunistic way of advancing economic conservatism, the cart may now be dragging the horse. In what is almost a direct criticism of modern capitalist culture, Weyrich quotes William Lind:

> In a "free market" of values, the limits, restraints and self-discipline traditional ways of living require cannot compete with aggressively promoted self-gratification, sensual pleasures, and materialism. . . .

While traditional conservatism sought only to limit government, Weyrich's new "cultural conservatism" would use government to enforce the traditional values of family stability, hard work, and sexual puritanism. Such a variety of conservatism, which would enlarge government in order to enforce certain styles of individual behavior, is inescapably reminiscent of fascism.

SOCIAL WELFARE AND THE CONSUMER CULTURE

If the consumer culture presents major obstacles, albeit usually unacknowledged ones, to the New Right's achievement of its social agenda, so does it also create problems and tensions for the right to exploit. The consumer culture holds out a powerful vision of abundance, but it also insists on our subservience to that vision. Ideally, from the point of view of American business, we do not question the intrinsic value of the multitude of goods dangled before us in advertisements, but only commit ourselves to work harder to acquire them. Thus, while the consumer culture promises freedom from material scarcity, it simultaneously demands that we relinquish some of our freedom as self-determining individuals. These contradictions necessarily bedevil our view of social welfare, if for no other reason than that it represents a potential mechanism for realizing that vision of universal abundance held out to us, daily, in the consumer culture.

First, in the most practical sense, the consumer culture subverts one of the most fundamental assumptions of liberal social welfare policy: that there are certain basic needs which can be met, when necessary, by an activist government, such as the needs for housing, food, clothing, education, and medical care. Attempts to define "basic needs" can be foolish and even cruel, as in the case of the calculated nutritional needs that still underlie federal definitions of poverty. But even critics of such penurious standards do not question the existence of basic needs, but confine their arguments to how they should be defined—more meat and less rice, safer housing, more personalized medical care, for example. The assumption is always that once properly defined, basic needs can be met, and that the ultimate result will be some measure of human satisfaction.

Meanwhile, the message from the consumer culture is that there *are* no basic needs, or rather, that all wants are needs and all needs are basic. The occasional product that rests its advertising claims on luxury status does not refute the drift of the omnipresent commercial text, which intentionally blurs any possible distinction between what one might want for purposes of prestige or self-enhancement and what one might actually require to get through the day. Furthermore, the "needs" defined by the consumer culture vary from year to year and season to season, both as a result of technological innovation (often on a very trivial scale) and of media-promoted changes in fashion.

The effect, at the very least, is to confuse our sense of what constitutes a real need and to compromise our notion of mutual obligation. We know that people made temporarily homeless by a natural disaster need blankets, canned goods, and shelter, and we are often extraordinarily generous in our response to them. But if they are dislocated for a longer period, do they also need television sets, clothes that meet current standards of fashion, beer, and cigarettes? If the problems of the poor at times seem to loom before us as a bottomless abyss that no amount of money can fill, the reason lies not in the improvidence of the poor but in a notion of human nature inculcated by the consumer culture. We have come to understand human needs as limitless, just as the cornucopia of goods and services offered by the market appears to be endlessly abundant. In this view, greed is central to human nature, and it is also fully consistent with the expectations of society.

But let us look a little more deeply into the notion of human nature that is both promoted and required by the consumer culture. On the one hand, it is an immensely attractive view of the human condition as no longer bounded by scarcity but open to perpetual improvement. If we were merely healthy, we can now be fit; if we were only presentable, we can become attractive; if we were tied down, a household appliance or a credit card can make us "free." Never mind, for the moment, that the consumer culture cannot actually provide the freedom we are offered in a sports-car ad, the conviviality portrayed in a beer commercial, or the erotic possibilities we are supposed to associate with certain brands of designer jeans. Even if the consumer culture can offer only commodities—lifeless objects—it holds out an optimistic, expansive view of the human condition.

Not coincidentally, this view is entirely consonant with the assumptions of familiar liberal ideologies. For example, Keynesian economics assumes that potential demand is unlimited and that it can be the basis for perpetual economic growth. Similarly, though in a very different vein, the most identifiably "liberal" psychological ideology—that advanced by the human potential movement and its derivative schools of therapy—assumes an unlimited human capacity for novelty and pleasure. In this view, which

needless to say is anathema to cultural conservatives, the aim of
life is "growth" to ever new plateaus of experience and pleasure,
and the mental states associated with traditional values, such as
guilt and repression, are pathological conditions requiring treatment.

There is, of course, a more negative side to the view of human
nature required and promoted by the consumer culture. Critics on
the left, as well as some genuine conservatives, have repeatedly
indicted the consumer culture for reducing us to a state of apolitical, childlike dependency on the next sensation or "revolution"
offered by the marketplace (Marcuse 1964). If our needs are bound-
less, insatiable, and, worse, defined by the very people who stand
to profit by them, then we are hardly independent beings, or even
individuals in the classical liberal sense; we are more like addicts.
At the very least, we come to sense that our autonomy is threatened by the constant imperative to consume, perhaps especially
when the seductions of the consumer culture conflict with the
traditional values still honored in our homes, workplaces, or
churches. The conflict between these values and hedonism, which
Bell attributed to capitalist society in general, becomes internalized as a source of personal anxiety.

This tension, we might speculate, is particularly strong among
the white Christian fundamentalists who have so far composed the
major mass constituency of the New Right. On the face of it, the
message of television evangelists like Jim Bakker, Pat Robertson,
Jerry Falwell, and Jimmy Swaggart is that there is no further need
for such tension: Christianity and capitalism are reconciled, and
the born-again believer will be rewarded with material success. All
of the leading televangelists explicitly reject asceticism as a sign of
grace, just as they refrain from criticizing the commercial culture
that surrounds them (with the exception of material deemed either
pornographic or "humanistic"). To a largely lower-middle-class
audience of believers, the practical import of the fundamentalist
message is not much different from that of the consumer culture
itself: Believe in yourself and your ability to succeed, get what you
want, and, in general, go for it.

But this cheery message never entirely escapes the gloomier

reverberations of the Christian heritage. Contemporary Protestant fundamentalism addresses a world in which Satan is still at large, and in which the alternative to salvation is not merely death but damnation. Even as genial preachers like Robertson and Bakker urge their audiences to enjoy life, they cannot escape a religious heritage that features suffering as the path to redemption, pain and deprivation as the prelude to eternal life. The result is a message that seems almost guaranteed to provoke anxiety in the believers: they are told to embrace the pleasures of this world, and especially the offerings of the consumer culture, while never relaxing their guard against sin. The ancient Christian insight that money and markets are the province of the devil cannot be entirely abolished, only repressed.

For most of us, religious or otherwise, the consumer culture is not an entity that can be distinguished from the rest of the environment we inhabit. We may resent its blandishments and demands on us, but our resentment must be deflected to clearer targets. Part of the success of the New Right must be attributed to its ingenuity in pinpointing peripheral targets for the anger that stems from a sense of consumer dependency or entrapment. One such target would be what the right sees as "pornography" in the mass media. If we cannot complain about the ad, or beyond that, about an economy that depends on our gullibility and willingness to consume what we do not need (or at least did not need yesterday), then we can at least complain about the use of sexual suggestion to enlist our attention.

In a larger sense, one could say that the project of the right has been to deflect this unspoken (and in current political discourse, almost inadmissible) resentment toward the welfare state. The connection is by no means direct or even rational; in fact, for many of us, contributions from the welfare state (such as social security) are necessary if we are to enjoy even minimal access to the consumer culture. But at another level, "welfare dependency" has come to serve as a condensed symbol for a much more common if not universal condition. Dependency itself is hardly a meaningful issue in an urban society with a complex division of labor, but decrying welfare dependency allows us to express a horror at having forfeited our own autonomy, judgment, and even dignity to remote and only superficially benevolent forces.

Furthermore, if nothing can be done about one's own dependence on the consumer culture, one can at least decry the hedonism of the new-class "welfare statists" and the foolish dependency of their beneficiaries among the poor. From this perspective, the common characteristic attributed to those two very disparate groups—a slavish self-indulgence—begins to make more sense. This is the characteristic we have come to dread in ourselves: it has the uncontrollable quality of an addiction; it binds us to unrewarding work; it conflicts, in many cases, with older notions of autonomy and selfhood. So, by the classic mechanism of projection, we are urged to find it in those we dislike or can come to see as marginal groups, social "others."

According to psychoanalytic theory, projection is a fundamental mechanism underlying racial and ethnic prejudice (see Kovel 1970). Historically, whites projected onto blacks violent and sexual impulses that were taboo in white Protestant culture; gentiles projected onto Jews a venality that was at odds with feudal and religious tradition. Projection externalizes the unacceptable desire, the despised trait, without, of course, actually eliminating it from the person who does the projecting. There is a comfort—or at least the right would like to offer it—in criticizing the new class for its sexual permissiveness, or the poor for their profligacy, when these are among the very traits the consumer culture seeks to inculcate in us all.

In the case of the poor, liberal ideology about the "culture of poverty" colludes with right-wing ideology to make the poor the ideal symbolic victims of consumerism. Those traits that liberals saw as central to the "cycle of poverty"—an incapacity for deferred gratification, a lack of self-discipline, and a lack of future-orientation—are, from another point of view, the traits of the ideal consumer. Nothing could be better for the consumer-goods industries, at least in the short term, than for us all to abandon our capacity for deferred gratification, and to become as suggestible and as addicted to sensation as the poor are supposed to be. Hence, through the mechanism of projection, the more lurid stereotypes of the poor: the "welfare-dependent" black mother wallowing in the illicit contributions of her many lovers; the flashily dressed black man driving a pink Cadillac. These are images of people who have abandoned themselves to consumerism and whose "dependency" is only incidentally upon the offerings of the welfare state.

The new class, or the "liberal elite," plays a slightly more complex role in the imagination of the New Right, having to represent both the product of moral degradation and, at the same time, the shadowy force that produces it in others. In this respect, one is struck by the resemblance between the new class as seen by the right and Jews as traditionally seen by anti-Semites. Both are "cosmopolitan" groups, portrayed as urban, sophisticated, and disdainful of more parochial values. Nazi anti-Semitic ideology portrayed Jews as sexually loose, even deviant, much as the new class is supposed to be sexually "permissive." Thus both groups embody the curious combination of schemes for domination (through the public sector in the case of the new class, through finance in the case of the Jews) with personal abandonment to hedonism.[6]

The new class is, in many ways, a logical target for the class resentments the New Right seeks to mobilize. Actual capitalists and the extremely wealthy are less visible in daily life than are members of the new class, who appear routinely in the media in every role from talk-show expert to the sophisticated consumer portrayed in commercials for upscale goods and services. As "Yuppies," new-class members are our society's hyperconsumers, pioneering the use of new products (such as personal computers) and introducing food fashions that others only gradually catch up with (such as quiche in the seventies and sushi in the early eighties.) And as I have argued elsewhere, the entertainment media tend to valorize new-class habits and life-styles while portraying those of blue-collar people as old-fashioned and obsolete (Biskind and Ehrenreich 1980; Ehrenreich 1985).

[6] Most of the New Right and the Christian right are, of course, officially opposed to anti-Semitism, in part because of their strong support for the state of Israel.

CONCLUSION

Perhaps the most surprising feature of the New Right's rise to national power and prominence is the degree to which its ideological assumptions have been absorbed or accepted within the moderate-to-liberal political mainstream. One of these assumptions is that liberalism is, if not elitist, at least inherently incapable of being populist. Thus, even as polls have repeatedly shown substantial and growing public support for social welfare (see chapter 2), erstwhile liberal politicians have persisted in the belief, inspired by the New Right, that social welfare advocacy is unwise or even suicidal. Even more pervasive is the New Right's assumption that *the* problem of American society is permissiveness, and that liberalism is inherently incapable of curbing it.

The New Right has been able to seize the moral initiative from liberalism, above all, because it has dared to advance a strong *qualitative* critique of capitalist society. Liberalism too once had the moral initiative, pressing for measures to bring the poor and racial minorities into the mainstream of American life. But liberalism offered no alternative vision of—or for—that mainstream. Just as business unionism has demanded "more" (Samuel Gompers's emphatic vision) for its constituents, the crusading liberalism of two decades ago offered "more" for the excluded, but without questioning the content or limits of such a demand. Morally speaking, liberalism was made vulnerable to ideological attack because it failed to address the meaning of "more" in a consumer culture that advertises unlimited acquisition and pointlessly commodified hedonism.[7] It is not that the old quantitative, redistributive demands of liberalism are any less urgent than they were twenty

---

[7] There had, however, been a strong undercurrent of liberal rejection of the consumer culture in the late fifties and early sixties. Many liberal intellectuals, for example, worried that the war on poverty would only create more of the "real problem," which they defined as "too much affluence." While that concern now seems ludicrous—and genuinely elitist—it did contain the germs of a powerful critique of capitalist society, not only for whom it excludes but for what it has to offer those it does include. Such a qualitative critique persisted in and was further developed by the New Left and the radical feminist movement of the sixties and early seventies, but mainstream liberalism decisively rejected these movements and their ideologies.

years ago. But they have been upstaged, so to speak, by a right-wing ideology that insists we do not need simply more of what there is to have, but a profoundly different way of living.

Like other right-wing movements of this century, the American New Right *does* offer an alternative vision to the endless disruptions and aimless individualism of bourgeois society. It is a vision of the future in which people will live in stable families within stable communities and will work hard and be sober and chaste. Authority will be firmly vested in adults over children, in men over women, and in ancient sources of wisdom, such as the Bible, over modern science and "humanism." If there is still poverty after such a moral reformation of society, it will be dealt with through individual or local charity rather than impersonal government mechanisms. In short, this is the traditional nostalgic vision of *Gemeinschaft*—of the organic community associated with small-scale agriculture restored, only in the midst of a technologically modern capitalist society.

Lacking an alternative vision, today's liberals have simply appropriated the most evocative themes and language of the right: family, hard work, the importance of replacing permissiveness with sterner values. While criticizing the excesses of the New Right, they have implicitly accepted its cultural polarity: permissiveness versus traditional values, hedonism versus repression—or as Samuel Francis might put it, Mick Jagger versus Jerry Falwell. As a result, liberalism itself has come to seem vacuous and yielding, not so much a coherent ideological vision as a surrender to the moral breakdown that the right proposes to address. It offers no new ideas other than the old notion of gradually amending the status quo, while the right offers a future—even if it is, manifestly, only the past, or a distorted version of it.

An effective response to the New Right would have to begin with an unambiguous rejection of its pastoral vision of the future. So far, feminists and civil libertarians have been in the forefront of the effort to counter the New Right's social vision, and they have done so on the grounds that it is a threat to individual rights—the rights of women and young people, and potentially the freedom of expression of all citizens. This kind of response is valuable and essential, for surely individual liberty ought to be one of the traditional values we hold most dear. But it is also a limited and inadequate response. First, it only reiterates the libertarian ideology which the New Right has effectively learned to associate with the "permissive," cosmopolitan interests of the new class. A response that focuses only on individual rights cannot allay either the anxieties or the class resentments which the right seeks to exploit. In fact, to counter the New Right with arguments that rest ultimately only on a liberal conception of individualism is to miss what is most powerful and appealing about the current ideology of the right: that it *does* dare to challenge the unrewarding individualism (coded as "hedonism" or "permissiveness") cultivated by the consumer society.

A more effective response to the New Right must emphasize not only what is distasteful about the right's vision—for example, from a libertarian perspective—but what is fundamentally duplicitous about that vision. As we have observed throughout this chapter, there is an inescapable contradiction between the New Right's stance on social issues and the (old or new) right's championship of unfettered free enterprise. The New Right's nostalgic vision of *Gemeinschaft* (or, some might say, a patriarchal version of fascism) cannot be achieved within the context of unregulated capitalism. It is not the new class that uproots communities and engenders pervasive anxiety even among the stably employed, but, in the most direct sense, corporations in search of lower labor costs and higher profits. And it is not the new class that foments the addictive materialism and self-indulgence of our society, but the consumer culture with its dynamic of endless expansion and ceaseless cultivation of "needs."

Ultimately, an effective response to the right must rest on a genuine critique of capitalist culture and on a genuinely radical alternative vision. This requires, first, that we transcend the right's false polarity of "traditional values" versus "permissiveness." The choices, as the basis either for society or for our lives as individuals, do not have to be self-denial or self-indulgence, repressiveness or what Marcuse termed the "repressive desublimation" offered by the consumer culture. There are alternative values that are, at least in American culture, every bit as traditional as, say, hard work and self-denial. And these are the old small-R republican values of active citizenship, democratic participation, and the challenge and conviviality of the democratic process.

A reformed and expanded welfare state could be organized to provide expression for these alternative values. An expanded welfare state must, of course, address the grave material inequalities of American society, and it must do so as its foremost priority. But a radically alternative vision of social welfare, and hence of our common enterprise as a society, must aim not only for a redistribution of wealth but for a fundamental revival of citizenship. We need to re-imagine the welfare state, not as an impersonal or "new class"–dominated mechanism for the distribution of goods and services, but as the social infrastructure for a revitalized democracy.

This means envisioning programs and approaches that tap the creative energy and communitarian impulses of ordinary Americans, the economically vulnerable as well as the poor. There are precedents for such an approach in the Great Society antipoverty programs that mandated "maximum feasible participation" on the part of the recipients; there are useful examples from other nations and from nonprofit private efforts in this country. In general, the huge need for human services—for the poor, for the elderly, for children—could be turned into an opportunity for widespread citizen involvement on many levels, much as the Peace Corps and Vista once mobilized the moral energy of America's young people.

Above all, we cannot let the attack by the right foreclose the task of envisioning what a just and democratic American welfare state could look like. Without a compelling alternative vision, it is difficult even to defend the inadequate programs we already have. Social welfare need not be a desperate or halfhearted measure taken in times of mass unrest and withdrawn, periodically, at the behest of economic elites. It could become a stable institutional mechanism for meeting fundamental human needs—including needs for participation and meaningful self-expression—that are ignored or distorted in our present society, and that would be denied forever in the utopia of the right.

REFERENCES

Bazelon, David. 1967. *Power in America: The Politics of the New Class.* New York: Simon & Schuster.

Bell, Daniel. 1976. *The Cultural Contradictions of Capitalism.* New York: Basic Books.

Bergmann, Barbara R. 1986. *The Economic Emergence of Women.* New York: Basic Books.

Biskind, Peter, and Barbara Ehrenreich. 1980. "Machismo and Hollywood's Working Class." *Socialist Review,* June,

Bruce-Briggs, B. 1979. "Introduction to the Idea of the New Class." Pp. 1–18 in B. Bruce-Briggs, ed., *The New Class?* New Brunswick, N.J.: Transaction Books.

Carter, Sandy. 1979. "Class Conflict: The Human Dimension." Pp. 97–120 in Pat Walker, ed., *Between Labor and Capital: The Professional-Managerial Class.* Boston: South End Press.

Crawford, Alan. 1980. *Thunder on the Right: The "New Right" and the Politics of Resentment.* New York: Pantheon Books.

Currie, Elliott. 1985. *Confronting Crime: An American Challenge.* New York: Pantheon Books.

Edsall, Thomas Byrne. 1984. *The New Politics of Inequality.* New York: W. W. Norton & Co.

Ehrenreich, Barbara. 1983. *The Hearts of Men: American Dreams and the Flight from Commitment.* New York: Anchor/Doubleday.

———. 1985. Review of *Twice in a Lifetime,* a film by Bud Yorkin. *Ms.,* November, p. 32.

Ehrenreich, Barbara, and John Ehrenreich. 1970. *The American Health Empire: Power, Profits and Politics.* New York: Random House.

———. 1979. "The Professional-Managerial Class." Pp. 5–45 in Pat Walker, ed., *Between Labor and Capital: The Professional-Managerial Class.* Boston: South End Press.

Ehrenreich, Barbara, and Deirdre English. 1978. *For Her Own Good: 150 Years of the Experts' Advice to Women.* New York: Anchor/Doubleday.

Francis, Samuel T. 1982. "The Message from MARS: The Social Politics of the New Right." Pp. 64–83 in Robert A. Whitaker, ed., *The New Right Papers.* New York: St. Martin's Press.

Gouldner, Alvin. 1982. *The Future of Intellectuals and the Rise of the New Class.* New York: Oxford University Press.

Gross, Ronald, and Paul Osterman, eds., 1972. *The New Professionals.* New York: Simon & Schuster.

Kovel, Joel. 1971. *White Racism: A Psychohistory.* New York: Vintage Books.

Marcuse, Herbert. 1964. *One-Dimensional Man.* Boston: Beacon Press.

Miller, Douglas T., and Marion Nowak. 1977. *The Fifties: The Way We Really Were.* Garden City, N.Y.: Doubleday & Co.

Moynihan, Daniel Patrick. [1972] 1979. Quoted on p. 2 of B. Bruce-Briggs, ed., *The New Class?* New Brunswick, N.J.: Transaction Books.

Murray, Charles. 1984. *Losing Ground: American Social Policy 1950–1980.* New York: Basic Books.

New York Times. 1985a. "Buchanan Labels Cuomo a 'Reactionary Liberal'." June 16, sec. A, p. 1.

New York Times. 1985b. "A Defender of 'the Welfare System.'" July 31, sec. A-1, p. 12.

New York Times. 1985c. "The Value of Workfare." November 12, sec. A, p. 35.

New York Times. 1985d. "A Liberal by Any Other Name May Get More Votes." November 24, sec. E, p. 5.

Oakley, J. Ronald. 1986. *God's Country: America in the Fifties.* New York: Dembner Books.

Paige, Connie. 1983. *The Right-to-Lifers: Who They Are, How They Operate, Where They Get Their Money.* New York: Summit Books.

Peattie, Lisa R., and Martin Rein. 1983. *Women's Claims: A Study in Political Economy.* New York: Oxford University Press.

Phillips, Kevin. 1979. "Political Responses to the New Class." Pp. 139–45 in B. Bruce-Briggs, ed., *The New Class?* New Brunswick, N.J.: Transaction Books.

———. 1982. *Post-Conservative America: People, Politics, and Ideology in a Time of Crisis.* New York: Random House.

Podhoretz, Norman. [1972] 1979. "The Adversary Culture." Pp. 19–31 in B. Bruce-Briggs, ed., *The New Class?* New Brunswick, N.J.: Transaction Books.

Scammon, Richard M., and Ben J. Wattenberg. 1970. *The Real Majority: An Extraordinary Examination of the American Electorate.* New York: Coward-McCann.

Rusher, William A. 1984. *The Rise of the Right.* New York: William Morrow & Co.

Tyrrell, R. Emmett, Jr. 1984. *The Liberal Crack-Up.* New York: Simon & Schuster.

Wall Street Journal. 1986. "Rise in Never-Marrieds Affects Social Customs and Buying Patterns." May 28, p. 1.

Weyrich, Paul. 1986. "The Cultural Right's Hot New Agenda." *Washington Post,* May 4, p. 1.

Witcover, Jules. 1972. *The White Knight: The Rise of Spiro Agnew.* New York: Random House.

INDEX

ABOUT THE AUTHORS

FRED BLOCK is a professor of sociology at the University of Pennsylvania.

RICHARD A. CLOWARD is a professor of social work at Columbia University and co-author with Frances Fox Piven of *Regulating the Poor* and *Poor People's Movements.*

BARBARA EHRENREICH's most recent works are *the Hearts of Men* and *Re-making Love.*

FRANCES FOX PIVEN is a professor of political science at the Graduate School and University Center of the City University of New York.